THE DRUMMOND
Girls

THE DRUMMOND Girls

A STORY OF FIERCE FRIENDSHIP BEYOND TIME AND CHANCE

MARDI JO LINK

GRAND CENTRAL
PUBLISHING

NEW YORK   BOSTON

The events described in these stories are real. And while all eight of my Drummond Girl sister witches are portrayed with their given names, I've given a few outsiders fictitious ones, for reasons that should become obvious. Be advised: While on Drummond Island, I was a pool player, a partier, a hiker, and a friend. Not a journalist.

Map of Drummond Island by the painter Kris Love.

All photos courtesy of the author.

Grand Central Publishing
Hachette Book Group
1290 Avenue of the Americas
New York, NY 10104

www.HachetteBookGroup.com

Printed in the United States of America

RRD-C

First Edition: July 2015
10 9 8 7 6 5 4 3 2 1

Grand Central Publishing is a division of Hachette Book Group, Inc. The Grand Central Publishing name and logo is a trademark of Hachette Book Group, Inc.

The Hachette Speakers Bureau provides a wide range of authors for speaking events. To find out more, go to www.hachettespeakersbureau.com or call (866) 376-6591.

The publisher is not responsible for websites (or their content) that are not owned by the publisher.

Library of Congress Cataloging-in-Publication Data has been applied for.

ISBN 978-1-4555-5474-4

To Andrea, Bev, Jill, Linda, Mary Lynn, Pam, and Susan—
I pledge with all my might.

*"First woman settler on **Drummond Island**, 1820– 1896; courageously she wrought, joyously she lived."*

—bronze plaque on a granite boulder,
South Water Street, Drummond Island, Michigan

*"**Girls**, US, Applied, often jocularly, to women of any age, especially in the form of address; used mainly by women."*

—Oxford Dictionary of Slang

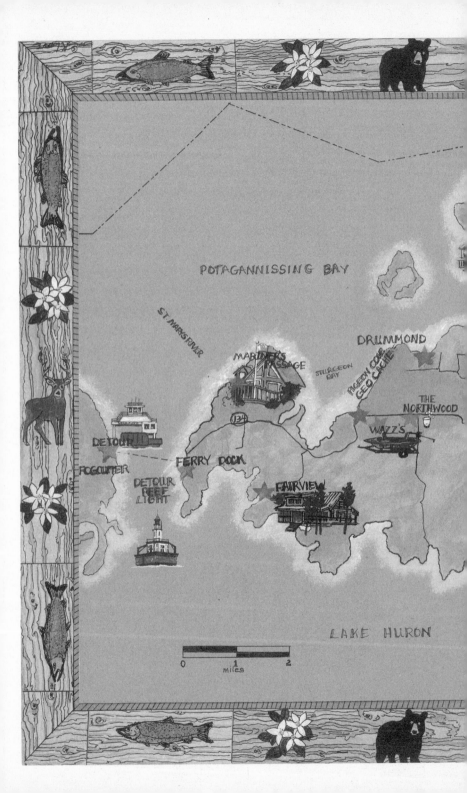

THE DRUMMOND

Girls

PROLOGUE *OCTOBER 2013*

*From left, me, with Bev, Jill, Andrea, and Linda,
outside Paw Point Lodge, 2013.*

Okay, so check us out. It's two o'clock in the morning and there we all are, eight bony, dark-rooted, and wide-awake women, sitting around the table at Paw Point Lodge.

If there exists a more improbable group of girlfriends, I don't know where you'd find them. Not on Drummond Island; we've already claimed that rock as surely as the Pilgrims claimed Plymouth. Not with buckle shoes or lukewarm beer from barrels, but with aerobics sneakers and shots of Absolut; otherwise, it's a pretty similar setup. A group of energetic misfits pools their resources, leaves their familiar confines in a huff, docks in a strange land, and parties like Vikings. (A historic liberty. I can't recall anyone saying they partied like Pilgrims. Ever.)

At the head of this table is Linda, busy counting the cash in our kitty. She started our trip more than twenty years ago with seventy-five dollars and a roll of quarters from her tip jar; when she arrives at the final sum tonight, it will have a comma in it. A pair of Kmart readers slips down her nose and a cigarette is notched between her fingers. An impressively long ash hangs from the end, but fall off? It would not dare.

Susan is in the kitchen, mouthing the words to a Van Halen song while also texting her husband, downloading a geocache coordinate, and mixing a cocktail. It might be her second Maker's and Caffeine-Free Diet; it might be her fifth. Two decades in, yet it is impossible for me to tell which.

Pam is smiling contentedly, simply being her relaxed and happy self. She's making a snack, scooping up a teaspoon of potato salad, but vowing next year to bring baby spinach with turkey-bacon dressing instead (3.5 carbs). Her cropped hair is a dozen shades of bronze, a style that would look ridiculous on the rest of us, but is the bee's knees on her.

Mary Lynn is here, yet not here, and I miss her. She was taken from us more than a decade ago by what her doctor called "a cardiac event." I am older now than she was when she died, and I silently vow to never get myself invited to one of those. Then top off my cocktail, eye a pot brownie, and go for a sloppy joe and a handful of corn chips. I can diet when I'm dead.

I take my place at the table then, across from the two women leaning in and whispering. Yes, the ones who look like they're plotting a revolution. Andrea and Jill, the youngest of the girls at forty-three and forty-seven. Put them in charge and we'll be kidnapping a cop, fixing a flat tire with nicotine gum, then popping into the Northwoods to sing covers with the bar band. It's late now, though—or actually really, really early—and most of us have our Cuddl Duds on, so those shenanigans will just have to wait until tomorrow.

"When did we start going on this trip, anyway?"

Sitting next to me with her perfect posture and that pretty, heart-shaped face is, finally, Bev, aka "the Polish Princess." She might insist on the senior discount and have a Medicare Part D card in her purse (if she can find her purse; dammit, it was just right here), but she's still got the cover-girl look. She could draw back the bow, aim the arrow, and be Bear Archery's poster girl tonight if she wanted to.

She doesn't. She just wants to know when the eight of us started going to Drummond Island together.

"Was it ninety-four? Or maybe...ninety-six?"

The room quiets and a few of us share a look. We've answered this question for her already, several times in fact. So I think I'm justified when I turn to her with *just a hint* of irritation and open my mouth to answer it again.

I lift my hand for emphasis this time, hoping my words will take. But then before I can utter a single one something in the gesture catches my eye.

Because, for the love of Christ, there's what looks like a two-dollar night crawler on the back of my hand, stuck under the skin. It's purple, it's tender looking, and it's big enough to catch a lunker bass if someone had the wherewithal to poke a hook through it.

Then I remember I'm wearing a pair of Lacoste boots—the pink plaid ones I bought just for this year's trip. Describing my footwear may seem like a random observation until I explain that inside their narrow toes my bunions are screaming the seven words you can't say on television. One of those words is *piss*. Not a bad option, as obscenities go.

In my head, I try it out: *Piss, my feet fucking hurt.*

Which feels satisfying for about one second. Because wait—is that my rotator cuff? And has it started throbbing?

The nerves inside the shallow socket rear up at odd moments since an ill-advised, backwoods horse race. Considering the heft of the dinner plate in my hand, the one holding my "snack," I probably just reinjured my shoulder by carrying it to the table.

I swing my arm in a circle to get some circulation going and narrowly miss Bev. She gives me a reproving look. Not for the arm windmill, but for the attitude. Considering my own maladies, is helping her remember the year she first came with us to the island really all that much to ask?

The other girls are looking at me that same way, too. Over her glasses Linda raises an eyebrow. Susan turns down the classic rock, and she and Pam make eye contact, say nothing, and take lady-like sips of their drinks instead. Even Andrea and Jill have stopped strategizing long enough to look my way.

I get the message.

Who am I, with my varicose hand, my horse-wrecked shoulder, and my squee-hawed feet to begrudge Bev a little memory lapse?

They're right, of course. They usually are.

There was a time when we believed we were immune from the passage of time. That we'd be young and sound forever. Today, we know different. And our once sacred pact to keep the details of our trips to the island a secret ("what happens over the Mackinac Bridge *stays* over the Mackinac Bridge") doesn't feel relevant anymore.

"When are you going to write our story?" the girls asked me.

There are eight stories, I reminded them, not just one.

"Fine," they said, undeterred, "then write yours."

That we ever became friends at all is miraculous. Within our group is every combination of married, divorced, remarried, and staunchly single. We've got graduate degrees but also high school diplomas barely and miraculously bestowed; world travelers and homebodies; Republicans, Democrats, and several who self-identify as members of the None-of-Your-Damn-Business Party. Besides Drummond Island, Michigan, the one thing we share is a puritanesque independence. And by that I mean that one Drummond Girl does not ask another Drummond Girl for anything very often. When one does, no matter what it is, you do not say no.

I'd do anything for these women.

I'd take a rubber bullet for them. I'd do ninety days at a minimum-security prison camp, plan a hostile takeover of a Caribbean beach resort, or even lift one of those little plastic dump trucks off a baby, and they'd do those things and more for me.

And Beverly, I'm sorry I became irritated with you that night at Paw Point. I remember exactly when you joined the Drummond Girls. It was 1995. I remember the two trips before you came along, and a good deal of what we've all shared since then, too.

So here goes. I'm going to start at the beginning and work my way forward. That's the only way I know how to tell our story. It's not just mine; it's ours. The girls knew I'd come around to that idea eventually.

I hope it helps you, Bev, and the rest of us, too, remember every single minute of it.

CHAPTER ONE   *1993*

Andrea, Linda, and Jill, with Frank, at Barb's Landing, 1993.

Mothers who hand sewed their kids' clothes, who read used Jane Austen paperbacks and stenciled checkerboards and hearts onto their kitchen cupboards, did not go away on weekend benders. Not according to my husband they didn't.

"This one does," I told him, tossing long underwear, a disposable camera, and a Led Zeppelin cassette tape into a denim duffel bag.

It was early October; I was a thirty-one-year-old wife and mother of two, a bar waitress with a college degree, and getting into Jill's red Fiero that morning was the most radical act I'd committed in years. My older son was three, the younger fourteen months, and I'd rarely been apart from them for more than a few hours. And yet when Jill backed down my driveway, that duffel bag and I were in her front seat.

My husband stood on the rickety front porch, our baby in his arms. Next to him squirmed our older boy, grasping his father's leg with one hand and solemnly waving good-bye with the other. I blew him kisses and waved back. Then watched out Jill's windshield as the three of them grew smaller and smaller. Inside my rib cage, guilt battled the anticipation of a girlfriends' weekend away.

I was leaving behind flannel sheets, family dinners, baby skin smell, and him.

I was leaving behind temper tantrums, dirty dishes, diapers, spit-up, and him.

It's going to be okay, I thought, *it's only for the weekend.* Then almost immediately my mind overrode that with *I've earned this.*

Jill drove the quick two miles to Peegeo's, the bar where we worked, and we met up with two other coworkers, Linda and Andrea. The plan had been to leave before sunup; we were racing the light and had fallen a little behind. The sun was crowning over the trees when Jill parked the Fiero at the back of the empty lot, and the four of us scrambled into Linda's Jeep. I knew the name of the place we were going—Drummond Island—and that we'd need four-wheel drive, but little else about the weekend.

By the time we'd crossed the Grand Traverse County line, it was daytime, and those girls and the island—not my guilt—won out. From then on, for that one weekend a year, no matter who was waving good-bye, the island would win. The island would always win.

Linda hit the gas hard and pulled out onto US 31 North, which for the next ninety miles would take us along the coast of the Grand Traverse Bay, then Little Traverse Bay, and finally the shore of Lake Michigan for our approach to the Mackinac Bridge. After we crossed it, another coastal highway, this one running along the northern shore of Lake Huron, would deliver us to the Drummond Island car ferry.

"Sure you're ready for this?" Jill asked me, when we were far enough from home to see the iconic bridge ahead in the distance.

"Clear your head!" Andrea hollered before I could answer. "And prepare your*self*!"

She held her fingers in front of her face and then slowly slid them apart like a security gate, illustrating exactly how I might go about clearing my head.

As for how to prepare myself, I had absolutely no idea.

But I was still young then. And boy, would I learn.

"There's no cops on the island," Linda said.

The tone of her voice made it sound as if that fact were a value-added selling point. I'd heard her use the same tone when she told customers at the bar that the fish was good and the salad dressing was homemade.

I was sitting in the backseat with Jill, Andrea had turned to the front, and the Mackinac Bridge loomed huge in front of us when Linda imparted that detail. The fish *was* good at Peegeo's, the salad dressing *was* homemade, so what she'd just said about the police was probably true, too.

"Drink and drive, baby!" Jill whooped.

The three of them had been to the island together once before, and even though I was so excited to be along I could barely keep a rational thought in my head, I was aware enough to be in awe of their friendship. When I was around new people, only a tiny percentage of what I was thinking ever came out of my mouth. And what I was thinking was that my presence in that car felt provisional. If I fit in, I'd be included. If I didn't, I wouldn't. On Drummond Island but back home, too.

I'd still have my waitress job, the four of us would still work together, they'd probably even still be friendly to me, but every woman knows friendly is not the same thing as friends.

No one came right out and said those were the stakes, but it was kind of a given. The three of them were the established group;

I was the untested one they'd decided, for some unknown reason, to try out.

Back then, friends were the one thing I'd wanted more than anything else. Not just any friends. I wanted *them*. Those three women were everything I'd wished I could be: tough, undaunted, independent. I hoped being a wife and a mother didn't preclude me from becoming those things, too. They had cool to spare. Once we were on Drummond Island, some of it just might rub off on me.

"Hey," Jill said, unbuckling her seat belt and reaching to the back of the Jeep. "Who wants a beer?"

I looked at the clock on Linda's dashboard. Eight thirty.

"Not till we're over the bridge," Linda said.

"Oh yeah," Jill said. "Right."

Her voice carried an unmistakable sigh of disappointment. But she turned back around, buckled her seat belt again, and busied herself with the air flowing by out her window. It was a familiar way to pass the time on a road trip, but when most people put their hand out a car window, they just cupped their fingers and rode the air currents, letting their hand swim easily along. Jill was full-on rock and roll when she did it, even that early in the morning. She punched the wind with her fist, then pumped her whole arm up and down to the beat thumping from the radio.

I'd been so absorbed in whether or not I was going to fit in that Linda's comment about the police hadn't fully registered. Jill's enthusiasm for drinking and driving did, and although I didn't say so out loud, I wasn't exactly sure what to think.

Linda had told me there were two bars on the island, plus we all worked in a bar, so I knew there was going to be drinking. Not a problem. I enjoyed a beer as much as the next college-educated waitress with two little kids and a grouchy husband at home.

The girls had also told me about the miles of dirt roads that crisscrossed the island—two-tracks, they called them—where we'd unroll the windows, drive for hours, not see another vehicle, and just enjoy the wilderness. That was why we needed the four-wheel drive, so I knew there was going to be plenty of driving around that weekend, too. I would have preferred hiking, but I was so happy to be along at all, I wasn't going to quibble about it.

I just hadn't realized we'd be doing the drinking and the driving at the same time.

When Linda said there were no police where we were going, she'd said it not with caution or warning, but with what today I can only call glee. That's what should have registered with me. Because Linda didn't do glee. She was too self-controlled and deliberate for a such girlish emotion. I didn't know her very well then, but I knew that. Everyone knew that.

Linda could be wickedly funny and was sometimes even animated, but she never gushed. Ever. She was a woman's woman, not a girly girl. And yet, she'd just said "no cops" with all the excitement of a cheerleader on her way to the big homecoming game.

What had I gotten myself into?

I was raised in an active family of outdoor enthusiasts. We'd camped, fished, hiked, sailed, canoed, swum, ridden horses, and backpacked all over Michigan, and I was absolutely certain the presence of law enforcement (or not) had never been a factor for me, my parents, or my grandparents when planning any of those excursions.

Yet despite having traversed much of my beloved state, I'd never been to Drummond Island. Not once. In my mind the island seemed mysterious and special, a land separate and secret from all those other places I'd seen and all those other things I'd done. Apparently, it was also the kind of place where no one in uniform, trained and obligated to help in case of an emergency, dared tread.

My husband was often irritated with what he called my "completely useless tendency to overthink everything to death."

I did do that, but it wasn't something I could control; it was just me, and I silently put the signature trait to use right there in that car.

No cops meant no parking tickets, no speeding tickets, no sobriety tests, no arrest warrants, no nights in a jail cell that smelled like urine and dirty feet. (I'd never been in jail but my brother had.)

Then again, it also meant no help with directions if we got lost; no free lockouts or jump-starts if Linda locked her keys in her car or her battery died; and no armed protection from thieves, gropers, flashers, rapists, wild animals, or serial killers. Drummond Island was not a population center, that much I did know. The demographics didn't seem very promising for a serial killer. Just perfect, though, for wild animals.

I'm levelheaded, I thought to myself, *and reasonably capable.* In stressful situations I wasn't prone to panic, freeze, or scream. When I was in college, a man in an actual tan raincoat *had* flashed me. I burst out laughing and he ran away. These women would have given chase and then beaten the crap out of that guy, I was sure of it.

No cops.

I wasn't going to celebrate it the way Jill had, but I could accept it. If anything bad happened on Drummond, we'd just take care of ourselves. What appealed to me more was another authority figure the island lacked: bad-tempered husbands.

Linda's tires bumped onto the metal grates of the Mackinac Bridge. I looked down at the water far below and watched fingers of wind shift direction and claw the steely surface of the Straits of Mackinac. The wind was actually blowing backward, from south to north. A thrill came over me so completely then that I could hardly sit still. It was the kind of feeling only a wife and mother, with responsibilities and worries back home, could feel. I might have only been going away for two nights, but I felt like I was on a grand adventure, the kind I'd only read about in books. My companions were unknown, the itinerary unplanned, the destination uncivilized, and the conclusion uncertain.

I leaned back against the seat, stretched my legs out long, and watched the Michigan I knew pass by hundreds of feet below. If drinking and driving was what was required, then drinking and driving was what I'd do. Come to think of it, after we crossed the bridge I was sure a cold beer wouldn't taste half bad.

I unfocused my eyes and aimed them toward an opaque horizon of land far to the north. Drummond Island was out there. It was going to be reckless and it was going to be wild. *We* were going to be reckless and wild, and there wasn't anyone up there to stop us.

Spanning an amazing five miles, the Mighty Mac connects Michigan's Lower and Upper Peninsulas and is the longest suspension bridge in the Western Hemisphere. California's Golden Gate is only a quarter as long, and when Neil Armstrong returned from the moon, he said he could see our bridge from space.

"Look how far you can see!" Jill said, sticking her head out the window and staring two hundred feet down, straight at the water.

I watched the wind trace patterns on the surface like gusts across prairie grass, and that day, even from so high up, the Straits of Mackinac looked solid, as if you could step off the shore and walk right out onto the water. Then I remembered the news story about that woman from Detroit. What happened to her was so terrifying, I was sure everyone in the whole state remembered it.

She'd been a waitress, too, thirty-something years old, and also headed up north on a weekend off. No one ever figured out why, but as she approached the apex of the bridge she drove straight into oncoming traffic. She'd been able to veer safely back into her own lane, but the police said she must have overcorrected because just like that, her little car flipped over the guardrail. It took a week for divers to find it. When they did, her body was still buckled in the driver's seat.

No wonder Linda had rules against beer until after we'd crossed.

"Those boats are, like, so tiny," Andrea said. Like Jill, she'd stuck her head out the window, too, and looked straight down. "They look like little bugs or something."

"Yeah," I said, locking my eyes on the horizon. "Bugs."

We passed the bridge's two main towers, started our descent, and about a mile and a half later, the syncopating grates under Linda's tires were replaced by solid pavement again. There's a tollbooth on the northern side of the bridge; in 1993, it cost $1.25 per axle for passenger cars. Linda slowed, threw some change in the metal bin, the traffic arm lifted, and we crossed into the Upper Peninsula.

The contours of both peninsulas are so distinctive, any student of geography could have easily pointed out our location on a map. But maps don't show everything. Our passage from south to north felt imbued with more significance than simply driving over a line of famous topography. We'd left Traverse City only two hours before and were hardly a hundred miles from home, yet it felt like days since I'd waved good-bye to my family.

Our state's peninsulas are twins of a sort, but fraternal, not identical, and we had just driven onto the wild child. The Upper Peninsula is as large as Connecticut, Delaware, Massachusetts, and Rhode Island combined, but only 330,000 people live there. It was a land dominated by old-growth forests, bedrock outcroppings, and a sense of arboreal vastness that had long ago vanished from much of the rest of the country. Less than 1 percent of Upper Peninsula residents lived in a village or town. Car accidents were more likely to be between a car and a deer than a car and another car. Even from the highway, bear sightings were possible. The Upper Peninsula was where one of my favorite writers, Ernest Hemingway, went when he wanted to disappear. I relished the idea that my new friends and I were about to become a lot harder to find.

So I was surprised when just five hundred yards past the tollbooth, Linda pulled into the parking lot of the Michigan Welcome Center, a rest stop on the outskirts of the town of St. Ignace. Bathroom break. As we walked in, a shock of yellow sunlight from an east-facing window shined directly in my face, and I saw something that froze me in the doorway. Standing in the sunshine was a full-grown wolf.

"Hi puppy," Jill said.

The angle of the light changed, moved past our faces and onto a glassed-in cube we had to pass by on our way to the bathroom.

Okay. So after a bathroom break, after being startled by a four-foot carnivore inside a taxidermist's display, and after chugging a shared can of beer in the parking lot, *then* we were about to become hard to find.

"Next stop, Drummond Island!" Linda said, when we were all buckled back in.

There were still sixty-something miles of lonely coastal highway to drive and a mile of open water to be ferried across before we'd reach our destination. For the first time I wondered where we'd be staying. Linda had said something about a cozy place with a water view, but that was all I knew. I hadn't wanted to be the annoying new girl who asks a bunch of rookie questions about something as trivial as a hotel room, so I hadn't asked any questions at all.

I thought about that stuffed wolf, and when we were back in the Jeep, I asked the girls about it instead. Three hundred miles northwest, on Isle Royale, another island in the Upper Peninsula, there were a lot of wolves. Did wolves live on Drummond Island, too? I was afraid of them, but I kind of hoped we'd see one. A photograph of a wolf would be quite the souvenir to impress my husband and show my sons.

Jill said we were more likely to see a bear. She'd read there could be as many as sixty—*sixty!*—black bears living on the island, and they were dumber, hungrier, and tamer than wolves. Which also made them more dangerous. Wolves avoided people; bears didn't.

"How cool would it be to actually *see* one?" she'd said, her blue eyes sparkling.

Packed in my duffel with the Led Zeppelin, the long underwear, and the winter jacket was a disposable camera preloaded with enough film for twenty-four pictures. The nine dollars I'd spent on it was something of an extravagance. My husband was a Head Start teacher and sold encyclopedias door-to-door. I was a night waitress. We'd just bought our first house—a dated one story with an unfinished garage—on a land contract deal. We didn't have any extra money. One of his arguments against me going had been the seventy-five dollars I'd needed to contribute to the trip's kitty.

Hearing Jill talk about bears made me wish I'd splurged even more. Bears were nocturnal. For another four dollars, I could have bought a camera with a built-in flash.

"Say 'Drummond Island Ferry'!" a whiskered crewman said, his arthritic finger poised on the shutter button.

"Drummond Island Ferr-eee!" we cheered as the flat-hulled vessel rocked, the horizon tilted, and the wind sucked our voices north.

There were about twenty other cars, trucks, campers, and boat trailers on the ferry, all packed in so tight that a few of the drivers couldn't even open their doors. It was windy, and even the passengers who could have gotten out of their cars stayed inside for the ride from DeTour Village to the island. Some didn't even look out their windows, but just read a newspaper or napped instead. The remote passage was so beautiful, and the only reason I could think of for anyone to ignore it like that was if they'd made the trip umpteen times before.

What a life that must be, I thought. *Living, working, and even raising your children on an island.*

It was an odd sensation to be sitting in a car that was stopped, with the engine turned off, and yet was also moving steadily forward over open water. The crewman had directed Linda to park her Jeep in a spot alongside the ferry's starboard railing. I rolled down my window, smelled fresh water, and felt the cold sun shining on my face. I put on my Ray-Bans, opened my door as far as I could, and squeezed my thin body out. I didn't want anything coming between me and my first sighting of Drummond.

I walked to the edge of the ferry and leaned out over the railing. A plaque said her name was the *Drummond Islander III*, and I wondered what had happened to *I* and *II*. But I was just curious; none of the gruesome thoughts I'd obsessed over when we were crossing the Mackinac Bridge entered my mind. I was terrified of heights, but I'd learned to swim about the same time I'd learned to walk, been on swim teams in high school and college, and swam across several inland lakes just for the fun of it. There wasn't an undertow, a current, or a drop-off anywhere in the Great Lakes that fazed me. Drop me into the swirling depths of DeTour Passage, and even in that cold water I'd pop back up and swim to shore.

The other girls came outside and watched with me as the ferry cruised within sight of a small lighthouse looking like it had been anchored there forever. After we passed I scanned the unfamiliar shoreline the captain was aiming us toward. Drummond Island was a sentinel hunk of rocky earth grounded in the unpredictable currents, just like that lighthouse. Except for a ferry dock and a limestone quarry, its coastline looked uninhabited. I saw nothing but waves splitting onto man-sized boulders, trees swaying in full fall color, and a hill behind them so dense with evergreens it made the island look almost timeless, like a prehistoric continent modern life had chosen to leave alone.

On the map I'd found under Linda's seat, the island was shaped like a big blue crab. The St. Marys River, the North Channel, and Georgian Bay bordered it on the north, and nothing but the open water of Lake Huron flowed to the south. Drummond was a chunk of rock, forests, dirt roads, and one little town floating within a slingshot of Canada. There was no bridge to the island, so the only way for people to get there was by car ferry, boat, or private plane. Deer, bears, and wolves might be able to swim there, and I'd heard that in the wintertime animals sometimes walked to the island over the ice. Drummond's crab claws faced due west, and on Linda's map it looked as if they were trying to pinch the shore of the mainland and hold on.

A woman could lose herself in there, I thought, shocking myself with how tempting that idea actually felt. *She could just walk on in and never walk back out again.*

"Who's up for a cocktail?" Linda said, shooing us away from the railing and back into her Jeep as the ferry docked.

"Me, definitely," Andrea said.

"Ab-sa-freakin'-lootly!" Jill agreed.

"We'll check into our place first," Linda said, "and then head over to the Northwoods. Sound like a plan?"

I didn't have a plan. If the three of them did, they sure hadn't discussed it with me. But that was okay. I could already feel myself adjusting to not having a schedule, a to-do list, or the slightest idea of what time it was.

Back home I didn't wear a watch, even though there were things to do and places to be at appointed times. I had a good natural clock inside me, and whether it was my sons' naps, bedtimes, mealtimes, or my shifts at work—I was never, ever late. When we docked on that island, I felt a mental click, as if a series of invisible gears was grinding to a stop. It was the timepiece in my mind turning itself off.

I'd first met Jill, Andrea, and Linda on a night I'd randomly fled to Peegeo's for a beer, desperate for a break from my second-born son. He was six months old then, and usually I could make it through his two hours of crying every evening, but that night it had worn me down to nothing.

I'd never been to Peegeo's before, and it was Jill who'd said hello when I walked in the door; Andrea who'd poured me a Bud Light draft; and later, when I noticed the HELP WANTED sign, Linda who'd handed me an application. I hadn't gone there looking for a job and didn't want to work at all if it meant leaving my sons with a babysitter or putting them in day care. Back then our family finances were as raw as my nerves, so the sign caught my eye.

I'd never waitressed before, but when Linda handed me the application, I filled it out on the spot.

My thinking was that by working nights I could not only make some extra money, but also solve the babysitter dilemma. If I worked at Peegeo's, I could be with my boys during the day, and they'd be with their father in the evenings. Linda hired me the following week. Four months later, she'd invited me to go to Drummond with the three of them.

Of our group, Jill was the youngest at just twenty-one, yet the only one besides me who was married. She was short, pretty, and after working with her, I knew she could also be what my mother would call "mouthy" but what I would call a survival adaptation when you looked like her and worked in a place like Peegeo's. The bar and restaurant wasn't rough or scary, just male dominated and economically diverse; it was not unusual to see a golfer in plaid pants, a biker in skull tattoos, and a salesman just passing through, sitting on adjacent barstools.

Jill had worked there since she was fifteen. She was so good at it that she could cover the bar, the window booths, the takeout orders, *and* the dining room all by herself. You could not rattle Jill or put her in a bad mood. Not for anything.

Andrea and her boyfriend had been roommates with Jill and her boyfriend, right up until Jill got engaged. She and Jill still joked about the house they'd lived in together. How ramshackle it was, but how that was also part of the fun of living there. No matter how big a party they threw, it couldn't stain, break, or damage a place already so decrepit.

As someone who actually owned a house, I almost felt sorry for their neighbors. Andrea's voice could've carried through concrete. She talked loud, laughed loud, and jokes seemed to launch from her mouth at random. When someone I was waiting on complained about anything, I'd apologize profusely, assuming whatever had gone wrong was somehow my fault, but that was not Andrea's style at all.

"I *smell* what you're steppin' in!" she'd say, then tell the complainers she'd fetch them one of two things: their bill or another round. Andrea apologized to no one. She was nearly a decade younger than me, and yet I was in awe of both her wit and her intensity.

Linda managed Peegeo's bar and the dining room. She hired and fired the waitresses and bartended every Friday and Saturday night, reigning from behind that counter of blue Formica like a cross between Wonder Woman and the Queen of Sheba. The fact most customers behaved themselves—no matter how late it was, how much they'd had to drink, or how different they were from each other—was largely because of Linda. Peegeo's owner was a mercurial man named George. He'd given Linda a nickname, and I still remember the night I learned what it was.

We had a regular named Dan, a tall, skinny housepainter who came in every Friday, sat at the end of the bar, and didn't get back up until he'd drank a good portion of his paycheck. Dan didn't like to run a tab—he thought Linda padded his bill—so he always paid with cash. As the evening wore on, the pile of dollar bills and loose change on the bar in front of him would first grow, then slowly diminish until he was out of money.

One night, when Linda's back was turned, he picked up a penny and threw it at her butt. Who knows why. I worked at that place five nights a week for four years and never figured out why drunk men do half the things they do.

The bar was full, and when Linda felt that penny, she whipped around, glaring at each customer trying to discern the guilty one. Dan's oblivious act must have been convincing because she failed to pick him out. Emboldened, he ordered another beer, took a swig, waited a few minutes, and then hit her with another penny.

Peegeo's was always packed on Friday, but it was particularly busy that night, and so Linda had been mixing drinks at a furious pace. Liquor bottles were stacked against the wall, her back was often turned to the bar, and she'd missed catching his second delivery, too.

But Dan had a fatal flaw. He could not quit when he was ahead. A few more minutes passed; he slid his hand over to a glass ashtray—heavy, gold, and trapezoid-shaped—and flung it, Frisbee-style, straight at her backside again. I'd approached the bar with a drink order just in time to see Linda reach behind her back like a circus juggler and snatch it out of midair.

Dan's face turned the color of his painter pants. Linda—all

five feet one inch of her—came around that bar, launched herself up onto her tiptoes, grabbed Dan's earlobe in her fist, and yanked him off his barstool. Everyone else sitting at the bar froze as she jerked him into a human question mark and marched him out of the building.

"You think they call me 'the Dragon Lady' for *fun*?" I heard her yell after him.

So those were my three new friends and my traveling companions. A mouthy beauty, a cocky comedienne, and a bartending dragon. As I rode happily along in the backseat of that Jeep, on my way to what I thought was a hotel on the water or perhaps even a log cabin, all I could think was *Man, am I ever lucky.*

Like Linda, I wasn't a girly girl, either. I wasn't picky, I didn't mind rustic, and I liked camping and being outside in the woods. Besides the coveted water view, I'm not sure what I'd expected of our accommodations.

I know what I didn't expect. I didn't expect Linda to turn her Jeep off the main road and into a place called Barb's Landing. I didn't expect a long muddy driveway, the smell of lake fish, or the sight of travel trailers parked on a patch of bleached gravel, either.

And I definitely did not expect Frank.

"Call the National Guard, the girls are back!" said a burly man in his sixties, wearing a blue-and-white golf shirt stretched to capacity over a cannonball of a belly.

"Here's your keys and towels, blankets are on the beds. Live bait's in the cooler, but don't put no guts in the water. You gals need a boat." He smirked. "I should have one freed up by tomorrow afternoon."

It took a moment, but then it dawned.

There wasn't going to be any lakeside hotel or cozy log cabin. This was a fishing camp for fisher*men*, with a bunch of old trailers for rent. I looked around for one molecule of evidence that a woman had ever set so much as a pinkie toe ring on the place, but that effort was in vain. To complete the shock, it seemed like our white-haired host was getting his jollies by making fun of us.

A flock of turkeys ran into the woods, then flew into the half-dead branches of a gargantuan pine tree. Ragged flannel shirts and white waffled long underwear hung from a nearby clothesline, their stained and saggy flies flapping open in the breeze. The voluptuous Mudflap Girl adorned the rear wheel wells of every vehicle in sight, and a fleshy scent hung in the air like a manly poltergeist. The trailers all came with fish-cleaning stations, buck poles, and charcoal grills, and somewhere nearby, forest meat was being charred.

I looked back at Frank. He had his arms crossed over his chest and was stifling a laugh. He knew we weren't there to catch fish, and it was pretty obvious to me he'd found our gender both helpless and amusing. Which made me furious.

The decision to leave home and spend a whole weekend away from my husband and children wasn't made carelessly or on a whim. I'd thought long and hard about it before I'd said yes. Getting into Linda's Jeep that morning and leaving town had been a big moment for me. On the way I'd accepted the "no cops" announcement, the drinking and driving plans, my own bout of bridge vertigo, the dead wolf in the display case, as well as Jill's bear population estimate.

I hadn't anticipated any of those things, yet offered no protest because I didn't want these tough and capable women to think I was a sissy la-la. Which was what George and my coworkers called someone they thought was a wuss, a wimp, a gutless wonder. At Peegeo's, the worst thing anyone could be in life was a sissy la-la.

The drive north had been majestically scenic, the conversation fun, and I'd expected our arrival at the prearranged lodging to be met with a warm or at least a polite welcome. I'd slept in sleeping bags under the stars, out on sand dune beaches, and on the hard ground in plenty of tents, so I really didn't mind staying in a travel trailer.

But that smirk on Frank's face struck me wrong.

I might have been just the new girl, but someone was still going to tell me what the hell had happened to Barb.

"So, like, where's *Barb*?" I blurted.

I'd seen the sign marking the turn into his muddy driveway, and it had said BARB'S LANDING. Next to those words, hand-carved animals frolicked under a cartoonish pine tree. Nothing had prepared me for burnt meat smell, long underwear, fish gut protocol, or being the subject of one rude old man's amusement.

"There ain't no Barb," the man said. "Not no more. I run the place now and I'm Frank."

His face broke into a genuine smile as he proffered a shovel of a hand for me to shake. My own hands were dirty, and I went to wipe them on the thighs of my jeans before I shook his. Looking down, I spied a brick-sized rock. It was gray and appeared to have fossils embedded inside of it. Worms and shells and what looked like creatures straight from a biology textbook. It was the kind of rock you might see in a museum display or a rock shop. I picked it up and brushed off the dirt.

Frank looked at it, too. It was a limestone fossil, he said. The island was full of them, but this was a particularly good one, and I could have it to take home with me if I wanted.

I held the rock in my left hand and met his palm with my right. Frank lived in the small bi-level across from the rental trailers. He was the first local I'd met on Drummond, and so his handshake—calloused, knowledgeable, and engulfing—turned out to be my official welcome to the island.

"Look at it this way, Mardi," Linda said later, as the four of us raised shots in a toast at the Northwoods bar. "It's right on the water, and we're still only paying fifty-five bucks!"

That was fifty-five dollars total, not each. Which was a good thing, because although we'd pooled our money—our one-dollar and five-dollar tips, a few twenties from savings accounts, and all of the change in our coin jars—we still didn't have much in the kitty. Three hundred dollars to house, feed, fuel, and quench the thirst of four wild women for a whole weekend. Well, three wild women and me.

That tight budget didn't stop them from toasting my Drummond Island debut with what seemed like every flavor of Pucker the Northwoods had on their shelf. I was just an occasional beer drinker, but after downing those shots of schnapps, I felt both loaded and loved on. My impenetrable exterior required lubrication to let those women in, and for the first time in years, I felt like I was becoming part of something. I wasn't sure what yet, but whatever it was, it was going to include me.

The bar, those welcoming women, and the island when it was still new to me would appear often in my memory, sometimes in almost microscopic detail. Externally, my world that night was small—the backseat of a Jeep, a car ferry loaded down to capacity, the inside of a rented trailer, and our little pinewood table at the Northwoods bar—yet it felt limitless.

I was getting to know them, they were getting to know me, and the longer we sat at that table, the less anything else about the trip mattered. Not the doomed waitress from Detroit who'd driven off the bridge, not Frank, not even the trailers. There I was, past thirty, a wife, a mother, a taxpayer, and a mortgage holder, an adult woman with goals and responsibilities, and finally being accepted by the cool girls.

I was too amped up for anything approaching introspection that night, but many times since, I've thought about that first year, of my all-consuming eagerness to fit in, of the angst I felt about being the new girl and how unnecessary it turned out to be. Whenever my mind goes back to those first hours inside the Northwoods, I feel the weight of my life and those heavy-bottomed shot glasses in our young hands.

Each of us had so many options for our lives back then, the years ahead were like an endless road map spread out before us, our futures akin to the unexplored two-track roads cracking through the surface of Drummond's crab claws. And we didn't even know it.

Thanks to what was in those shots, by 2:00 a.m. or sometime thereabouts, we at least knew it was time to leave. Not because of the late hour—up there no one cared, or for that matter even knew, what time we'd finally get to bed—but because our bar tab totaled an unimaginable eighty-two dollars. More than a night in one of Frank's trailers and way beyond our meager budget.

"Keep it between the ditches, girls!" the bartender cautioned as we pushed out the plywood door and swirled together into the dark.

I scanned the parking lot and spied the red of Linda's Jeep, a bright and happy square to aim for among the dozens of dark and shadowy vehicles. Had there really been that many other people in the bar?

"I'm married!" Jill shouted randomly to the night sky, her pretty head thrown back, her warm breath floating like lace in the cold black.

It sounded to me like Jill was trying to convince herself that she really was a newlywed. She did seem so young, and while I didn't know her well, at least not yet, I had a hard time picturing her as someone's wife. A year before, Linda and Andrea had surprised Jill a few months before her wedding with a trip to the island. Their weekend away had been her bachelorette party, a reminder that they had a history that didn't include me.

Andrea wrapped her arms around Jill's waist and swung her in a lopsided orbit. They lurched and weaved, this way and that, floating around the parking lot like the last stubborn seeds on a dandelion head. Together, they could defy geography, time, and apparently even gravity, too, because when they were stationary again, they were also miraculously still upright.

I stood to the side and listened to their voices harmonize in a throaty laugh. The sound made something uncontrolled expand inside of me. They might have been friends before I came along, had adventures and shared memories, too, I thought. But that was last year. This was now; I was here, the night was clear, and when I looked up, I saw that every star in the sky had come out. There was no one else around, so all those stars must have been shining up there just for us.

"I'm married," Jill said again, when the spinning stopped. But she said it in a monotone that time, instead of a cheer. "To one of those," she added, pointing.

We followed the angle of her arm and saw exactly what she saw. Through the shadows and the cold and even the liquor, we saw.

Pickup trucks. The parking lot of the bar was full of them. Dirty, rusty, bashed up, and dented. Bald tires, cracked windshields, and matted pairs of fuzzy dice hanging from rearview mirrors. Most had ridiculously high lifts and giant CB radio antennas sticking straight up from bent hoods. I marveled at the number—I'd been so focused on being with the girls I'd barely registered there'd been men inside the bar, too.

Some of the drivers' side windows were open a crack, and we thought we could even smell their stink: generic cigarette smoke, paper sacks that had once held cold lunches, but now only abandoned crusts of meat, and the mildew of work clothes and stale sweat.

Back home, I'd met Jill's husband a couple times. He was a slight and handsome smooth talker who drove a puke-green rig that would fit right in.

You could always divorce him, I thought and was dizzy with the shock of it. Was that really my first instinct? One disillusioned comment from Jill, and bam, I was ready for her to just chuck him? It frightened me to allow the word *divorce* into my consciousness. Once I did, there was no telling what might come of it.

I thought of my own husband. The father of my sons who was home with them, and caring for them, so I could come here. What did I have to complain about? He might have been in a perpetually bad mood (especially, it seemed to me, when his pot ran out), but he worked hard and drove a Chevy Cavalier station wagon, not a junky pickup. Whatever my opinion of marriage was back then—of my own, of Jill's, or of marriage in general—it did not include divorce.

I wouldn't have felt comfortable giving relationship advice, not to Jill or anyone else for that matter. Linda and Andrea had to have heard the tone in Jill's voice, but they must have shared my reluctance to acknowledge it because they kept their thoughts to themselves, too.

Linda was thirty-seven then and Andrea was twenty-two. Neither was married but both had steady boyfriends, and so you would have thought that we'd have discussed our men. And yet that first year not one of us did. Love was still a mystery to us, its own strange and mostly unexplored island. Perhaps we didn't want to admit we knew so little about it.

If you'd have asked me back then was I content, I wouldn't have known how to answer. I couldn't have articulated that being a mother was what I'd really wanted, while having a husband felt like a necessary step toward fulfilling that desire. Within months of my own wedding, I was self-aware enough to recognize I'd become a lonely bride, but I thought that would fade as soon as I'd had children. It hadn't, not all the way.

Linda joined Andrea and Jill and was now swinging in circles with them around the parking lot. As they giggled, then tried to catch their breath, she untangled herself and cupped her hand to her ear.

"What's that?" she said, suddenly serious and alert.

"What's what?" we asked, looking beyond the parking lot and into the dark.

"Don't you hear it?" Linda asked, and we listened again, harder.

I expected the sound of something foreboding. A wolf's howl, the stick snap of a backwoods kidnapper, or a bear growling and charging at us from out of those black woods. When all we heard was wind, trees, and foghorns—normal sounds of the Great Lakes at night—the three of us shook our heads no.

"The two-tracks!" Linda hollered, running for her Jeep. "And they're calling our names!"

The lopsided twirl around the parking lot seemed to take Jill's mind off her marriage, and while two-tracking was probably not the most traditional way to bolster a girlfriend's spirits when she needed encouragement, that was Linda. A woman made of equal parts instinct and action.

She'd seen rough times herself, far rougher than any of us knew back then, and had little use for hand-wringing, mulling over, or excuses. As it turned out, the two-tracks—unmarked and rudimentary vehicle trails meandering through the woods—were exactly what Jill needed.

"Shotgun!" she called, dashing to the Jeep on her short legs and beating both Andrea and me there by at least a full stride.

People who have never been to the Great Lakes state hear the word *Michigan* and probably think of big lakes or the industrialization of Detroit. But three-quarters of our state is actually covered by trees. We have more state forest property than any other place in the country, and much of it, including 53,000 of Drummond

Island's 83,000 acres, is interwoven with two-tracks and accessible by car. (Of course, by "car" I don't mean Cadillac sedan on a Sunday afternoon drive. I mean something with 4WD that you don't care all that much about the paint job on.)

I have no idea whether other American women in their twenties and thirties liked to two-track, but boy, we sure did. Back home, I'd gone with Linda a couple times and knew Jill and Andrea had, too. From our houses or from Peegeo's, it was a bit of a drive to access the rugged dirt roads that twisted through the woods. On Drummond, two-tracks were around every corner. On Drummond, two-tracks *were* the corner.

Branches brushed across the Jeep's hood, the lights of the bar faded, and soon it felt like we weren't only in the woods, we'd become part of the forest itself. That was the lure of two-tracking for me. Yes, we were inside a vehicle, but all of our windows were rolled down, so that didn't preclude being overtaken with a sense of eternity and I felt wild with the independence of it.

We weren't on any tracks Linda or the other girls knew; we were on a frontier. We were exactly like the women adventurers of old, crossing the prairie in our one-wagon wagon train. Well, exactly like those women if they'd traveled at night, with their 4WD engaged, their forward motion fueled by gasoline and blues-rooted, guitar-driven rock and roll. *Did eastern red cedar trees dig Led Zeppelin as much as I did,* I wondered, giggling. *How about creeping juniper? Did it "Ramble On"?*

With Linda at the wheel, we charged through those woods, bouncing up and down over rocks and sticks at forty miles an hour, her tape player blasting my Zeppelin in darkness so complete, headlights were just pinpoints in a vast black universe.

It had rained recently and mud splashed onto the windshield and into my open window, and yet I was still able to identify the native flora. I couldn't decide whether my college botany professors would have been proud of my retention or aghast over the circumstances in which I was using it.

"Copper beech!" I hollered out the open window. "Tamarack pine! Prairie sedge!"

An hour or more must have passed like that before partial sobriety returned, we slowed down, and Linda turned off the music. We didn't need Robert Plant to tell us *we* were the girls so fair, driving around in the darkest depths of Mordor, although we could've used an autumn moon to light our way. Without the music, it grew eerily quiet inside that vehicle. No one said much because the scenery veering in and out of the headlights had remained disturbingly constant.

Trees, shrubs, mud, night.

"Where *are* we?" Jill finally asked.

I'd started wondering the same thing but hadn't wanted to say so. Linda seemed to know her way around the island so well I'd started thinking of her as a human compass. Even as the woods closed in, the trails led nowhere, and the scenery took on a disconcerting repetition, I'd been taking it on faith she knew where we were going.

After Jill asked the question, no one spoke at first, probably because not a one of us, not even Linda, knew the answer. We thought we were somewhere west of the ferry dock and the Northwoods bar, on state-owned land, in Michigan's Upper Peninsula, the USA, North America, Earth. But as far as our specific location was concerned, a precise point on the planet, we were lost.

Only moments before, I'd been feeling mighty proud of my plant identification abilities, but when it came to navigation, I didn't have any skills at all. None. My sense of direction was so bad, I'd sometimes find myself lost in my own town. As my sons grew, this became a running joke among their friends. It didn't matter if we were only going across town, add an extra half hour if Mrs. Link was doing the carpooling. On Drummond, I felt wholly dependent on Linda to find our way back to civilization. I may have started to worry if I hadn't remembered something germane.

Yes, we were lost.

But we were lost *on an island*.

All we needed to do was keep going, as straight as the two-track would allow, and we'd eventually come to the shoreline. Barb's Landing was *on* the shoreline.

The thought struck me funny, but I did my best to stifle the impulse to laugh. Sure, I'd downed every shot of Pucker those girls had put in front of me, but I was still present enough to realize that most women, and (as tough as they were) probably these three included, didn't want to hear maniacal giggling coming from a coworker they didn't know all that well, while she was sitting in the backseat of their car, lost in the woods at night.

Linda leaned forward, stared straight ahead, gripped the steering wheel, and drove on. Andrea lit a cigarette, exhaled out the window, and Jill turned around and leaned toward me.

"You okay?" she asked.

I knew she was just being nice, but I felt my grin fade as I considered the subtext of her question. She thought I was worried, or worse, scared. She thought I was a sissy la-la.

I'd been so focused on the fact that I didn't know Linda, Andrea, or Jill very well, I hadn't considered our acquaintance from their perspective. The truth was, they didn't know me all that well, either. They knew I could handle the Friday night crowd at Peegeo's, but they didn't know I'd backpacked through the Porcupine Mountains with my family when I was only twelve. They didn't know my grandpa and I once missed a trail turnoff at dusk and had to swim our horses through a river cresting over our saddles in order to find our way back to camp. Not one of them had children, so they didn't know what it felt like to give birth the old-fashioned way, in a regular bed without an IV, a beeping monitor, or so much as an aspirin. Then, two years later, to *choose* to do it that same way again.

They didn't know me at all. Because I hadn't let them.

"I'm good," I told her, and she turned back toward the windshield and the witchlike arms of trees reaching for us out of the headlights.

Jill didn't seem scared, though, and neither did Andrea or Linda. More like curious, excited, and alert. I wanted to prove to these women they were *definitely* my people and I, theirs.

"Let's just think about this for a second," Linda said, her voice steady. "Let's just stop right here and get our bearings before we run out of gas."

She stepped on the brakes right there—no need to pull over and let the traffic go by, because there wasn't going to be any traffic, ever—took her hands from the steering wheel, and turned off the ignition. Without branches passing by the windows or the constant sound of grass and weeds whipping by underneath us, we could have been anywhere. Visibility was so absent we could have been crouched in a cave or floating in the vastness of outer space.

"We could sleep in the Jeep," Andrea said, her voice chipper. "Find our way back in the morning."

"No *way*," Linda said. "We paid for that trailer and we're sleeping in it."

Drummond's unknowable darkness closed in, but the emptiness of it wasn't frightening to me, it was intoxicating. A month before I'd read in the newspaper that NASA had lost contact with its Mars Observer. The space probe had been on a one-year interplanetary cruise and only three days from reentry when it disappeared. I pictured it without power, locked out of orbit and catapulting through space.

Next, I remembered visiting Mammoth Cave with my family as a kid, and how when we were as far down into the earth as the tour went, our guide had switched off the overhead lights. Inside that darkness my little girl's body felt like both nothing and everything at the same time. The only sounds were the dripping of cave water and my mother's soft breathing.

Being in the blackness of Drummond Island felt just like that. It was damp and chilly, and the only sounds were the *tick, tick, tick* of the engine cooling down and the soft exhales of my companions.

I wasn't only someone's daughter, someone's wife, or even someone's mother anymore. I was a person in my own right, a woman who had real friends now, a woman who was part of a silent, woodsy sisterhood. The even breaths I heard going in and out sounded like they were coming from something bigger, something older, than four sets of young female lungs. That night, for those few moments, they could have been coming from the earth itself. Like my mother's had, from inside that dark cave.

Just then there was a rustling in the leaves. Perhaps it was a trick of the dark, but the sound seemed big and only inches from the outside of the Jeep. *Bear?* I reached in my jacket pocket for my camera. If Linda turned her headlights back on, even without a flash there might have been enough light for a picture. But my pocket was empty, and I had the sudden image of the camera I'd just *had* to have, sitting right where I'd forgotten it. On the gold-speckled table back inside our trailer.

The rustling might have been a bear or maybe even a wolf, but I'd spent enough time outside in the woods at night to know everything sounded bigger in the dark.

The mystery of something wild and alive in those woods was still thrilling. I'd found a sense of what I'd been craving—real wildness—and whether I could get a photograph of it or not, I felt a surge of ferocity I wanted to capture and take with me when we went back home. It was a primal vibration resonating beyond expensive bar tabs, past men-only fishing camps, and deep into the island that was just the four of us.

I thought about my husband and how he hadn't wanted me to go and how he was back home, sleeping alone. I thought about my sons. At that moment they'd be sleeping in their beds, too. I thought about the cozy log cabin and the clean lakeside hotel room I'd once imagined, before ever setting foot on the island. Then I pictured Frank's old travel trailer parked on a square of gravel with the plastic lawn chairs we'd arranged in a half circle nearby. And I longed for them. I longed for the chairs and the bare light-bulb in the trailer's galley kitchen, and the teeny bathroom with the chipped plastic accordion door, and the bedsheets that smelled like cigar smoke and mothballs.

"I say we just keep going," I said, offering up my first real suggestion of the weekend.

"Works for me," Jill said.

It wasn't a particularly brilliant idea; it was just the obvious choice and the only way we'd ever get back to Frank's before daylight. But it would still become our motto. Continued motion—sometimes even paced and steady, other times hell-bent—would be the operating mode on all our future trips to Drummond Island. But it would guide our mainland lives, too. Our sisterhood would grow; four more women, including Bev, would join us on our annual sojourn north, and no matter what fate put in our way, we'd travel in one direction: forward.

Linda said she thought we might be somewhere near the center of the island, and she started the Jeep, put her foot on the gas, and a few minutes later we spied a diamond-shaped light blinking in the distance. It was slim and bright, its shape reminding me of wolf's eyes, but it couldn't be that. It was too high up, too big, and was going off and on in a reassuring rhythm.

Linda was the one who figured out what it actually was. The

beacon of the DeTour Reef Light, the old lighthouse anchored in the St. Marys River, not far from the ferry dock. Which meant we weren't in the center of the island after all; we were out on its southern claw and no more than four or five miles from Frank's.

It must have been after 4:00 a.m. when we pulled down his driveway. The light in the front window of his house was still on, and a face appeared in the glow. We knew it was his by the pine-cone of a nose practically pressed against the frosty glass. The light clicked off as we drove by.

Linda parked next to our trailer, her headlights passing over the lawn chairs, the awning, a square planter of fall flowers, a log picnic table I hadn't even noticed before, then illuminated the steps leading up to the door. I had to duck my head down a little when we entered. The thrill of braving the night woods faded into exhaustion and once we walked inside I felt a collective sigh exit our bodies as one breath.

The next morning, Jill made an absorption-platter breakfast using groceries we'd packed in the cooler with the beer and brought along with us. Eggs, green peppers, shredded potatoes, cheddar cheese, and ham all cooked together in a cast-iron pan. We ate outside on the picnic table, all of us wearing souvenir sweatshirts over our pajamas. We'd shopped for them the day before—I couldn't afford the expensive one with the zipper and the hood and had bought a simple gray pullover instead, but on my chest it still read, "Drummond Island, Gem of the Huron."

"Clear your head!" Andrea had hollered before we'd even left town.

It wasn't possible she'd offered that advice to me only forty-eight hours before, was it?

So much had happened since then. And yet, when we drove back over the bridge, when I completed my reentry to earth and my husband asked me what we'd done on the island, I already knew that no matter what I told him, it would seem insufficient.

Found a fossil? Downed shots of Pucker at a bar? Drove around in the woods? Ate breakfast outside? None of those activities sounded life changing yet my head felt clearer than it had in years.

The sun was out and shined its thin and vernal light upon us, reflecting off our waxy paper plates. We ate fast so our eggs wouldn't get cold. When we were finished, Jill's voice turned serious and she said she wanted to ask us something.

I thought of those dirty pickup trucks, of everything that remained unspoken the second time she'd said, "I'm married," and I braced myself. I was certain she was going to ask for some advice on her marriage. Dark woods didn't frighten me, but that did. She was my friend now, I was the only other one of the girls who was married, and yet I had no advice to give her.

"Can we come back here?" she asked. "I mean, I don't just *want* to come back next year. I *need* to come back."

Jill hadn't wanted advice, she'd wanted a promise.

None of us could predict what was going to happen in our lives between now and next October, she explained. Maybe she'd decide she wanted a baby. Maybe Linda would move in with her boyfriend, Kenny. Maybe Andrea would get married to her boyfriend, Steve. Maybe I'd get one of the stories I was always working on published. The island didn't care about anything that happened on the other side of the bridge, Jill said. The island cared about us, when we were on it together.

"Can we all promise, right now, that we're coming back next year?" Jill asked, looking around the table at each of us.

Can I promise? I thought. *Does a wolf shit in the woods?*

I thought of my husband, and his irritation at both my presence on the island and my tendency to overthink everything, and worked out next fall's scenario. I'd start saving my money as soon as we got home. I'd get a black permanent marker and X out "Drummond Island, 1994" on the calendar. Starting in September, I'd make a bunch of dinners ahead of time and freeze them so my family would have healthy meals to eat while I was gone. And I'd make sure I had enough money to buy the more expensive disposable camera. The one with the flash.

I'd had the impulse to shriek, "Yes! Yes, I can promise you!" To get up and hug Jill, slap Linda on the back, high-five Andrea, and run around the table in my bunny slippers.

"I don't know about the rest of you," I said, faking a yawn, "but I'd probably go."

In or not, I didn't want them to know how desperate I'd been for friends. If there was anything that marked you as a sissy la-la, it was desperation.

All three of them looked at me, tried to keep a straight face, but then started giggling. They'd seen right through my act—that's what happened when you had friends. They knew the real you, let you be yourself, but called you out on it sometimes, too.

"We're not just coming back next year," Linda said. "We're coming back *every* year."

"Unless we're pregnant," Jill added.

"Or dead," Andrea said.

We'd all laughed out loud at that. On the outside, we were adults; but on the inside, we really were just girls back then. And girls were immortal. Death wasn't real for people like us; it was a punch line.

"We're the Drummond Girls now," Andrea said, extending a clenched fist. It was the first of several such gestures, rituals even, that she would originate. We all touched her fist with our own, and that's how our pact was made. On a Sunday morning in October 1993, sitting outside on Frank's wobbly picnic table, under an endlessly clear sky and within sight of the million-dollar view we'd paid fifty-five dollars for, it was decided. The four of us would come back to Drummond Island together every year on the first weekend in October unless we were either pregnant or dead.

Of all the possibilities fate might decide to heave in our direction, those were the only two we could imagine keeping us away.

CHAPTER TWO   *1995*

Bev and me, exploring Drummond Island's eastern shore
sometime in the 1990s.

Who can predict the circumstances required for a new friendship to begin? The next two years passed for the Drummond Girls uneventfully—no babies, no weddings, no publication, nothing out of the ordinary at all.

Then I met Bev.

It was just another night shift at Peegeo's when Bev's trajectory crossed with mine. The pact between Linda, Andrea, Jill, and me had stuck and in less than a month I'd be making my third trip to Drummond Island. I needed to make some extra money so I'd offered to be first in, which meant covering the bar (and keeping the tips) until a bartender arrived. I'd just punched in and there she was: blond, skinny, wearing a dress with big abstract splotches, and perched on a barstool like a tropical bird. Beverly Cynthia Mary Marsha Wojciechowski (pronounced, I'd learn soon enough, like *where's your house key*).

"Bud Light draft is a dollar nine, right?" she'd said, pushing a procession of coins my way with a bony index finger.

An exchange of money and conversation over a blue Formica bar now seems as likely a place as any other to meet your best friend. Like me, Bev lived only a few miles from Peegeo's. She was a frequent customer, and while I'd seen her often, I had never really talked to her before that night.

She may have forgotten much of this now, I don't know, but I remember how, over that border of blue, we shared the details of our lives.

I was married with young children; she was divorced with grown children. I worked nights as a bartender and waitress; she worked days as a legal secretary. I'd gone to college after high school; she'd gone to Texas after her divorce. I was thirty-three; she was fifty-one.

"You're a Sagittarius, aren't you?" she'd asked me.

I didn't put much stock in astrology, yet was impressed she'd guessed me right on her first try.

"Me, too!" she'd said, slapping the bar in triumph. "We're *exactly* alike."

It would be months before I would reveal this to Bev, but before I met her I'd felt a bit friend incompetent. Linda, Andrea, and Jill were solidly in my life, yet it was still my way to keep everyone, even the three of them, at a distance. There were reasons for that, blips I thought of as unavoidable grooves worn into the friend-making receptors in my brain.

My family had moved around a lot when I was growing up—every year, in fact, for one long stretch—so all of my early friendships had been temporary. Colleen, Doreen, Joleen; Carrie, Mary, Sherry—my childhood friends had blended into a hazy summer carousel of braids, cutoff jeans, and banana-seat bicycles. In junior high I was so inseparable from Mike (neighbor girl who shunned the glam of "Michele") that instead of knocking on her front door,

I'd stand inside her open garage and call out her name. I was a year older than she was, which matters when you are twelve and thirteen, and high school eased us apart.

As a freshman, I was skinny and shy, but by senior year I was a tall, curvy, wide-eyed floater with fashionably feathered hair and a love of books. I studied in the library with the brains; made varsity in two sports with the jocks; talked boys, music, and clothes with a few of the popular girls; snuck beers with the partiers and joints with the burnouts. I let anyone who wanted to copy off my test papers and was certain I fit in everywhere.

Then one Saturday night the most popular of the popular girls arranged a sleepover to confront an unacceptable person in their midst. I was thrilled to be invited. I remember feeling mystified by the gathering, yet mindlessly in favor of it, too. I can still smell the Aqua Net Super Hold in that cavernous bedroom. Casey Kasem was counting down to the number one song of 1980. He announced what it was with great fanfare—"Call Me" by Blondie—just as my own life bottomed out. Because—*psych!*— I actually fit in nowhere. It was me; I was the unacceptable one. Too selfish, they said, too self-involved, and I lived too much in my head.

As Debbie Harry's voice raged from a boom box, those girls told me I didn't know how to be a friend. The tiny table the radio sat on had looked so perfect, even if it was just two milk crates draped with a musty lace tablecloth. The girls I'd thought were my best friends would not be calling me anymore. I called my mom instead to come and pick me up. I'd changed my mind, I'd told her over the phone, and wouldn't be spending the night after all. My kind and lovely mother had been a popular girl, too, and so even in the disguising dark of our family's Oldsmobile, I'd felt too ashamed to tell her what had happened.

Those girls would befriend me again, I'd act as if nothing had happened, yet all through college, then after I'd rented my first apartment, even after marriage, babies, and jobs, because of that sleepover I still believed the part of me that made friends was defective.

That's what being included on the Drummond trips had meant to me. Acceptance. Not in spite of who I was, but because of it. Linda, Andrea, and Jill had given that gift to me. By the time I met Bev, I was ready to let someone else in. I had my Drummond Girls, and I had Bev; the two were separate, but that didn't matter. I had *friends*.

Weeks before we were to leave for Drummond that year, Andrea's boyfriend proposed and she'd said yes. She planned her own all-girl celebration, and I can still hear the surprise in her voice the night she asked me, "You brought your *kid* to my *bachelorette*?"

I was then, and still am, an obsessively devoted mother. Besides the Drummond trips and my shifts at Peegeo's, when my sons were young I was always, always with them. I had a journalism degree and probably could have worked during the day at a magazine or a newspaper, but I'd taken on some contract editing assignments and continued to waitress at night instead. My boys may have handled hours in day care just fine, but *I* would not have survived it.

That does not mean I was nutty enough to bring a three- or a five-year-old to a Drummond Girl's bachelorette party. To Andrea's credit, I did have my arm around someone. He was thin, much smaller than me, and I held him protectively against my hip.

Had Bev been the one who'd first thought of Earl? She hardly knew Andrea then and so wouldn't have been invited to the party. And yet, probably she had thought of him. It was just the kind of thing she loved. Funny, goofy, attention-getting, and a little bit lewd.

It was a Saturday in August, late, and already dark outside as my guest and I rounded the corner of the porch at T.C. Traders. Andrea had left Peegeo's for a job at the nautically themed restaurant, hoping to make more money, and inside a dozen people were already celebrating. T.C. Traders had closed for her bachelorette party, and the front door was locked when I'd arrived. Pounding on the porthole hadn't worked, and my date and I were just heading for a side door when Andrea appeared.

"Definitely not cool," she'd said, eyeing my dual outline.

Among Andrea's other friends—and as the life of any party, she had many—I was the only one with young children. Although motherhood was a big part of my life, I'm still not sure I would have considered it my defining characteristic. Andrea did. In her mind, even standing on that porch at 10:00 p.m., dressed in a short red romper dress and high-heeled sandals was not enough to remove me from that role. No matter the location or circumstance, if someone four feet tall was accompanying me, it had to be one of my sons.

I walked my companion toward the brass entry light and waited for her exasperation to morph into a full-face grin. Because my date had not come from my womb; he'd come from my wallet. "He" was a vinyl blow-up doll wearing nothing but inked-on curls of black chest hair and a gold lamé G-string.

"Andrea, meet…um…," I said, thrusting his weightless body forward. I'd bought him but had forgotten to name him.

Andrea squinted, pursed her lips, and cocked her head to the side.

"Earl," she declared. "You are definitely an Earl."

Andrea wasn't a large woman; she was slight and fine boned. Her laugh was full-throated, though, like a big wave capable of engulfing everything in its path. When I'd presented her gift, one of those laughs rolled out of her body, off that porch, and drifted into the night. She grabbed Earl's free hand and pushed the restaurant's heavy door open. Rock music thumped from speakers near the bar, I heard the sound of happy women celebrating, but just for a second, the three of us stood there, awash in the pale light.

My Lee Jeans, beer T-shirt, no makeup, hiking boot–wearing friend was a bride-to-be. And in that moment, she'd been transformed. For one thing, she had on mascara (*mascara!*), but it was more than just that. It wasn't the ruffled blouse or the tight flowered miniskirt or even the nylons that made her seem so different. It was how she carried herself, how she moved, the proud set of her shoulders.

Usually so boyish, for the first time ever Andrea seemed not like a girl at all but a grown-up woman.

The moment lasted for only a second, but I knew even then I'd remember it later. Even though she was years younger than me, when we were together I'd often catch myself admiring her "jump first, look later" attitude. And the way she managed to remain unscathed by the consequences. When you were her, there never seemed to be any.

Other times, though, I'd feel maternal toward her, and now that she was getting married, I hoped she would escape making the same mistakes I had. In love at least. My marriage had started out fine, then faltered into disappointment. My husband never seemed happy and spent most of his free time sleeping. And I'd grown tired of asking him what was wrong.

I knew growing up when I saw it. And felt lucky to have been standing on that porch with Andrea when it happened to her. That the other witness had been a male blow-up doll wearing a perpetually surprised expression and pair of underwear appropriate for a traveling male stripper did not take away from the tenderness of the moment.

"Earl is one lucky man," I told her, meaning it, before the three of us walked the gangplank into T.C. Traders, the door swinging closed behind us.

*   *   *

Buying Earl was so out of character for me, he had to have
been Bev's idea. I told her everything back then, and even though
I was thirty-three and not thirteen, by the end of that summer, my friendship with her reminded me a lot of the one I'd
had all those years ago with Mike. I didn't stand in Bev's garage
and holler her name—Bev lived in an apartment; she didn't even
have a garage. But I had no qualms about showing up unannounced for no other reason than I simply enjoyed her company. She was enough older than me that I often considered her
life a kind of preview for mine, and I liked what I saw. Bev was
proof you could be a mom and be middle-aged, yet also be vibrant
and fun.

Andrea and Bev's friendship would come later, though Earl was
just the kind of wacky gag she might have suggested. I do know I
was scheduled to work at Peegeo's the night of Andrea's party, so
I knew I'd be late getting there. My plan was to compensate by
making a big entrance with a funny gift. It was probably Bev who
told me about Traverse City's erotic lingerie store, Ravissant. They
had just what I was looking for—a four-foot Partyboy Doll who
could be mine for $28.95 plus tax.

In 1995, Bev was single, worked as a legal secretary, and her
children were grown so she had no one to provide for but herself.
She was frugal, but that kind of expenditure may not have seemed
all that prohibitive to her. I was a waitress with two young children. My average tip was five dollars a table, so for me, Partyboy
was expensive—the equivalent of waiting on at least six tables.
Money I could have used to buy groceries, gas, or put toward our
electric bill.

I held up the box and pictured myself walking into Andrea's
party with it. In this daydream a hush fell over the room and
Andrea shrieked with laughter and gave me a hug. She also tossed
all her other gifts aside the second she saw mine. Her other friends

might have been on time for the festivities, but they'd also wished they'd been clever enough to think of a blow-up doll.

Bev may have been vaguely aware of my insecurities where friends were concerned, though I'd never confided the reason. The right time for such a conversation had never presented itself. When you were a grown woman, how exactly did you say to another grown woman, "I'm really glad you've agreed to be my best friend because I haven't had one since I was thirteen"? You just didn't.

It was strange, I'll admit, to be surrounded by garter belts, velvet blindfolds, and vibrating harnesses, yet engaged in a fantasy not about my husband, not about any man, but about making points in a platonic friendship instead.

I didn't care. I pulled out my waitress bankroll, peeled off thirty one-dollar bills, dug around in the bottom of my purse for some change, and bought Earl. Later I decided not to wrap him up, but to have him arrive on my arm instead, fully inflated and wearing the G-string.

Once Andrea, Earl, and I were inside T.C. Traders, she introduced us to the dozen other women she'd invited to the party, then hooked her finger into the elastic of Earl's underwear, stretched it away from his abdomen, and looked down.

Earl was the economy model—no bells, no whistle.

"So tell us," Andrea probed, a talk show hostess now, playing it for laughs, all drama and fake sympathy. "Do you ever get that 'something's missing' feeling?"

Bev was at home, Linda was out of town, and so except for Jill and the bride-to-be, all the other women at the party were strangers to me. But funny was funny. One woman spilled her drink and another yelled, with admiration, "Who *brought* that?"

We left T.C. Traders soon after, all of us and Earl packed inside an RV. Although Andrea's parents were helping her pay for her wedding, she and her fiancé, Steve, were still on a tight budget.

The vehicle she'd hired to convey us from bar to bar wasn't the kind of RV you saw in television commercials or gleaming on the show floor of a camping expo. It was a bus. I don't mean it was big like a bus or boxy like a bus, I mean it was an *actual* bus. An old Blue Bird school bus its mullet-haired driver had gutted, outfitted with camper seats, spray-painted a splotchy blue, then stenciled with fauna native to the Northern Hemisphere. Canada geese in flight, deer with ridiculously large antlers, black bears standing on hind legs.

The rear windows and the emergency exit underneath them were blacked out, and a bumper sticker offered this advice to tailgaters: "Don't Laugh, Mister, Your Daughter Might Be in Here."

Andrea had been in love with Steve for as long as I'd known her. They'd met when she waited on him and some of his friends. It was an instant sense of like between them that had quickly turned into love. She hadn't dated anyone else since, and she said she did not want to memorialize the end of her single life by seeing some oiled-up stranger half-naked. She'd made both Jill and me promise: no stripper. She thought they were creepy, not sexy.

Jill might have been disappointed. I acted like I was but inside felt only relief.

I didn't have much experience with the opposite sex. When other girls my age started dating, I was still playing kick the can, streetball, and building forts in the woods with the neighborhood boys. Even my best girlfriend, Mike, went by a boy's name. I'd married a man I'd met when I was only nineteen. Just the idea of a male stripper gave me a shuddery feeling, the same sensation that came over me whenever I'd left a chicken breast in the refrigerator too long.

Earl, however, was safe. Nothing could have made him sexy, but he sure made those women I didn't know funny.

Who blew up the skinny yellow balloon and stuck it into Earl's G-string? I don't remember. Did one of Andrea's friends just happen to have a balloon stashed with her cigarettes, lighter, and lipstick inside her night-out purse? If not, what was a balloon a parade clown might use to twist into a wiener dog doing inside that crazy bus?

As the driver careened through town, those women fondled Earl's dachshund in a display much cruder than anything they would have attempted with a real live stripper. Andrea had indeed ignored her other presents after I'd presented her with Earl, and after each place we stopped, he'd become more infused with our group. By the end of the night, Earl was simply one of us. A foil to our exaggerated laughs, a silent participant to our elaborate toasts, a dance partner for our bumps and grinds.

If he had been Bev's idea, he was a good one.

Even though she wouldn't have known the other women along, either, she must have known a fake man in a sagging G-string would be silly fun for anyone. What no one could have anticipated was how other people would react to him.

"What's with the fag?" some guy in jeans and a rodeo belt buckle wanted to know.

"You're an idiot," Jill told him, putting her face aggressively close to his until he walked away.

"Baby, I been lookin' for you all night," said a middle-aged red-head, inside Traverse City's only dance bar.

Both reactions had fascinated me. Socializing in large groups with people I didn't know did not come naturally to me, so I concentrated on observing people instead of obsessing over my own awkwardness. Today, I'm more comfortable with it, but that night I said little—easy to manage when the music is loud enough to erase the history of human speech—and instead watched how strangers reacted to Earl.

An idea began to form. I put my hand on Andrea's shoulder

and decided to share it with her. "Earl should go to Drummond," I yelled over the music.

She stopped moving in her chair for a second, looked at me, and her eyes grew wide. Then she hurried out onto the dance floor. The redhead protested when Andrea yanked Earl away, but the house lights went up soon after, and the music was turned off. Even in my temporary deafness, I registered a sound.

Andrea had popped open the valve on Earl's back. We both massaged him, and once he was deflated, she packed him away in her purse.

A week later, Andrea was standing up straight, sober and lovely at the front of the church. Her alabaster dress contrasted with her black head of curls above, and what was easily a good half acre of red carpeting below. The dress had been her mother's, and she looked stunning in it. I'd already seen it once—at the seamstress's house for her final fitting—but it sure hadn't looked like this. Regal, tight, perfect. "Something old *and* something borrowed," she'd said, proud of her own practicality.

The pews inside Christ the King had filled with guests; then Jill and three other women from the bachelorette party lined up along the communion rail, beaming as Andrea and Steve prepared to take their vows. Jill was the maid of honor, and she and the other bridesmaids wore strapless black dresses, heavy black gloves stretching all the way to their elbows, and white pearl chokers.

I'd arranged a babysitter for our two boys; the wedding was like a date for my husband and me, and we were seated in a pew near the front. He had a fresh haircut and looked so handsome in his pressed white shirt. Then the bridesmaids turned sideways, angling their bodies toward Andrea, and he caught sight of their shoulder tattoos. There was a butterfly on one shoulder, a half-naked Tinker Bell on another, and a long-stem rose with several of its petals detaching on a third. Next to me, I felt him stiffen.

When I looked over at him again, he didn't look quite so handsome anymore.

"Carny rats," he griped under his breath, scowling.

Exceptions were made for war veterans, but otherwise he didn't think much of people who had tattoos. Duty, he understood. Female emotion expressed with a needle and permanent ink, he did not. I just hoped none of my friends had heard him.

There were all sorts of people he dismissed—country music fans, cigarette smokers, Republicans, hunters, fishermen, high school dropouts, heavy metal music fans. His prejudices were so specific I shared none of them and at the sight of those tattoos only remember thinking, *Something blue!*

Philosophical differences like this between my husband and me always seemed to present themselves on special occasions. Was it okay to watch football and eat Thanksgiving dinner at the same time? (Him—no; me—yes.) Should our children be able to pick what they wanted to wear on school picture day? Even if that meant a pajama shirt with their favorite superhero on it? (Him—no; me—yes.) Was it okay for him to arrive stoned at my family's annual Fourth of July gathering, just so he could endure all that togetherness? (Him—yes; me—no, no, please, God, no.)

As usual, when he grumbled too loud at Andrea's wedding, I sat quietly next to him, not wanting to cause a scene. The church lights made Andrea and her bridesmaids glow, and I focused on that instead. Later, Andrea would confess she and the other women weren't exactly radiant; they were perspiring like wrestlers in the ring. Being surrounded by carpet, velvet, and satin on a humid August afternoon had made them so overheated that all during the ceremony a river of sweat had cascaded from their foreheads, down between their boobs, and trickled all the way to their knees.

Sitting in the third pew back, all I saw was beauty, happiness, and skin decorated with tiny blue wings and blue flower petals floating on a blue breeze.

At the reception, I was in charge of the guestbook and made sure everyone signed, even the popular DJ hired to play dance music. The guestbook from my own wedding had been a strange net-wrapped contraption created from two pieces of glass by an artist friend of my husband's. Our guests took one look at its sharp edges and were afraid to touch it, let alone sign their names. No real record existed of who came to my wedding, and I vowed Andrea and Steve would not suffer the same fate.

The next day, they drove to New York City for their honeymoon, by way of Canada and Niagara Falls. Neither of them had been out of the country before and had no idea what to expect at a border crossing. After they came home, Andrea told us what happened when Steve pulled up to the Canadian line.

A guard in full regalia approached their car, bent at the waist, and peered into their window, his nose barely an inch from Steve's startled face.

"Citizenship?" the guard barked.

In Andrea's retelling, Steve stared straight ahead. "Yup!" he confidently replied.

She heard the assurance in her new husband's voice and a great rush of love plunged through her. When she met the officer's eyes, though, a giggle attack took over, along with a urinary close call.

"That'd be a great one to tell our kids someday, huh?" she'd said, imagining the headline: "Bride Pees at Border Crossing, Causes International Incident."

The officer had wanted to know what country Steve belonged to, not whether he belonged to one at all.

"The United States of Andrea" is how he could have answered, because he belonged to my friend now.

*   *   *

While Andrea was away on her honeymoon, Linda was busy making final plans for our third trip to Drummond. Our departure date was in less than a month, and she called Frank, finalized our trailer reservations, checked on the price of gas ($1.20 a gallon), and watched grocery store fliers for a sale on ground chuck. Sloppy joes were easy, filling, traveled well, and Linda had her own secret recipe.

By cooking some of our own food instead of always eating out, we'd saved enough money on our two previous trips to carry a balance from year to year. It was only thirty or forty dollars, but Linda deposited it into her savings account, where it made a couple bucks interest and was waiting for us when we needed it. Having a little something in the kitty before we even left town bolstered our pact and gave our trip an added sense of continuation.

"Have you talked to Jill?" Linda asked me one night at work.

"Not since Andrea's wedding," I told her.

Jill and her husband, Marty, had rented a house, moved to a neighboring town, and she'd left Peegeo's to work at the Hoffbrau, a bar closer to their new place.

"I ran into her in Kmart," Linda said, "and it doesn't look good."

It was the end of the night when Linda told me that, and we were working through our cleanup list. We were both in the kitchen and I had a dozen ketchup bottles stacked and balanced, mouth to mouth, "marrying" the contents. The caps soaked in a dish of piping hot water while the red paste dripped from the bottle on top into the bottle on the bottom.

Jill and Marty were not doing well, and although she assured Linda she was still planning to go to Drummond—she needed the trip more than ever, in fact—the encounter worried Linda. She was concerned about Jill, but also about our trip's finances.

Since the beginning, she'd budgeted our money as carefully as she could, but even with her knack for money management, the only way for us to afford everything—gas, groceries, the bridge toll, the ferry, two nights in the trailers, and our bar tabs—was if all four of us went on the trip and paid our share. If anyone dropped out, or couldn't come up with the full amount, it would put our whole trip in jeopardy.

I was worried for Jill, too, yet still never above indulging in a little overthinking.

"Was that why you first invited me along, for the *money*?"

"Yeah," Linda said, "partly."

Something in me knew that was going to be her answer—Linda didn't lie, ever, not even to spare someone's feelings—but the easy way she'd agreed still landed in my gut with a sickening thud. I couldn't fault her for telling me the truth; it was one of the things I admired about her, yet I was glad I hadn't asked her back then. It would have devastated me. It caused a twinge even now, after we'd become close friends.

"Why can't things just stay the way they are?" Linda said then, oblivious to how her answer had affected me. "Why can't everyone in my little world just agree for five frickin' minutes to keep their shit the same?"

After we'd finished our cleanup, after all our customers had cashed out, after we counted our tips and took off our waitress aprons, we sat down at a table in the empty dining room with tubs of clean silverware hot from the dishwasher.

A new government regulation said that for hygienic reasons, a restaurant's silverware had to be wrapped in a napkin. That meant an extra hour tacked on to the end of our shifts. The rule at Peegeo's was that waitresses would be paid regular wages for the hour if you weren't drinking while you rolled; if you had a cocktail in front of you, you rolled for free. Linda sometimes grabbed a Scotch first, sometimes not; it depended upon how stressful her night had been. I needed the money so bad that I always rolled dry.

With Linda sitting across from me, I opened a napkin, smoothed it flat, laid a knife down in the center, balanced a fork on top, rolled the implements up tight, and wrapped a self-sticking strip of colored paper around the bundle. The new regulation was different, but it wasn't the kind of change Linda was talking about when she said she wished everything would stay the same. She was talking about Jill and her husband.

Linda worked constantly at adjusting the variables in her life until everything was exactly the way she wanted it. I'd always supposed that her attachment to the familiar was just who she was and how she was raised. Besides the time her dad was posted overseas, Linda had lived in the same house with her parents from infancy through high school. Waitresses and bartenders were known to job-hop, but she'd worked at Peegeo's, in the same position with the same schedule, for eight years. When we went to the island, we went the same weekend, stayed in the same place, did the same things. She didn't like change and went to great pains to avoid it.

When I was growing up, my family had moved six times before I was eleven years old. I'd hated it. Yet as an adult, I hadn't become any more predictable or stationary. By the time Linda hired me, I'd attended three colleges, lived in five states, and had worked for wages at everything from newspaper reporter to seamstress to tree planter. Change had become something I didn't mind all that much, and yet when it came to our annual Drummond trip, the consistency of it was comforting.

Everything in my life that was supposed to be secure, most notably my marriage and my finances, felt unpredictable. My weekend away with the girls had started out as just a chance to party without interference from anyone, an opportunity to go somewhere to escape our responsibilities for a little while. But it gave me something to look forward to, and had begun to feel more stable and certain than any other part of my life.

I say we just keep going had been my advice to the girls that first year when we'd become lost in Drummond's dark woods.

By 1995, I'd started to feel lost inside my own life, and yet had somehow kept going, kept working, kept mothering, and stayed married. I wasn't aware of all that then, but I still knew Linda was right. We needed to do something to make sure our trip wouldn't collapse if someone's personal life did.

In those few weeks between Andrea's wedding and our departure for Drummond, something unexpected happened. Our boss, George, fell in love with his new girlfriend. His googly eyes whenever he looked at her made me feel even more cynical about my own relationship with my husband, but surprisingly it was Linda who withheld judgment and instead observed him with interest.

George smiled when he came to work, even if the day waitress was late. He smiled when the prep cook called in sick. He smiled if an ornery customer complained about something ridiculous. Say, a pizza with too much cheese or a bar crowd that was laughing too loud and having too much fun. He let a few of the people he'd once banned from Peegeo's for their bad behavior back in his good graces. Even, for a while, Dan the ashtray hurler.

And—this was the real giveaway—he even smiled whenever Linda or I approached him during the Friday night dinner rush, saying, "I've got a little dilemma." Which was waitress code for "I really screwed up." (Considering that Peegeo's was such a small place, there sure were a lot of ways to err: Forget to put in a drink order. Illegible handwriting. Push the wrong button on the cash register. Bus your tables too slowly. Spill, drop, or break something. Trip.)

Even today, Linda and I both remember those charmed weeks fondly. George would fix our mistake or solve our problem, make a point of looking us kindly in the eye, and, in all seriousness, ask if there was anything else we needed. Anything at all.

No sarcasm, no ridicule; he'd actually seemed interested in our answer.

George had to be in love, we told each other; that or alien possession were the only possible explanations, and as far as we knew, no one had seen a spaceship. A few years prior, George had survived an ugly divorce; it had made him understandably bitter, and the fact that kindness and patience were becoming normal behavior for him was a miracle. The miracle's name was Susan.

I liked Susan well enough and was happy for George, but Peegeo's already had a set group of regulars. With Susan added to the mix, the late-night vibe of the place had shifted. It wasn't bad, it was just different and another change for Linda to rail against. It certainly never occurred to me that Susan's appearance in George's life would ever have anything at all to do with the longevity of our trip to the island. The ability to put those two things together was an example of why Linda was in charge of it and not one of the rest of us.

"We're doubling down on Drummond," she informed me one night.

Another hectic Friday had come and gone; another pyramid of wrapped silverware grew on the table between us.

"Whatever that means," I said, my voice weary from a full day with my sons, followed by nine hours of working the all-you-can-eat fish fry.

For those willing to wait in line for a table, their reward was a plate of deep-fried cod, steak fries, homemade coleslaw, a dinner roll, two pats of butter, and a pickle spear for only $5.99. The fish was (and still is) delicious, so an awful lot of people were willing to wait for it, and they lined up out the door and sometimes even down the front steps.

"You know, college girl," Linda said, lighting a cigarette and waving away the smoke. "Economies of scale."

She looked at me as if I should have known what those words

meant, but I didn't. Fiscal terms whizzed past my ears like deerflies someone carelessly let into the kitchen. After working the same shift I'd just endured, her eyes didn't look tired at all; instead, they'd gleamed. The same three words that had sounded boring and unfamiliar to me—*economies of scale*—hummed with potential for her. When it came to budgeting what little money any of us had for the trip back then, she was not only good at it, she even seemed to find it *fun*. No decision was too small not to have some research and thought put into it.

"A plan might not be shit," she'd told me once, "but *planning* is everything."

That sounded familiar, and while I was pretty sure I'd heard it somewhere before, I didn't know where. I've since looked it up. Dwight D. Eisenhower said it, without the cuss word, when asked to account for his successful invasion of Germany in WWII. When organizing four waitresses for a party weekend, Linda's strategy mirrored that of the supreme commander of the Allied forces (and our thirty-fourth president).

She explained it made sense to keep track of our expenses, since even though many of them were preset and beyond our control, they were also relatively constant. The distance from Peegeo's parking lot to Drummond Island (188 miles), the price of gas ($1.20 a gallon), the toll for the Mackinac Bridge ($1.25 per axle), the ticket for the car ferry (fourteen dollars), and the rent on Frank's trailer (fifty-five dollars a night). That year, the four of us had pledged $125 each to the kitty; fifty dollars more than what we'd needed in 1993, an increase Linda said would hopefully secure and even build on the amount we carried over from year to year.

I wished all of that had made sense to me, yet the truth was whenever talk turned to money, my concentration went somewhere else. Fiji maybe or Guam.

"Cost per unit?" Linda said, snapping her fingers in front of my face. "Hello? Anyone home?"

When I didn't respond with intelligent discourse or even an imbecilic nod, she made an effort to explain what economies of scale, cost per unit, and doubling down had to do with Drummond Island. If we invited additional women to go with us, she said, it would create a more robust kitty in relation to our fixed expenses. When I *still* didn't get it, she translated again.

"Eight girls can party harder on eight hundred dollars than four can on four hundred dollars."

That I understood. Even if Jill and Marty worked things out, that didn't mean our trip was safe from cancellation. Jill and Andrea were still in their twenties and someday soon, they probably were going to want to start a family. That might not take them out of the trip entirely, but they'd probably miss a year. "Pregnant or dead" had been a joke, but Drummond Island—at least, the way *we* did Drummond Island—was no place for a pregnant woman. Plus, something unforeseen or unavoidable might someday waylay one of us, too. With four more women, our trip would be better situated to withstand an unplanned absence.

Linda's obsession with money had often been the source of amusement. She used glass jars for budgeting big-ticket items— one for her car payment, another for firewood, a third for our trip, etc. Yet I had to admit, this time I was impressed by it.

When I looked around the restaurant and considered the other waitresses I worked with, I realized that all of them, me included, had financial problems. When you're paid in cash, often in one-dollar bills and handfuls of change, it spends pretty easily, often disappearing before you've realized where it went.

Linda made her money the same way I did, yet she had just bought a used Ford Explorer, only a couple years old and with no rust; financed a new bedroom set and paid it off early; and probably had more in her savings account than Andrea, Jill, and me combined.

She didn't have a college degree in economics—she didn't

have a college degree in anything—and yet she knew more about money management than all those white-haired men who came on my TV and droned on and on about the deficit.

I imagined the dialogue if CNN interviewed her instead of them: "The dumbasses in government just need to get themselves some really big jars. Problem solved."

I grinned just thinking about it. My shyness was slowly disappearing, partly because it was a handicap for a waitress and partly because of my friendship with Linda, Andrea, and Jill. That and my growing closeness with Bev had given me some much-needed confidence and I actually liked the idea of doubling the number of women on our trip. It meant we'd have more money and I'd make new friends, but it meant something else, too. I wouldn't be the new girl anymore, a status unimaginable to me only two years before.

I watched as Linda set the last silverware roll on the pile and then took a sip of her Scotch. I tried to picture eight women up on the island together instead of just four and started to imagine who we'd invite. There would probably be a discussion, we'd each make suggestions (I'd suggest Bev for sure!), and then we'd take a vote. I wondered if any of the other women I knew, like the mothers of the children in my son's kindergarten class or a neighbor I'd recently become friendly with, would want to go along with us.

"Susan, Mary Lynn, Pam, and Bev," Linda said, putting her head back and exhaling a tidy line of cigarette smoke toward the ceiling.

"What?" I'd asked, confused yet again.

"That's who I'm inviting."

Since she'd included Bev, it was hard for me to be too irritated, but I still thought all four of us should have been in on the decision. I knew or knew of the three other women: Susan was George's girlfriend, Mary Lynn was a regular customer, and Pam was a bartender at a nice restaurant downtown.

Susan and Pam seemed like good choices—young, outgoing, and fun—but I couldn't figure out why Linda had chosen Mary Lynn. She and her husband had three grown children between them and they came into Peegeo's almost every weeknight for dinner; I'd waited on the two of them a lot and even grown to appreciate Mary Lynn's cranky sense of humor. But with her teddy bear sweatshirts and hunched posture, she'd seemed old. It wasn't just her age—Bev was a lot older than me but I didn't think of her as old—it was her mind-set. I just couldn't imagine Mary Lynn keeping up with the rest of us.

Neither Andrea nor Jill had any problem with Linda's decision, but the realization I wasn't going to have a say in choosing any of the new girls continued to grate on me. I couldn't argue with her planning or budgeting ability, but I had noticed a tendency in her to decide things for other people and then neglect to tell them about it until the last minute.

"Do *they* know they're going?" I'd asked her.

"Nope," she said happily. "But they will."

Only now do I understand how much thought and care Linda put in to her selections. It's not every woman who can hike, two-track, happily sleep in a trailer, and be willing and even proud to be known as a "girl" years after the literal definition applied. The eight of us, so different, would turn out to be amazingly well suited for not just our weekends up north, but for the lifelong friendship that resulted. Linda was the one who'd had a sense of that, even all those years ago.

The first year the four of us went to Drummond Island together had probably seemed like a novelty to the men in our lives. The second year had been tolerated. By the third year, not one of them was looking forward to October with the same gusto we girls were.

I'm not entirely sure how Marty or Steve felt, but neither

Linda's boyfriend nor my husband were in favor of us leaving town and doing who knows what, who knows where. As for George, he'd never objected in theory, but Linda and I were both strong waitresses, reliable and competent, and he didn't like having us both gone from work at the same time. Our men were one thing, George was another, and adding people to the trip wouldn't necessarily solve the problem. Unless they were the right people.

George was a hands-on boss, and I'd never met anyone who worked harder than he did. He arrived early and stayed late. He was smart, often generous, and sarcastically funny—most nights he'd have a running commentary on politics, NASCAR drivers, snowmobile trail grooming, and the foibles of customers' lives in a kind of one-man painfully observant floor show. He was also a stick of emotional dynamite and my condolences to the waitress or customer incompetent or unlucky enough to be in close range when he blew.

Linda understood George's mercurial nature. She knew it was difficult for him when both of us took the same weekend off. Peegeo's was a family. A dysfunctional family, but a family nonetheless. Even people in dysfunctional families want approval, and there was no more visible way to give ours to George's girlfriend than by inviting her to Drummond. Plus, how could he get irritated at us for leaving if Susan and some of his own customers were along with us?

Linda's mastery of organization, finance, and even human resources obscured the thing that should have surprised me. The woman who abhorred change, who worked the exact same schedule every week, who parked her car in the exact same spot, drank the same drink, smoked the same brand of cigarettes, wore the same hairstyle, and even sat at the same table to roll silverware after work, had voluntarily made the biggest change our trip would ever encounter.

*   *   *

"Say your good-byes, sisters, 'cause we're off like a bride's panties!"

I was pumped full of coffee but still sleepy and dawn was at least an hour away. As far as Andrea was concerned, that was no reason not to crank up the Metallica.

Up ahead, Susan, Mary Lynn, and Pam were riding with Linda in her new Ford. Inside the Chuck Truck, Andrea's name for her little Bronco II, were Bev, Jill, and me. For weeks I'd been so focused on the eight of us, how we'd get along with each other, whether the new girls would instantly love the island the way I had, I'd totally forgotten our possible ninth traveler.

Then when Andrea pulled into my driveway that morning, and I'd opened the hatch to toss in my duffel bag, there he was, inside a Ziploc freezer bag, flattened and folded with his feet near his ears. Earl had not only survived the final hours of Andrea's bachelorette party, he was resting comfortably for his ride.

Andrea always remembered things like that, enjoyed being the author of the grand gesture, whether that gesture was a fist bump or a blow-up doll. There was also a cooler of beer, two bags of Wild Berry Jell-O shots, a fifth of Popov, a bag of sour cream and onion potato chips, a deck of cards, a boom box, and a CD case bulging with hair metal packed in the back with him. Drummond was going to be epic.

I closed the back hatch and looked up the hill at my little white house. In order to squeeze every moment out of our three days off, Linda always had us leaving at what she referred to as "the ass crack of dawn." It was hours before my sons were due at the bus stop but they knew I was leaving and were already up. I'd given them breakfast and turned on cartoons but when I tried to wake my husband, he'd just mumbled something about there being no need for him to get out of bed that early. So there wasn't anyone seeing me off that year but our two dogs, and I remember their windshield wiper tails waving in unison behind the sliding glass door.

Wanting the good-bye to be different wouldn't make it so, and once we were on the road, I tried to forget about my husband, to stop wondering why the care and kindness once at the center of our marriage had faded, and instead allow the now familiar transformation inside of me to begin.

For the next three days there'd be no one's little hand to hold; no one to carry on my hip or hug; no one to criticize my housekeeping, fall asleep in front of the TV, then climb onto my body in the dark. For the next three days my body would belong only to me.

I leaned against Andrea's backseat and looked over at Bev. She was sitting as far forward on the seat as she could, staring out the windshield even though we'd barely left Grand Traverse County. Surely the scenery was familiar to her, yet I knew that kind of excitement. Like me on my first year, she'd never been to Drummond Island before, either, and she was filled with anticipation, wanting to catch sight of the place as soon as she could.

"Are there any decent-looking guys up there?" she'd asked.

I cringed.

"*What?*" Andrea squawked. "No, there aren't. Well, I don't know. Maybe there are. But that's not why you came...is it?"

"No," Bev answered. "Jeez, I was just asking."

Over the years, our relationship statuses would change, then change again, but that year Bev was the only one of us who was single. She and her boyfriend had just broken up, though even while she'd been dating him, men were a constant source of amusement and interest to her. Big or small, old or young, in suits or coveralls, it didn't matter. Bev liked them and they liked her. She also liked to travel, so I knew she hadn't agreed to go with us specifically to meet men. Bev was just being Bev. Her interest in men wasn't calculating, it was just innocent fun. Sometimes, though, her enthusiasm could be misunderstood.

Now that there were eight of us instead of just four, and now that we didn't all see each other regularly at Peegeo's, Linda scheduled a planning meeting a week before we left. She told her boyfriend, Kenny, he had to find something to do away from home for a couple hours; we all met at her house, and she handed out our assignments.

Ground chuck did go on sale, and Linda said she would bring her sloppy joes, already cooked, and ready to be heated up when we were hungry. Andrea was to bring hamburger buns; I'd bring coffee, bagels, and cream cheese; and Jill would bring the rest of the breakfast food and a case of beer. The new girls had their assignments, too. Pam made homemade potato salad to go with the sloppy joes; Mary Lynn brought all of the ingredients for Bloody Marys; and Bev brought along two rolls of toilet paper, one for each car, in case we found ourselves stranded far from any facilities.

Linda wondered how we'd communicate with each other on the way up now that we'd be in two cars instead of just one, but Susan said she had the solution. Cell phones were nonexistent in 1995 and even car phones were still a novelty, but George had a set of walkie-talkies and Susan said she'd bring them along. That would be her contribution.

Her idea was a good one, but our execution of it left a little to be desired. We were so unaccustomed to having two cars that when we drove out of Peegeo's parking lot and headed for US 31 North, both handsets were still inside Linda's Explorer. An oversight none of us even noticed until we crossed the bridge and pulled into the parking lot of the Michigan Welcome Center in St. Ignace.

"You guys, wanna play a game?" Susan asked, handing me one of the handsets. "I've got an idea for something fun we can do with these things."

It was a variation on Twenty Questions, with our pasts as the unknowns to be guessed at. Susan explained that someone in one car would depress the talk button and describe something crazy, funny, illegal, or just plain strange someone in the car had done, and if not regretted, then at least felt lucky to have survived. The girls in the other car had a minute to discuss it together off the air, but then had to depress their talk button and guess who it had been. Only the first guess counted, though we wouldn't keep score, and there wasn't going to be a winner, because that wasn't the point. The game was just to pass the time, Susan said, have some fun, and get to know each other a little better.

"Who spent thirty days in jail for selling pot?"

"Who painted 'Class of 1980' on the roof of their high school the night before graduation?"

"Who got kicked out of a bar with her friends and retaliated by picking up the owner's sports car and leaning it against the front door?"

"Who was an archery company's pin-up girl, and did it for free?"

No one matched the right girl to any of the first three questions, but even back then we all knew immediately who had posed with a bow and arrow. Only Bev had the personality and the looks to pose like that, plus the naïveté to do it for free.

"Hey, I was really young then, it was my job, and I didn't know women could get paid for that kind of thing," she said.

The game lasted from St. Ignace until we lined up for the crossing in DeTour. Once on the ferry, a crewman directed us to park right next to each other and we took it as a good sign. Every crossing is different depending upon what kinds of vehicles are in line, whether there are any trucks or boat trailers or campers, and fate could have had us parked far apart. Incredibly, there was a tugboat docked near shore with the name *Linda Jean* painted in big black letters on the stern. Our own Linda shared that same middle name.

We unrolled our windows, talked back and forth, and Linda pointed out the lighthouse, the ferry dock on the Drummond side of the crossing, the size of the dolomite boulders, and the working limestone quarry. Not as ordinary landmarks, but as our own precious discoveries.

The view was becoming familiar to me by then, yet it never failed to excite my senses. As we approached Drummond's shore, a certain clear watery light that only ever shines in the north made the island appear to pulse and glow. A canopy of scarlet maples was surrounded by the ropy twists of weather-stunted cedar trees, and I watched the calm water lap over those man-sized rocks just offshore. They were smooth as skin and looked to me like ancient mermen, perpetually surfacing, their muscular and rounded backs breaking through the waves over and over again.

I nudged Bev. "There's your hot guys," I'd said, pointing.

"Where?" she asked, craning her neck to see, and I had to laugh at the sincerity of her effort.

Bev had seemed so cosmopolitan to me back then. She loved to travel and had been to Europe, the Caribbean, Latin America, and of course all over the United States. She was from Michigan, too, but had once lived in Houston, a city far larger than anyplace I'd ever lived. She had a relentless curiosity about the world and enjoyed telling me odd details about the places she'd been. That year it was fun for me to approach Drummond Island with her and be the one talking about a place I'd been before, and loved.

A thousand-foot Laker—one of the hundred or so freshwater-only commercial freighters that sailed the Great Lakes—rested a quarter mile to the north, waiting patiently just outside the channel for our ferry to cross.

"I used to see those when Scott and I drove up north together," she'd said, remembering a camping trip she'd taken with her boyfriend before they broke up. "I always wondered where they were from and where they were going."

Her boyfriend had been much younger than she was. I didn't know if the other girls knew about the reason for their breakup but Bev had confided in me that he was childless and often agonized about it. Bev was fifty-one, her son and daughter were both grown, and she'd been honest with him. If he wanted children, it wasn't going to be with her.

"Tell me something about the island," Bev said.

I told her that those bright red trees, and the forest they belonged to, sustained a rich world of wildlife, from birds to voles to bears, and there were more deer on the island than people. I told her that in a few minutes the sun would be overhead and if we were lucky, the freighter would pass by, and we'd be able to see her stern and read her name and her home port. It might be Chicago, but it might be Istanbul, too. And I told her she'd better eat something. Tonight we were going to the Northwoods and maybe to Chuck's Place, too, and while the wildness of Drummond looked pretty now, its mudholed roads and wavy horizon were hell on a hangover.

I reached in the back, rustled around, and put my hand on the bag of potato chips.

"Chip?" I asked her, my own mouth soon full of salt and grease.

She wrinkled her nose. "Too salty," she said.

I felt the motor of the ferry downshift as we approached. For the past three years it had felt like Drummond belonged only to the four of us. Even when times at home had been difficult during the rest of the year, having memories of the island made me feel rich in a way that was difficult to describe. It was as if we all possessed something or maybe just *knew* something or *felt* something you couldn't bag, box, or buy from any store, no matter how much money you had.

That feeling of reclaiming our wild selves wasn't for sale, not at any price, and yet there were four new women along who we were happy to share it with for free.

Well, not for *free*, free, but for $125 in any denomination, including coin-wrapped rolls of quarters and stacks of one-dollar bills, deposited into the trip kitty; some snacks, toilet paper, and bottles of booze, with no penalty assessed if they'd been opened and were already half gone; a set of walkie-talkies with a five hundred yard range; and a two-quart Tupperware container of homemade potato salad.

I looked at the shrinking shore of the mainland and thought, *Yeah, we'd willingly share Drummond Island with you for that.*

"Is that a *camper*?"

Mary Lynn had just seen Frank's trailers and her features contorted into an expression I knew well. One of my daily tasks at Peegeo's was to write the dinner special on the chalkboard. On Wednesdays, it was barbecue beef ribs, which always smelled savory and rich to me, and were really popular with most of the regular customers, but not with Mary Lynn.

"Nothing but strings and gristle," she'd said, time and again, while pursing her lips and tilting her body as far away from the chalkboard as she could.

I'd been sure Mary Lynn wasn't going to be able to keep up with us, yet we'd barely arrived on the island and it was already apparent to me I'd been wrong. By the time we'd pulled into the muddy driveway at Frank's, Mary Lynn had slurped a Jell-O shot at the Welcome Center, made friends with Beth, the infamously goofy bartender at Northwoods, and even whizzed in the woods. Not one of these experiences had seemed to faze her.

One look at the trailer, though, and she'd balked. Pieces of junk held together by bungee cords, she'd complained, dismissing our accommodations the way she had the beef rib special. Mary Lynn was a fingernail-polishing, hair spray–spraying, fanny pack–wearing, cigarette-smoking, gin-sipping lady. Her favorite pastime was playing cards, euchre preferably, and doing it inside, at a cushioned table and sitting in a cushioned chair. Relieving herself in the woods aside, she was not a woman who roughed it.

"Didn't I *say* I don't camp? Didn't I make that *perfectly* clear?"

Mary Lynn was short—a half inch shy of five foot—and when she was worked up, her voice sounded like she'd just taken a hit off a helium balloon. Behind her back, some of the Peegeo's regulars called her "Gnomie." They wouldn't have said it to her face, though, unless they enjoyed receiving a barrage of grief in that ear-puncturing shriek. When Mary Lynn aired her grievance about the trailer, birds took flight; the wind stopped blowing; and while we hadn't seen Frank yet, I pictured him running inside his house, with those giant hands over his ears.

"Don't judge it until you see the inside," Linda told her, with more kindness than she ever would have shown someone younger. "They're really not that bad."

"Think of it as an *adventure*," Bev added, striding to the louvered door and pulling it open.

"An adventure in yuck," Mary Lynn snapped.

One good thing about the trailers: They were clean. Once Mary Lynn smelled the Pine-Sol, she relented. We divided ourselves into the two trailers the same way we'd divided ourselves into the vehicles: Linda, Mary Lynn, Pam, and Susan in one; Andrea, Jill, Bev, and me in the other. We unpacked, put our groceries in the little propane refrigerators, and then met back outside to decide what the rest of the day would bring.

Bev and Susan both said they wanted to see more of the island. From onboard the ferry, the approach to Drummond was scenic, yet revealed mostly just trees and rocks. We had stopped at the Northwoods, but the bar wasn't too far from the ferry dock, and on the drive there it'd just been more trees. Frank's was farther up the coast but reached via the main road, which was inland, so trees again.

"What about hiking trails?" Bev asked. "There's got to be a good place to get *into* the woods instead of just driving past them."

I loved her for saying that. I'd been longing to get my feet out into those woods from the moment I'd seen them. The other girls had preferred two-tracking to hiking, and I hadn't wanted to suggest something different if I was the only one who'd felt that way. With two of us, even if no one else wanted to hike, she and I could go together.

I doubted Mary Lynn was a hiker or a regular exerciser; I didn't know about Susan; and Andrea, Jill, and Linda got their heart rates up by hoofing platters of food and trays of drinks from the kitchen to the dining room eight hours a day. I did that, too, but I *loved* the woods.

Bev worked in an office all day and sat at a desk. On the weekends, she went to the gym, took an aerobics class, or went for a long walk in the woods near her apartment. New girls were going to mean new activities, something Linda had already planned for.

"There's this place we could check out," she said. "It's a preserve or something called Maxton Plains."

"Huh," Mary Lynn huffed, skeptical. "Sounds like a field."

"No, it's an *alvar*," Linda corrected.

"What's an alvar?" Andrea asked, looking to me, not Linda, for the answer. I was the writer. I was the one with a ready and understandable definition for even the weirdest-sounding word. *Providential?* Lucky. *Effrontery?* Shameless. *Indefatigable?* Us. But an alvar? I had nothing.

"An alvar looks like a field, but the plants are actually growing out of rock," Linda explained. "They're super rare. There's only a few in the whole country, and the one up here is supposed to be the biggest. It's new. We've never been there."

"Yeah," Mary Lynn grumbled. "Like I said. A field."

Linda patiently explained that whoever wanted to walk could walk, whoever wanted to hang by the cars could hang by the cars, but Mary Lynn rolled her eyes at that, too. Usually, that would have irritated Linda no end, but she let it go, and I figured it was just Mary Lynn's way. Every group had a curmudgeon, and Mary Lynn was going to be ours.

Bev was the first to get ready, and once inside Andrea's Bronco she bounced her legs up and down like a little kid. Mary Lynn was the last, grumbling all the way to Linda's Explorer, but then when we drove the few miles down South Maxton Road to the edge of the preserve and parked, she raced Bev to be the first one out.

All eight of us were struck silent by what we saw.

Before us was an ancient place, a flat circle of silver and gold a half mile across and surrounded by florescent evergreens. The silver came from the concave, unbroken expanse of flat rock under our feet, so damp with dew, fog, or mist that it gave off a metallic sheen. The poplar leaves, the grass blades, the yellow of fall-blooming wildflowers, and even the wings of birds and insects merged together in the sun, creating an airy layer of gold.

For once the wind was nonexistent and none of us spoke; cicadas celebrating that they were simply alive was the only sound. Bev took a breath and marched off in hiker mode; Mary Lynn stayed right next to Linda's car, but she was just as awestruck by the sight as the rest of us were. If silver could be spun from rock and gold from grass, what else was possible on this enchanted island?

"It's *beautiful*," Andrea said in an uncharacteristic whisper. "Linda, how did you even know about this place?"

Maxton Plains was out on the island's remote right claw. No electricity, no houses, no people, and no roads beyond the one we'd taken to get there. Although today there are all sorts of Internet sites about it, you couldn't Google the preserve in 1995. You couldn't Google anything in 1995. Linda only knew about Maxton Plains because years before she'd come to Drummond Island to hunt deer with her boyfriend and they'd stumbled upon it. Someone had told them it was a good place to get a buck—a wildlife preserve that allowed hunting in order to cull the island's exploding white-tailed deer population. She hadn't shot anything, but the site had made an impression on her, and so when Bev said she'd wanted to hike, Linda remembered it.

"Most alvars are remote, so it's rare to even be able to see a place like this," Linda said.

She pointed to a series of interpretive signs, worn down by time and weather. Everyone else had walked right past them. More than a thousand acres of the alvar had been preserved by the Nature Conservancy, and although Linda had said it was a "new" place, it was actually only new to us. A glacier created Maxton Plains, and the rare combination of surface rock, endangered wildflowers, and stunted trees wasn't new at all, it was prehistoric—at least ten thousand years old. Limestone and bedrock extended as deep as two full miles. At ground level, some of the rock was covered with soil, but it was such a thin layer even small trees couldn't take root. The hardy plants that could grow there were grasses and wildflowers usually native to the Arctic tundra—prairie smoke, Indian paintbrush, Houghton's goldenrod, and dropseed. In some places, especially near the center of the alvar, the flat stone plates were exposed, and other hardy plants like juniper and moss grew in the rain-collecting cracks between them.

"I take it back," Mary Lynn said, staring. "Not just a field."

For all her grumbling and exaggerated pessimism, she apparently didn't mind admitting when she'd been wrong. In my own life, I found that a particularly difficult thing to do, and I liked her more for being so willing to. It wasn't easy for Mary Lynn to walk on the alvar or in the woods, especially when there wasn't a trail. She had a slight stitch in her gait, and we weren't sure if it was from a childhood accident, a birth injury, human wear and tear, or something else, but that day she went just as far and explored the place for just as long as the rest of us did.

Well, for as long as everyone except Bev, who'd marched off without a care, a backward glance, or an invitation for me to come along to parts unknown. She'd returned, though, rosy cheeked and smiling.

Bev was an anomaly—the oldest of our group yet often the most energetic. The one who wore dresses, heels, and nylons to work, but was comfortable in the woods. A woman without a man, yet who seemed to generally like them more than we did, and who'd lived for more than half a century yet back then seemed untouched by age or time.

Mary Lynn appeared just the opposite to me, and I couldn't help but compare her to Bev. In contrast, she seemed old beyond her years, set in her ways, closed off to most new experiences, or at least often highly critical of them.

When I remember how I viewed her back then, as someone behind the times enough to just be dismissed as old, it makes me cringe. Why had I been so judgmental? So what if I was younger than she was. So what if I thought she should have been as energetic as Bev. Except for her nightly visits to Peegeo's, and to wonder why Linda had invited her along, until that day on the alvar, I'd barely given Mary Lynn a passing thought.

For someone who supposedly wanted friends, I certainly wasn't very compassionate to people I didn't understand. When Mary Lynn went to the island with us that first time, she'd been only forty-four. Almost a decade younger than I am now. I knew nothing of her life or of its difficulties. I thought everyone could and should be just like Bev.

Late the next afternoon I was sitting outside our trailer in a lawn chair, noticed the faint odor of stale beer drifting by, and looked around for its source. A screened-in shed back at the wood line. Other than that, Barb's Landing was unchanged from the previous year and the one before that. Frank hadn't fixed the dock, replaced the old trailers, or weeded the gravel, but he had built a shed to store the trash and returnable cans.

Just then Susan walked out her trailer door holding an insulated coffee mug I was pretty sure didn't have any coffee in it but rather whiskey and Diet Coke. A straw angled jauntily out the sip hole and her ponytail bounced in the breeze.

"So?" she'd asked, perky and expectant. "What kinds of stuff do we do when we're up here?"

Several of the other girls had also claimed one of Frank's lawn chairs and we'd arranged them in a half circle. Next to me, Linda leaned back and raised an appraising eye.

"Ah, you're pretty much doing it," she'd said.

Our lodgings' interior was tighter than I'd remembered, and although Susan had spent a long time getting dressed, fixing her hair, and putting on makeup, Bev and I had been anxious to get outside. It was a warmish fall day, fifty degrees and sunny, and we'd gone for a walk down to the dock to look at the lake. From the northeast side of the island where we were staying, all you could see were other, smaller tufts of forested islands, the occasional freighter, and open water. Miles and miles of open water. It looked cold, but also beautiful.

"Doesn't that make you want to get in a canoe!" Bev had said.

When we walked back and joined the girls, most of them had gathered outside together in the lawn chairs. With such tight quarters and an unseasonably warm day, the gravel rectangle between our two trailers had been turned into a sort of outdoor living room. No TV, no couch, and no fireplace, but there was a well-stocked cooler next to the picnic table, a nice fire crackled in the fire pit, and an orange extension cord powered Andrea's boom box.

"So then what, we just sit around and drink?" Susan had asked, looking from Andrea to Jill to me for an answer. We stared back and she took our silence as a yes.

"Okay." She'd shrugged. "Cool beans."

Afternoon drinking has since lost its novelty, but back then it was the only way we knew how to relax and leave all our worries of home behind. Susan hadn't sounded the least bit surprised, and seemed just happy to be along. If afternoon drinking was what was required, then afternoon drinking was what she'd do. I knew the feeling. I hadn't regretted one second of time with the Drummond Girls, and was starting to feel like she wasn't going to, either. It looked like for all his bluster and boldness, George had met someone pretty great, and I was glad for him.

I'd met his ex-wife when they were still married and she'd been nothing at all like Susan. His ex could be funny, but she could also be coarse, bad mannered, and sometimes even mean. After their divorce, all the women who worked at Peegeo's felt a bit protective of George. Our place of employment might have been a backwoods bar in the middle of nowhere, but it had good food, a great atmosphere, and through long hours and hard work George had built it into a successful business—making him tantalizing bait for the wrong kind of woman. The more I got to know Susan, the more I could tell how much she cared about George.

She jogged down the trailer's stairs then and sat down in the circle like she belonged there. She wanted to join our group not because it would make a good impression on George, but because she liked us for our own sake.

"I think we're going to see a bear this year," Jill said randomly. "I feel it in my bones."

"Well," Susan sang out, "just in case that doesn't happen, I brought Pictionary!"

Linda glanced my way and raised an eyebrow. Her look said, *Board games? On our party weekend she wants to play board games?* Before I could return it with a look of my own, Frank appeared. None of us had seen him coming, but then there he was, same white hair, same big belly.

"Got a surprise for you girls," he'd said.

His arms were tucked behind his back, and he was smiling as if what he was hiding was something unusually good. Linda introduced him to the new girls, and Bev hopped up to introduce herself.

"And who might you be?" he asked.

"I'm the Polish Princess," she said.

Frank's gruff exterior softened, and I could tell he was charmed by her, the way a lot of men were. By then, my opinion of Frank had changed and I felt genuinely happy to see him. He was one of the only people we knew on the island, and although I'd wanted this kind of welcome my first year, that kind of familiarity wasn't just given away here. You had to earn it.

He still sometimes struck me as paternalistic, but I could tell he was also fond of us. To him, I think we were somewhere between paying customers and distant daughters, and whatever he was holding behind his back must have needed two hands because he didn't reach out to shake Bev's.

Frank wouldn't have bought us anything from a store, so whatever was behind his back was probably something he'd made himself. A plank of the smoked lake trout or whitefish the Upper Peninsula was known for? A jar of wild blueberry jam? Some hand-carved thingamajig? We all turned in our chairs to see.

"The recipe was real good this year, but I saved this one just for you all," he said, thrusting a bottle of oily liquid toward Linda.

Homemade jam? Really? I should have known. The previous winter I'd checked some books about Drummond Island out of the library. The Ojibwa who'd been the region's first inhabitants had called the island Potagannissing, but when Canadian settlers and military officers arrived, they'd ignored the native history and renamed the island after one of their countrymen, Gordon Drummond, a lieutenant colonel in the British army.

The British had control of Drummond Island during the War of 1812, but the Treaty of Ghent solidified many sovereign borders, and that was when the island became part of the United States. It took fifteen years for the British to leave, a delay I could well understand. When the U.S. military officers arrived to inspect the fort, the first thing they did was get liquored up on "copious draughts" of rum the British had left behind.

Drummond Island's history was built on booze, not fish and not jam. It was a tradition that apparently still dominated nearly two hundred years later because in Frank's fist was the neck of a Jack Daniel's bottle that someone had soaked the label off. Inside was a watery gold liquid the color of grizzly bear fur and the greasy consistency of gasoline. A fifth of his very best, Frank declared, arching his back, sticking out his gut, and handing the gift to Linda.

She held the bottle up to the light and offered to open it right then so we could share a taste of it together, but Frank said he had Barb's Landing chores to do and would regretfully have to decline.

"Probably shouldn't smoke near it, though," he suggested, eyeing her cigarette.

Before he left us, Frank said he'd overheard Jill mention wanting to see a bear. For our own safety, he thought we should know about the "Megabear" that had been terrorizing the island in recent weeks. According to Frank, this bear was so destructive and dangerous there was a $1,000 bounty on him. He was bold, hungry, and unafraid of people. He (and by the size of it, Frank said it had to be a he) was big, perhaps more than 350 pounds, and for the last several weeks had been ransacking Dumpsters, prowling through the island's campgrounds, and scaring campers and tourists.

The news was intended to scare us, I'm sure, but it had the opposite effect, at least for Jill. At the word *Megabear* Jill's face lit up. An expression that Frank did not seem to be immune from. He looked like he'd put the bear on a leash and walk it around his resort if she would have asked him to. She didn't, of course, but he gave us a suggestion anyway.

"If you want to see him, just wait until dark and then drive on over to the dump. He's down there feeding almost every night."

There was no place in the world like Drummond Island, I'd remind myself again and again. No place with the same combination of rocky cliffs, fresh water, remote wilderness, and tough, friendly people. No place where eight otherwise perfectly sane mothers, wives, girlfriends, waitresses, bartenders, and one paralegal on a weekend vacation would enthusiastically choose to sit in a car at the gate of the town dump and hope, with all their might, to catch sight of a dangerous predator on the lam.

That was just fine by me. After another year of housekeeping, bill paying, and fried fish order taking, I was with the girls on Drummond again. Having Bev along only added to the magic of the place and at that moment, lying in wait with her, Jill, and the rest of the girls for a menacing bear on a garbage pile in the dark seemed like a great idea.

"There's supposed to be sixty-some bears on this island," Jill said, when we were on our way. "Shouldn't be too hard to see one."

"Bear! Bear! Bear! Bear!" Andrea chanted.

The dump was only two miles from Barb's Landing, and so we'd all squeezed inside Linda's new Explorer for the drive. Andrea was loud, and sounded as if she were cheering from the wide-open stands at a football game, instead of crammed into the back of a two-door SUV.

Some of the girls didn't care whether we saw a bear or not and were just along for the ride. But Andrea and Jill could talk of little else. Of the eight of us, they were the real thrill-seekers, and in three trips to the island we'd yet to see anything more dangerous than the deer that sometimes leaped out of the woods right in front of our cars.

If Frank was right, then nearby was more than three hundred pounds of sharp teeth, long claws, and wild eyes. There was something oddly comforting in knowing large and independent animals thrived on the island and could happily exist season to season, year after year, mostly invisible, and yet within shouting distance of people.

No matter how dangerous he was, I wasn't just along for the ride. Like Andrea and Jill, I wanted to see a Megabear. In theory, I suppose I could identify with him, because *I* often felt invisible, too, though not always by choice. But it wasn't legit to believe you identified with something you hadn't even seen.

There were bears living in our own area of Michigan; you'd hear stories of them knocking down bird feeders and getting stuck in Dumpsters, but with thousands of miles of land to roam, they mostly stayed away from people so it wasn't likely we'd ever see one back home. The island was different. On the island, a bears' innate wildness was present but also geographically contained. Kind of like ours.

"We're not going to see anything," Mary Lynn said, dismissive of the entire effort.

"I'm telling you," Jill repeated, "we're seeing one. I've got good intuition and I can feel it in my bones."

"That ain't intuition," Linda quipped. "It's Frank's secret recipe."

She knew how to break the tension and everyone laughed. After talking to us about the bear, Frank had retreated from our circle to do his chores but we'd passed his bottle around anyway. One sip was enough to cure bad posture and remove your tonsils, and Linda had quickly screwed the cap back on and put it away.

So that's how locals made it through a winter on Drummond, I thought.

Traverse City is right on the 45th parallel and winters there were bad enough, but winters on Drummond Island were the stuff of legend. Ice storms from November through May, seventy-mile-per-hour winds, and blizzards that downed what few power lines the island had, cutting residents off from the outside world more than they already were. I'd often wondered how anyone could live there year-round, but I'd wonder no more. Down a bottle of that stuff, and you'd endure a furnace blast of searing heat, then be down for months of complete hibernation.

We arrived at the dump but saw nothing that looked like a bear. I thought of Earl, back in Andrea's Bronco, tucked into his Ziploc bag; of Frank's ancestors holed up in their log cabins for the winter, nursing a fresh batch of bootleg, and I wondered if Megabear was already hibernating. It was only the first weekend of October, but the temperatures in the Upper Peninsula were already starting to dip and there'd even been a dusting of snow. But Jill said black bears wouldn't "den up" for at least another month. They should be busy now eating as much as they could in preparation for winter, even if the food they found was just garbage from the town dump.

"Don't tell me that," said Pam, who was so tenderhearted she couldn't stand to hear about any animal's discomfort, let alone real suffering. To her, the image of such a majestic being eating garbage in order to survive qualified as both.

Jill and I were squeezed way in the back, pressed in next to each other scanning the outside terrain, and while Linda and Mary Lynn teased Pam about the bearskin rug she had in her living room ("It was a gift! I hate it, but we couldn't say no"), I asked Jill how she knew so much about bears.

"I'm going to take it as a sign," she'd said, as if I'd asked her something else. Something a lot more personal. "If I see one, I'll know everything is going to be okay. I'll know I'm going to be okay."

Andrea was squeezed in the back with us, too; she gave me a look and shook her head no. I think by then all of us knew things weren't going well for Jill, that she and her husband were about to split up, but I wouldn't have asked her about it then. Linda's car only sat five, but all eight of us were mashed in and doing our best to stay quiet. I'd been known to ask a personal question or two, but that was not the moment for it, and even *I* wouldn't have chosen to probe into Jill's marriage right then.

Dusk was fading into dark, and in the glow of Linda's parking lights we could just make out the center of the dump—a steep pile of ragged newspapers, unraveling blue tarps, and the smeared bulges of waterlogged magazines flapping in the wind.

"There's one!" Mary Lynn whispered, pointing frantically.

Of course, I thought, *the naysayer* would *be the one to spot the bear,* and then like hypnotized cartoon characters with spinning eyes, we all stretched our necks toward the windshield and looked as hard as we could look. Halfway down the trash hill was a large and puffy black shape. And it seemed to be moving.

It wasn't *the* bear, the shape was much too small for him, but in the beam of our stares, it did look like an older cub—was there such a thing as a teenage bear? There had to be, and this one appeared hunched over some prized morsel and "feeding" just like Frank said. Its rounded back was toward us and muscles rippled under its glowing fur. Huh. Maybe a diet of garbage wasn't so bad for bears after all. Maybe that was why there were so many of them living on the island.

We watched it arch its back, then relax. We held our collective breath and waited for the animal to turn around, lift its head, and stare into Linda's headlights. I'd remembered to keep my camera in my pocket this time, and I pulled it out and pressed down on the little button that warmed up the flash. Even the girls who hadn't seemed to care one way or the other watched intently.

Inside the car, it was as quiet as if time had stopped to take a breath. If our eyes had been lasers, there would have been sixteen holes burned clear through the windshield.

"That's a *garbage* bag," Linda said, appalled, and we shrieked with laughter. Some nature girls we were, mistaking an orb of lumpy plastic for a real live bear, and the giggling lasted for several minutes.

"C'mon, we've got to be quiet or we'll scare them away!" Jill finally hissed.

She was still holding out hope that her intuition knew something the rest of us did not. Mostly for her, we stayed parked at the dump's gate for maybe another half hour, but not one deer, crow, chipmunk, or so much as a mosquito ventured into view. Eight women squeezed into one car in the dark after an afternoon of drinking, when at least half of them need to pee, is not a good formula for silence. It didn't take long before we had to unroll the windows for air. If Megabear had been at the dump that night, there's no way we would have seen him.

"What now?" Linda asked, her hands in their familiar ten-and-two position on the steering wheel.

"I don't care," Jill said, slumping against the seat, defeated. "Anything's fine."

A bland-sounding round of "me, toos" filled the vehicle. The excitement of our second night on Drummond together felt like it was over. No one suggested we go back to Chuck's, and Northwoods seemed too far away—eight or nine miles at least. Two-tracking was out—I'd sensed we all wanted to exit that stuffy car, not spend more time inside of it. It was much too early to call it a night, though, and too dark outside by then for even Bev to consider a walk in those unfamiliar woods. Linda started the drive back to the trailers.

"Don't forget," came a cheerful voice from the middle of the car. "I've got *Pic*tionary!"

For all the island's wide-open beauty, it's surprising that my memories of those early years often center on compact indoor spaces. The inside of Linda's and Andrea's cars, the snug quarters of Frank's trailers, the circle of lawn chairs, and the tables at Chuck's and Northwoods we all gathered so tightly around. Back in Traverse City, I'd often longed for "space"—at work when trying to squeeze through the bar crowd to get to the kitchen, and at home, too, when I craved even a little time to myself.

When I was on Drummond Island with the girls, it was just the opposite. I reveled in the closeness we'd created, both emotional and physical. My friends didn't want anything from me; they just wanted to be with me, and I felt the same toward them. As someone who was claustrophobic about putting on a turtleneck sweater, on the island I actually *liked* the feeling of being squeezed into Linda's car with everyone else.

When the last of the natural light faded that night, it took every bit of warmth from the day along with it, and when we returned to Frank's, the wall heaters inside the trailers had already kicked on. Pam, Bev, and Mary Lynn called it a night, but Susan talked the rest of us into playing her board game. The double bed next to the galley kitchen slid away to make room for a dinette table and the five of us gathered around it. If Linda, Susan, and I scooted in tight and Andrea used a cooler for a stool, we could all fit, and there was even a little room for Jill.

Susan pulled a rectangular blue box from her bag, unfolded the playing board, and handed out pads of paper and freshly sharpened pencils. Jill was antsy, though, and even after the rest of us had sat down and were ready to play, she stood in front of the open refrigerator and looked inside. I thought she was contemplating a snack. She was, but not for herself.

"If we can't go to the bears," she said, "I'll make the bears come to us."

"Oh, give it up, Jillsy," Linda said.

Linda might have been the first to doubt the suitability of a board game, but that had been hours ago. Since we'd left Traverse City the morning before, she'd spent a lot of time driving, and now she was just happy to be out from behind the wheel.

We left Jill to her own devices, divided ourselves into two teams, and Susan shuffled the word cards, put them in the center of the board, and handed out the category cards. Some of the words were difficult to render, such as *prophet* or *virtue*, and others were easier, like *sit* or *iron*. Susan was about to turn over the top card when Jill pulled something out of the refrigerator, turned toward us, and held up her selection.

"Bear bait," she'd said.

In Jill's hand was the white plastic container of Linda's sloppy joe meat. She spooned a small hill of the beef, green pepper, and ketchup mixture onto a paper plate, opened the trailer door, and walked down the steps.

There was probably a knack to baiting a creature as large and wild as a full-grown bear. Especially one with a $1,000 bounty on its head. I was close enough to the open door to see down the steps. From that vantage point it looked like all bear baiting entailed was setting a paper plate of meat on the ground one inch from the bottom step, then dashing back inside the trailer and slamming the door.

Jill's giggle was infectious. In a few short hours, Megabear had become more legend than actual animal. He wasn't real to us anymore, though Jill must have believed if anything could change him from a spirit bear into a real one, it was the sweet, sticky comfort of Linda's secret recipe.

"Ground beef isn't free, you know," Linda said, sounding both annoyed and amused.

Jill ignored her.

"Now," she said, "we just have to sit back and wait for nature to take its course."

Her task complete, Jill was content to let us absorb her into the game. It was Andrea, Jill, and Susan against Linda and me. Someone mixed the drinks, someone else opened Frank's bottle again, just for a taste, and as the sand in the game's little timer sifted down, we considered each word through the aperture of Drummond. The cards offered up images and actions that seemed ridiculous and silly, yet somehow preordained, too. *Baby, wedding cake, adventure, confusion.* It was as if a board game most of us hadn't even wanted to play was now telling the story not just of our trip, but of our lives.

I'm usually so competitive, but that night it was just fun to guess, and I don't think one of us even thought about trying to win the game. After our first turn, the very idea of teams faded away and together we guessed every word right. When it was Susan's turn to guess, she made a big show of covering her eyes. Andrea pulled a card—*punt*. Besides me, Bev was the only other real sports fan of our group, and as the sand timer funneled the seconds away I wished she'd have stayed up with us. I couldn't think how to show that kind of kick with a drawing and wished I had Bev there to help.

It might have seemed like just a game, yet between the five of us we'd so far guessed every word on every card that Susan had turned over. As the night wore on, all those correct and speedy answers had taken on a deeper meaning. They weren't just part of some late-night fun, they were a reflection of how well we'd gotten to know each other, of how much our group had jelled after only a couple of days. I don't know if the other girls felt that, but I did. To me, those answers were evidence of a commonality, a wavelength, a bond that hadn't existed when we left Traverse City, but did now. The walkie-talkies had shown us how little we knew about each other's pasts; the game that night proved we knew everything about the present.

The pressure was on to get Susan to say that word. The rest of us tapped our pencils, looked at the ceiling, and closed our eyes, just trying to think of something, anything, to draw, but papers stayed blank.

When a tiny divot of sand was all that was left inside the timer,

Jill leaned back, set her pencil down, and clasped her hands behind her head. She glanced at the card one last time, looked Susan in the eye, and with complete impunity broke the most important rule of the game. Instead of drawing her clue, she said it, right out loud.

"This word rhymes with George's ex-wife."

Susan's eyes flew open. "Punt!" she blurted.

The trailer shook with laughter. Andrea tipped backward off the cooler, rolled out the door, and down the steps, escaping injury and also missing the bear bait by inches. The game completely dissolved after that, Susan folded up the board and put it all away, and when we'd all calmed down, she and Linda returned to their trailer and we all went to bed.

For the longest time that night I couldn't get to sleep. At home, my struggles with insomnia were frustrating, but I didn't mind them on Drummond. I actually enjoyed just lying there, wide awake, replaying all the joy and silliness of the previous two days. The ride up, being able to share that first view of the island with Bev, the rare beauty of Maxton Plains, and then how warm and welcoming the inside of the trailer had felt. In that darkness, the tiny bedroom I shared with Bev felt safe. Like a familiar den.

Way too early the next morning I awoke to the sound of empty aluminum cans bouncing over on gravel.

"The *hell*?" Andrea groaned from somewhere up front.

It had been late when we'd finished playing, and I was surprised to hear her stirring so early. The noise outside was kind of loud, but Andrea could usually sleep through someone cutting sheet metal with a power saw during a thunderstorm.

After Susan had put the game away and she and Linda went back to their trailer, Andrea and Jill had removed the table, pulled the mattress back out, and slept in the double bed up front. I'd slept in the back bedroom, and it looked like Bev had moved to the pullout bench sometime in the night. I didn't think anyone in the other trailer was up yet, so I tried to relax, turn off my brain, and go back to sleep.

In a perfect world, the Jack Daniel's bottle from Frank would've been full, I would've grabbed a few more hours of sleep, and breakfast would've still been hours away.

But ours was an imperfect world. Where black bears dined on garbage at the town dump, marriages that had started happy and loving turned so gloomy and secretive that when you packed up in the early morning to leave for three days, that didn't mean your husband would get out of bed and hug you good-bye.

It had been so great to have the new girls along, but by Sunday morning I missed my sons, and was half-glad we'd be on our way home in a few hours. I heard Andrea and Jill stirring so I got up, too. Andrea wrapped a blanket around her shoulders, and she and Jill and I rambled outside in our pajamas to investigate the source of the sound. Linda was already up and standing just outside the other trailer. The noise we'd heard was coming from the shed at the edge of the woods, and we walked over to have a look.

Hunched in the doorway with his back to us was Frank.

He was bent over, he was cussing, he was gripping a rifle, and he was wearing nothing but sagging tighty-whities and a pair of knee-high rubber boots.

The last man I'd seen in his underwear who wasn't my husband had been Earl. Each of these sightings—Earl's triangle of gold lamé and Frank's Fruits of some aging and bedraggled Loom— would now be combined and forever branded onto my retinas.

"Bear!" Frank growled when he saw the four of us.

The shed's screen door had been torn off its hinges. Scattered around the inside of the small building and between our two trailers were beer cans, food wrappers, soggy brown grocery sacks, and fish guts. It looked like a fairy-tale monster had clomped in from the woods, torn the door off, then grabbed several garbage bags in each claw and hopped around, shaking them to death. I could have retrieved my camera and taken a picture, but a man in his underwear carrying a gun and running down empty beer cans was not the native wildlife I'd had in mind. In what type of album would I have glued such a photograph?

Yet the same way that quarterbacks sometimes want to have a bad throw back, I think I'd like to have that moment back. In a do-over I'd look through the lens of that drugstore camera, depress the shutter, and develop the photograph, just to assure myself it all really happened exactly the way I remember it. Once the ball leaves your hand, though, it's gone for good.

Those trailers were anything but soundproof and you would have thought at least one of us would have heard something. Without Frank's hibernation helper, perhaps we would have. I wished the destruction had woken us up; at least then Jill would have seen her bear, but no one heard anything.

Andrea, Linda, and I stood there like posts, but Jill walked around, kicked at the grass, then peered into some bushes. After a minute, she picked up something thin and white in each hand and held the two items aloft. The torn halves of a paper plate, each with a big orange grease spot.

"I knew it, I *knew* it!" she hissed, whispering so Frank wouldn't overhear. "I *told* you we were going to see a bear."

Andrea and I rewarded her with our shock faces: jaws down, front teeth forward, but Linda wasn't so easily impressed.

"Ah, maybe I missed something," Linda said, "but we didn't actually *see* anything."

Jill just smiled, waving the torn pieces for emphasis. "Mega-bear. Was right. *Here*," she mouthed.

It didn't matter to Jill whether she'd seen it with her own eyes or not, Megabear had still walked past our trailer sometime in the night and taken the bait. It was Jill who'd had the feeling we were going to encounter a bear that weekend, and Jill who'd made it come true. It was also Jill who had ignored the one fast rule of the board game, and that morning those two acts of will seemed related. I didn't know what was waiting for Jill back at home but I believed whatever it was, she could handle it.

Frank stomped over and marveled aloud what an amazing coincidence had befallen Barb's Landing. The same night we'd wanted to see a bear, a bear had decided it wanted to destroy his new garbage shed.

"That was us," Andrea confessed. "But hey. You gave us the moonshine. We can't be responsible for anything that happened after that."

Andrea declined to mention we'd engineered the shed's destruction on only two sips apiece and that the bottle was still three-quarters full. She couldn't tell him that. It would have made us look like sissy la-las.

Frank seemed unmoved by her confession and said nothing but held the garbage bag open for Jill. She disposed of the evidence, he tied off the bag, tossed it back inside his ruined shed, then opened his mouth as if he were going to growl at us some more. Not a sound came out, though, and he shook his head and walked away.

I watched him go. His shoulders lifted and relaxed, lifted and relaxed, as if he were laughing, even though one hand was pressed to a spot on his lower back and the other was using the butt end of his rifle as a cane.

"It's a young man's game," he grumbled.

I didn't know if he meant women were a young man's game, renting out trailers to eight of them was, or defending your turf against Megabear. Maybe he'd meant all three.

The four of us headed back inside our trailer. The other girls weren't awake yet, but they would be soon, and we decided to get breakfast started. Linda and I offered to help Jill cook while

Andrea folded up the bed, reinserted the table in its place, then wrapped herself back up in the blanket.

"Drummond just keeps getting better and better," she said dreamily. "I'd sure like to see ahead to next year. Just to know how we're ever going to top this one."

Maybe that was just a figure of speech, but I didn't understand why some people wanted to know the future. I never really understood the point of crystal balls, tea leaves, or palm readers. As the smell of eggs, ham, and peppers filled the trailer, it was the certain but unknown changes ahead that seemed delicious to me.

I didn't see how we were going to top ourselves, either, but in the months ahead, when the wind would pin me inside, when there'd be several feet of snow on the ground, and I'd be spending my nights washing greasy fish platters and my days trying to balance a teetering checkbook while my husband argued with the TV news, I sure planned to enjoy imagining the possibilities.

CHAPTER THREE 1997

Pam, aka "The Sheriff."

My thoughts of snow materialized not too long after we returned home in 1995, and winter came early two years in a row. The blizzard of '96 lasted well into '97 and was lumbering and destructive. Roofs were caved in by heavy snow, tree limbs broke under the weight of ice and landed on power lines, and schools were closed for days on end.

Pregnant with my third child, I'd left my waitress job at Peegeo's, found work as a freelance editor, and many days that winter I remember standing with my sons at our living room window, as snowflakes the size of pennies tumbled past the beam of our porch light. Behind us, three pairs of mittens steamed in front of the fireplace while their father slept on the couch.

On one of those evenings I stood all alone at the kitchen counter instead, and dug my fingernails into the butcher block. Hours later my third son arrived—a breech and beautiful blue-eyed present. I was thirty-five then, an "older" mother, and my husband stayed with me all through the difficult birth. Afterward, he only left the hospital once—to buy me flowers. When he returned, he asked the nurse for a vase so he could arrange the three blue carnations and one red rose into a bouquet for my nightstand. He was making an effort, but I didn't get it. Every woman knows there's nothing in a florist's case cheaper than carnations; I'd thought he'd been trying to save money, not trying to say something.

Who could have predicted it'd be me, the "old" mother of two, and not the childless and much younger Jill or Andrea, who'd be the first to make use of the Drummond Girls' "pregnant or dead" clause?

"At least it was the former!" Bev had said when I replayed for her the details of my emergency C-section.

She'd come by with a twenty-four pack of Luvs, Rose's lime juice, and a bottle of Absolut; we'd been in a gimlet phase when I'd gotten pregnant. Now that my son was here, and healthy, she saw no reason not to return to it.

Sitting on my living room couch, Bev oohed over my perfect baby, assured me that sons were easier than daughters, then kindly but firmly suggested I put the difficult birth behind me. I should think only positive thoughts and just accept that Y chromosomes were going to dominate my life for a while. When I pointed out that she couldn't possibly understand what I was going through, that it had been a quarter century since she'd cared for an infant, she readily agreed. That was no reason for me to act so depressed or refuse her offer of a cocktail. So what if it was the middle of a weekday afternoon; even modern babies took naps, didn't they?

I found her logic crazy, quirky, and impossible to argue with. Our friendship grew, even though with three sons I had less free time and felt frustrated by Bev's habit of trivializing serious topics. If anyone wondered what could possibly overwhelm my optimistic, goal-oriented, and indefatigable self, by that spring I knew the answer. Three sons under the age of seven, an emotionally absent husband, a new career as a magazine editor, a wardrobe of clothes that still didn't fit, and a longing for Drummond so acute it felt like physical pain.

"Don't worry," Bev assured me, "you'll go this year and it will be great. Like you never even missed."

In the weeks that followed, she'd often call or stop by unannounced, the way I had stopped by her place when we'd first become friends. She frowned whenever I complained of exhaustion or told her I didn't think my husband was doing enough to help me. She preferred to talk about her favorite television shows, all her guy friends at Peegeo's, and how absolutely enjoyable platonic relationships with men could be. She'd found a new aerobics class to attend and liked the music the instructor chose to accompany the routines.

None of those things interested me, but she did, and her visits cheered me up in spite of myself. Pessimism was not my natural state of mind. It bothered me that my family, and even my mother, assumed I had it together. Probably because I couldn't bring myself to tell anyone that I didn't. That would have meant I'd have to ask for help, something I'd always been loath to do. Bev was the only person who'd recognized I was struggling, even though she never came right out and said so.

"You need some Mardi time," she advised late that spring. "Not in October. You need it now."

It took me weeks before I had an opportunity to take her advice, but then one weeknight I said I'd meet her at Peegeo's after my children were in bed. By the time I got there, it was quiet, most of the customers and even Linda had gone home, and it was just George and Susan at one corner of the bar, and Bev and me at the other.

It was the first time I remember her stepping out from behind that sunny exterior. In March, her mother had died of cancer. Until that night, Bev hadn't talked much about her, at least not with me. Part of my assessment was right—she did shy away from negative or difficult topics. Not because they didn't exist, but because there wasn't anything she could do about them. She couldn't bring her mother back. She couldn't make my marriage happy or help me earn a living while also raising three growing sons. Spending what time she could with me had been her way to forget what was sad or out of control. She wanted our time together to have the same benefits for me, too, and what I called working things out, she called dwelling.

But sometimes I *wanted* to dwell. What made me feel better wasn't pretending everything was fine, but rather knowing there was someone in my life who cared about me enough to listen to me. Even when I was sad, overwhelmed, or felt invisible.

That night at Peegeo's, Bev explained she'd been an unpredictable daughter who'd both enjoyed and suffered through a tumultuous upbringing in a large Polish-Catholic family. Her father owned a cab company in Southfield, a blue-collar city a sideways glance from Detroit. He wielded immense power over his clan, and in my imagination, he'd become this big, hulking ogre. But the next time I went to her house, I saw a single grainy photograph of him on her bulletin board. He was slim and photogenic, just like Bev. Handsome even, with a smile like Frank Sinatra's.

Bev had two brothers and one sister; her father had been controlling toward all of his children, she said, even after they'd become adults, and to wriggle out of his grasp, she'd married at nineteen. Bev's mother stayed loyal to her father, and by the time of her cancer diagnosis, Bev was divorced, her own children were grown, and she invited her mother to move in with her. The experience had been challenging and fulfilling for both of them. Atonements were made, mistakes forgiven.

"But what about your father?" I'd asked her.

"Heart attack," Bev said. "Took him out like a sledgehammer. Hey, did you know I have a canoe?"

As time passed I would become if not comfortable, then at least familiar with Bev's sudden breaks in logic. They were both part of her charm and what could happen when your best friend had almost two decades on you. By then I knew to expect that when she didn't like where the conversation was going, she'd change the subject. Abruptly.

No, I had not known Bev had a canoe. Or that she kept it chained to a tree at a rarely used public access on nearby Spider Lake. The following Saturday morning, I asked my husband if he'd watch our boys for a couple hours.

There were few places I'd felt more at home than sitting in the stern of an aluminum canoe. Being on the lake with Bev reminded me of when my mother and I would slide my grandparents' canoe out early, when the sun was just waking up but Duck Lake and everyone else in the house was still sleeping. We'd catch turtles, sneak up on blue herons spearing frogs, and pick a single water lily—only one, my mother always said, so there would be water lilies for other little girls' breakfast tables. We'd usually let the turtles go but bring back our single flower. She'd trim off the stem and set the white bud in a clear globe vase, and it would slowly open into a white star that would last for several days.

Bev had a strong, assured stroke; she sat up straight and, like my mother and me, knew not to bang the gunnels with the paddle blade. It made an awkward and out-of-place human noise that would scare everything wild away. She and I were in unison that morning, her vessel balanced us naturally in the water, and our practiced strokes felt as if they were being made by two women who'd canoed together for years.

"I was adopted," I blurted. "When I was a kid, we moved around a lot. And I didn't live near my relatives like you did."

Anyone raised near water knows that sound travels over the surface of it quickly and in unpredictable ways. Someone could be standing on their dock humming, and people across the lake might hear it clear enough to recognize the tune. I knew that, but on our shoreline paddle, Bev sat in the bow and I told her straight back how those high school girls had dumped me. Eighteen years had done surprisingly little to dilute the memory, and it took that moment in her canoe for me to realize I'd subconsciously aligned the two. It probably wouldn't have seemed related to anyone else, but being given up for adoption and being asked to leave that teenage clique had wounded me in similar ways.

Bev didn't say anything right away, but she didn't jump out of the canoe and swim to shore or suggest that I should, either. She didn't tell me I was crazy, that I needed therapy, or to stop complaining and count my blessings. No rogue wave swamped the boat, no lightning bolt electrified us in our metal seats. I'd dared to share a hunk of my damaged soul, out loud, with another woman. And survived it.

"It hurts to be a girl," Bev said after a few minutes of easy silence.

Then, "Is that a stick poking out of the water or a turtle's head?"

Summer ended, my two older boys went back to school, and when it came to Drummond, Bev turned out to be right. I'd been stashing money away and baby or no baby, when the girls left for the island, I planned to be with them.

That was not entirely amenable to my husband, however. What exactly did I think I was doing, a mature mother of three now and yet still planning on some juvenile, irresponsible weekend up north? My husband did not come right out and ask me that, not in so many words, but I could feel him thinking it. I called my mother and asked for her advice. I could only dream of having a marriage as strong as my parents did. She told me she thought the rest of the girls and I must have rocks in our heads to do some of the things I'd told her about. But she and my dad would drive to Traverse City, stay for the weekend, and help out my husband while I was gone. They'd make dinners, carve Halloween pumpkins, change diapers, catch me up on laundry, and do whatever else needed doing.

When my first son was born, I'd somehow managed to repel the new mother guilt that television commercials (bathe baby morning, noon, and night); women at the food co-op (baths dry out the skin); my mother, my aunt, and my grandmother (baby needs more formula); the breast-feeding bullies (baby shouldn't have *any* formula!); and even my father-in-law (let baby wail or baby will be a spoiled brat) aimed my way.

I didn't have a sister or any girlfriends with newborns, and so the first infant I'd spent any time around was my own son. It was mostly ignorance, not confidence, that allowed me to disregard all that conflicting advice and trust my own instincts. In 1990, childbirth, babies, and parenting didn't attract the hand-wringing preciousness they do today. When my second son was born, two years of personal experience worked even better at stiff-arming the meddlers.

Then I had to go and give birth to son number three.

There were frightening delivery complications and something must have happened to my own brain in the process because all of my calm assurance evaporated. Over twenty harrowing minutes spent under the lights of an operating "theater," I became a worrier. I just knew my baby slept too long, but that he also didn't sleep enough. I was sure I'd squish him in our bed or he'd stop breathing if left alone in his crib. He looked too chubby one day, too skinny the next. He was hyper; no, he wasn't, he was slow.

The truth was, he was perfect—healthy, willful, and cute. As he grew, I let some of my anxiety go, but with three sons to care for, my physical needs, my emotional desires, and even time to think my own thoughts were eliminated in favor of caring for my children. My devotion wasn't extraordinary; it was just what mothers did. Not because a television commercial or a lactation consultant or a family member told them to, but because of an innate and exquisite craving to care for one's own pink, plump, drooling, and smiley kin.

Worry, though, had turned me into an insomniac. I would tiptoe into my sons' rooms, one after the other, and watch them sleep. A half hour in this one's, another half hour in this one's, a third check in that one's. I'd hear their even breathing and feel the weight of their lives heavy upon me. I needed to set that weight down for just a bit. I needed Drummond. I needed the girls.

In September I confided to Bev that I was afraid if I went to Drummond, I might never want to come home again. She told me not to worry.

"You won't go one night without saying how much you miss them," she'd said.

I searched my dark and selfish heart for a sign she was right. I didn't find one and worried some more. What if there wasn't anything there to find?

Two weeks before our departure, Linda called me with some bad news. Jill wasn't going.

"Is she pregnant?" I asked; when you are a new mom, it's hard to believe that any other state of being exists.

"No, thank God."

It was just the exact opposite. Jill and Marty were getting divorced.

"That's an even better reason to *go*," I said.

"That's exactly what *I* told her," Linda agreed.

I could believe Jill was getting divorced. I couldn't believe she wasn't coming to Drummond. The very woman who'd inspired our sacred pact was going to break it. She wasn't pregnant, and she definitely wasn't dead, but she also wasn't going to Drummond. The bear-baiting woman who'd been so bold and brave was gone,

Linda said. The woman who'd taken her place was subdued, hesitant, and troubled.

I barely knew Marty, and the few times I'd seen him in Peegeo's he'd acted like Mr. I'll Buy the Drinks. Jill's husband was friendly, had twinkling brown eyes, freckles, and an infectious smile that seemed to dwarf his small frame. And now I hated his guts.

It was official, Jill told Linda when she'd stopped in to pick up a to-go pizza. She and Marty didn't even live together anymore. Jill hadn't said where she was living and left so quickly that Linda hadn't had the chance to ask her. Maybe she just needed to talk. Maybe if one of us encouraged her, she'd find the will to come along exactly *because* life at home could sometimes be so tough. But I couldn't get in touch with her even if I'd wanted to, so if encouragement was all she needed, it wasn't going to come from me.

How could I not have her phone number? How had I not made a point of staying in touch with her, especially since I knew she was going through difficult times? Maybe those girls from my high school had been right. It apparently didn't matter that almost two decades had passed since I'd slunk my tall frame out of that bedroom. I'd been so wrapped up in my own problems I hadn't taken the time to ask Jill about hers. Eighteen years since that night, but right then it felt like I'd learned exactly nothing in all that time about being someone's friend.

That year, Linda still owned her silver Explorer, and planned to drive like always, but Andrea had sold the Chuck Truck and was in between vehicles. I didn't have an SUV—I drove a red, mom-friendly Subaru station wagon—but it was roomy and the girls asked if I'd be the second driver. Once on the ferry, I viewed Drummond's coastline again, this time from my new spot behind the steering wheel. I'd felt both happy and daunted by my new responsibility and the moment revealed something I hadn't consciously acknowledged before.

Bev was sitting next to me, Jill wasn't even along, we were in a different vehicle, and I'd missed a year. Time was passing. Our lives were changing. And yet, up ahead of us, there was our island, in the same place and anchored as solidly as always, not a rock out of place.

I remembered when its forests were a green mystery, wild and tantalizing. I remembered imagining myself fleeing into those woods and escaping from my own life. Now, that seemed unimaginable. What had I been thinking? That I'd raise my *children* in those woods?

I had a new baby at home; escape, for longer than this one weekend, wasn't an option. Had never been an option, regardless of how disconnected I felt from my husband. He was unhappy, too. With me, with himself, with life. He needed constant reassurance, fussing over, and pampering, and I wasn't the pampering type. When the island came into view that year, I didn't even get out of my car.

"What's the name of that bar—Northern Lights? Northerly?" Bev asked, laughing at her own forgetfulness. "The North Pole?"

"North*woods*!" Andrea and Pam called from the backseat.

Without Jill, our collective energy felt a little diminished, but we made our traditional stop there, toasted our traditional toast ("Drummond Girls, long may we reign!"), and later that night, the seven of us really did escape. Back home, my car was just a mom-mobile, a grocery-getter, a car-pooler; but it did have a red button in the middle of the stick shift labeled "4WD," and that night, I pushed it. We rode deeper and deeper into those woods, I drove faster and faster and let the island's wildness engulf me once again.

This time, though, *I* was at the wheel and felt more than free; I felt unleashed.

Linda, Mary Lynn, and Susan soon tired of rambling through that dark forest, but I continued to navigate its curves and switchbacks with abandon. Bev, Andrea, and Pam didn't mind and even cheered me on. We dipped down into mudholes and bounced up over tree limbs, jerked one way and dodged another, shrieking over the music, over the sound of my tires in mud, over the gears working harder than they ever had before. It felt like nothing would dare try to slow us down that night.

Then my chest grazed the steering wheel and I felt more than saw the heads of my passengers, my best friends, the women I was responsible for, whiplash forward and then back and then forward again. We'd hit a rock. Not head on, but underneath.

There was a pause, and for a few seconds all I registered was the sound of heavy bass from the stereo.

"We're stuck!" Andrea hollered, and the rest of us laughed as if that were the funniest thing we'd ever heard.

It should have been frightening, but we could hardly catch our breath. A station wagon didn't have the clearance of an Explorer or a Bronco, and I hadn't seen the rock beneath the tall grass. The front end had become lodged on a flat boulder, and try as I might, I couldn't go forward or back. My passengers got out and lifted my whole car, with me in it, off the obstruction, then posed like they'd just raised a flag on the moon.

I can still see Bev, standing in the gleam of my headlights, her foot on that boulder, her fist held high in triumph. She still had her long hair then, and in the light her blond waves reached all the way to her shoulders. She looked beautiful and capable and even sophisticated to me, despite what she was wearing: an oversized sweatshirt with tabloid-yellow text on the chest that read "Beer Contains Vitamin P."

The *P* stood for pee, of course, an apt statement from the woman whose contribution her first year had been extra rolls of toilet paper. But right then it could have stood for propel, promise, or even purge. Maybe that's what I was on that night, vitamin P. Maybe that's what we were all on. It was two or three o'clock in the morning, yet the exhaustion I felt all the time back at home was gone.

"I miss my baby," I'd said later, when we were back and settled in for the night. "I miss my boys."

I wasn't talking to anyone in particular. For once, what I was thinking had just come out of my mouth, easily and with no forethought at all. Bev wasn't usually a hugger or physically demonstrative, a trait I appreciated because I wasn't either. But my longing to hold my son in my arms was like missing a limb, and I remembered her assuring me I'd feel just like this.

Everyone was busy taking off coats and shoes and putting on pajamas and I didn't think anyone heard my lament. Or, if they did, they didn't let on. Then Bev put her hand on my shoulder and squeezed.

"Holy crap," Bev said, pointing. "What *is* that?"

It was late the next afternoon, and we were just pulling into Wazz's Party Plus to restock our coolers when there in the parking lot was a watercraft that looked like it could've navigated the bubbling waters of hell. It was hunter green, spray-painted over with amateurish black squiggles. In the belly of the vessel was a compact tentlike thing covered in netting. On the side facing us was a man-sized flap with fake foliage stapled onto it.

"That's what I love about this island," Andrea said, after I'd parked between Linda's Explorer and the vessel. "We could come up here for a hundred years and still not know what we're going to see."

The island itself had seemed so constant. It was the people who changed. Us, but the people around us, too. I think that's why we tried so hard to re-create the same experiences year after year. Not all the changes we'd experienced had been bad or difficult. Many of them weren't, and some we even celebrated. George and Susan had gotten married, I'd had a baby, and Andrea had left waitressing and opened a preschool. Yet good, bad, or just plain different, I think we were only beginning to accept the randomness of life, and we redoubled our efforts at keeping our Drummond Island weekends exactly the same.

Which was, of course, impossible. Just because it was an island, remote, and situated on the northern border, that didn't mean it was wholly immune from time, weather, people, or anything else, no matter how much we wanted it to be.

Andrea was right—we couldn't be sure what would happen on Drummond, who we'd become there or what we'd see. And that crazy-looking boat symbolized all those feelings.

It was small—perhaps only a dozen feet long—and someone had propped it haphazardly in the extended bed of a pickup truck. Even stationary it looked aggressive, as if that canvas flap could open at any moment and reveal something lethal. A speargun, the barrel of a cannon, or even a whaling harpoon.

Linda, Bev, and I volunteered to brave our way past it and go into Wazz's for supplies while the rest of the girls stayed in the cars and mixed drinks. Our annual afternoon of two-tracking deep in the primeval core of Drummond awaited, but we needed to be iced up first. Venturing into the forest on the more rarely traveled car paths and over to the side of the island that had no electricity, no plumbing, no paved roads, and no human habitation was, Bev said, no reason to settle for a warm cocktail.

Wazz's Party Plus was a gas station, deli, video rental store, to-go pizza shop, and package liquor outlet all in one. It was centrally located on one of the island's two paved arteries, East Channel Road, six miles past the ferry dock and a half mile before the Northwoods bar. The place was often a hub of activity, yet none of us could remember seeing it quite that busy. Every parking spot but the two we occupied were taken by pickup trucks, most with boat trailers attached, laden with vessels altered to look like swamp grass or bog shrubbery. Shotguns in gun racks obscured the back windows and many of their radio antennas were disguised to look like cattails.

I didn't hunt and neither did my husband, but my brother did, and from him I knew that fall in Michigan was the start of deer, black squirrel, fox, bear, and coyote season. What I didn't know was which animal the owners of those boats could possibly be preparing to kill. As far as any of us could tell, no one had collected the $1,000 bounty on Megabear, and perhaps *he* was their quarry. Yet I also thought bear hunters used dogs, not camouflaged rowboats, so that didn't fit.

Wolves were taken off the endangered species list in 2012, and since then Michigan's legislature has toyed with the idea of a legal wolf season, but back then it was still illegal to hunt them, so the rigs weren't for that. They had to be for stalking something that lived in the swamps. Moose? Elk? Muskrat invasion? Rabid beaver pack?

As far as the U.S. government was concerned, a "frontier" was a population unit and not a mind-set. Another thing I'd learned from my brother. The term was used as a census designation, a holdover from pioneer days, and any region in the United States with fewer than six people per square mile qualified. When I'd checked out those library books about Drummond's history, I'd looked at its current population density, too. Five point six people per square mile, so it just qualified. Maybe the truck and boat combos belonged to the last of the great hunters: men and women who stalked their prey by boat, shooting the creatures down when they came to the shore to drink.

"A hundred bucks says I can guess which guy owns that thing," Linda said, jerking her chin toward the vessel.

"How do you know it doesn't belong to a woman?" I'd countered, inspiring Bev to give me a high five.

"Look around, Gloria," Linda said.

When we'd waitressed together, she had sometimes called me

that in sarcastic homage to Gloria Steinem. I tolerated it. "I could launch that thing right here, right now, if I wanted to," I told her.

"Go for it," she'd said.

If I could have gotten it to the water, I have no doubt that I could have piloted it, but I was bluffing and she knew it. I glanced inside the truck's cab and spied a panting dog in the driver's seat and a Cabela's catalog on the dashboard. Crammed into the passenger seat were a sawed-off canoe paddle, a life jacket, and a small trolling motor.

"It's like *Mad Max*," I said, looking the boat over, "but with bath toys."

At the mention of one of her favorite leading men, Bev became even more interested in the boat. She didn't just like the men she knew and could talk to; she liked the Hollywood ones, too. The character was played by Mel Gibson, and he navigated a low-budget, post-apocalyptic world of mutant machines, violence, and danger. He also did it in tight leather pants, which was probably why he was one of her favorites.

Bev stopped abruptly then, and jutted her arms out as if Linda and I were about to cross a busy street without looking.

"Wait," she'd hissed, thinking for a minute. Then, "Maybe Mel's here *filming*!"

Her expression was initially dreamy, but then darkened. "Never mind. He's married."

Bev had many endearing qualities and one of them was that her thought process could often be followed in real time because she would say out loud exactly the things other people might keep to themselves. Linda was the exact opposite. She usually thought things through before speaking, and sometimes their personality styles clashed. When that happened, Linda gave Bev "the look."

Shoulders back, chin dipped to the side, mouth in a clamp, and eyebrows scrunched tight as fists, translated "the look," communicated one very simple concept: Don't be a dumbass.

"C'mon, Bev, *think*," Linda said. "What does that boat look like it's *for*?"

Bev considered, then braved a guess.

"Keeping Mel away from the paparazzi?"

At fifty-three, Bev was still single and still boy crazy. She'd been married, been single, she'd dated, stopped dating, had men who were friends, men she'd wished were more than friends, lost men, dumped men, longed after men. She just hadn't found the right one yet. And no one was going to convince her that a famous actor was out of her league. Unless, of course, he was married.

While Linda gave her the look, I looked into the truck's window again, and my eyes rested on the catalog sitting on the dashboard. I liked to know the proper names for things and that camouflaged boat had stymied me. I could not imagine what something like this might be called, but—in yet another legacy from my brother—I knew Cabela's probably would.

A subconscious urge propelled my hand through the open window, past the dog's long strings of slobber, and soon I was flipping through the catalog's pages. There in the boating section was a photograph of the vessel before us.

"It's a Beavertail Stealth twelve hundred," I said, as if Linda and Bev should feel as satisfied to have acquired that information as I was.

"It's for duck hunting," Linda said, nonplussed.

Two decades prior, Linda had moved to Michigan from Florida and one of the first things she'd bought when she arrived was a hunting rifle. Rumor had it she'd once opened the sliding glass door on her patio, leveled her new rifle in the opening, and shot an eight-point buck through the heart without so much as nicking her chaise longue. So, although she hadn't known the boat's actual name, she did know what it was for. I could have bypassed larceny from a vehicle and just asked her.

"Hunters hide inside that tent," she explained, "float their decoys in the water, and wait for ducks to fly over. When they do, they blast 'em."

Bev and I both stared at her, open mouthed, and a gory scene took shape in my mind. Broken wings, bloody feathers, limp necks.

"Oh. My. *God!*" Bev blurted. "Mel's on our island to do *that*?"

We both laughed out loud.

I'm not against hunting—deer, turkey, pheasant, I'd eaten them all. But those animals had speed, camouflage, or both going for them, so it seemed like they had a chance, even against high-powered weapons. I'd eaten plenty of wild duck, and liked it, but I'd never considered how the duck in my salad or my stir-fry had been hunted.

Even though she was naïve, Bev still had a point. Not about Mel (apparently, I was on a first-name basis with him now, too), but about the ducks. All the camouflage, firepower, and testosterone in that parking lot wasn't for facing the claws or hooves of some worthy opponent like a swimming bear, a wading cougar, or a rampaging moose. It was so full-grown men could sneak up on a duck. Right there in our midst was an aficionado of leading men, and yet we'd somehow stumbled into a meeting of the Elmer Fudd Fan Club.

Just like Bev had predicted, I'd missed my sons terribly that weekend. Seeing those hunting boats and shotguns, remembering all I'd learned from my brother, made me wonder if my sons would be hunters, too, when they grew up. Was there something innate inside men that made them want to kill things? I thought of the three sweet faces back at home with their father, I imagined their block towers and their happy chatter, and it was impossible for me to picture any one of them aiming a gun. And yet, the men who owned those boats had once been toddlers, too.

Later, I'd asked my brother why we'd never seen all those boats on the island before. He explained that Michigan's Department of Natural Resources had developed complex rules for hunting waterfowl, with different seasons for ducks, mergansers, coots, and geese, and different start dates for the state's three geographic zones. That year, not only had opening day of duck season fallen on a weekend—*our* weekend—some of the other waterfowl seasons had been combined and, for the first time in a generation, overlapped with duck season.

"Ice?" Linda reminded us, pointing to the store.

That one word encapsulated what, deep down, Bev and I knew to be true: Ducks were going to die that day on Drummond Island and forcing the girls to endure a warm cocktail wouldn't do a thing to spare their lives.

The fact that the boat *could have* belonged to a woman was only semantics. Inside Wazz's, not one of the other shoppers looked female. Unless you counted the Labatt beer poster of Pamela Anderson on the wall above the fire extinguisher, the only women in the place were the three of us. It was just camouflaged men, who belonged to the camouflaged trucks pulling the camouflaged boats, who were carrying shopping baskets filled with six-packs of Bud Light, bags of beef jerky, and pine tree air fresheners on a string.

"Do you think we should tell them we can see them?" Bev whispered out of the corner of her mouth. "Or just let them go on thinking they're invisible?"

Linda counted out a few dollars from the kitty, and Bev and I paid for the ice while Linda perused the snack aisle. From behind the chip display she gave each hunter the once-over. The one-hundred-dollar bet she'd proposed for matching the boat with its owner was just a figure of speech. I didn't have that kind of money to wager with and neither did she.

"And?" I asked her, when the three of us were outside the store.

"I dunno," she grumbled. "They all look alike."

"Well, duh!" Bev said. "They're all in that camo crap, *hello*?"

Linda gave Bev the look once more. She didn't mean the men in the store looked alike because of their clothes; she meant they were all tall with dark hair, mustaches, and beards. The standard groom for northern Michigan males. Considering every single one in the store had been sporting this, it would have been impossible for anyone to connect man to watercraft.

"Jack Pine Savages," Bev said with a dismissive wave. Where vocabulary was concerned, the trip to Wazz's had been amazingly productive. Beavertail Stealths were the boats hunters used to outsmart ducks and Jack Pine Savages were tall white men in scraggly facial hair.

"See that really, *really* tall one?" Bev was saying. "He goes with the teeny-weeny boat."

As if on cue, the really, really tall one exited the store, cool stepped past the three of us, opened the door to his truck, shoved the dog over, slid inside, and drove away. Linda and I both looked at Bev with newfound respect. Even back then, there were not that many things that could hold Bev's attention for long, but beefcake in camo was certainly one of them. We didn't even have to ask her to explain how she'd guessed the owner because I'm sure the question was plainly on our faces.

"I saw the shortest guy get into that thing over there," Bev explained, indicating a truck-and-boat combo at the far side of the parking lot with considerable girth. "So, doesn't it just figure the tallest guy would be in the little dinky one?"

Her successful deduction rendered the bet irrelevant. Not to be outdone, though, Linda took immediate charge of our afternoon plans.

"Let's follow him," she said.

While Linda could sometimes be stubborn, and Bev could be naïve, I certainly had my quirks, too. I often lived in my head, and unless something jarred me out into the world, I could be oblivious to what was going on around me. That year I was just beginning to notice a few of the island's most startling contradictions. For example, bounty hunters looking for Megabear needed only a bow, an arrow, and a hound, yet the men we'd just seen at the party store required a boat, a trolling motor, a truck, a tent, a trailer, spray paint, decoys, a dog, camouflage outfits, a paddle, a six-pack of Bud Light, and three shotguns to bag a duck.

Such contradictions weren't limited just to other people, though. I'd thought one of the reasons we were on the island at all, besides to be together, to be outside, and to explore the woods, was to get *away* from men. That Linda wanted to follow one was confusing to me. But there we went, bouncing down a two-track, following Bev's Jack Pine Savage into the woods.

After only a mile or so we arrived at a public boat launch and because the idea of contradictions was already top of mind, it came as only a small surprise that the facility revealed another one. Only on Drummond Island would a nationally recognized waterfowl sanctuary be located adjacent to a duck hunters' public boat launch. Surveying the area, I thought I could even hear the island's imaginary planning and zoning commissioner, whoever he or she was, explaining things: "Over here, you got your hippie-dippie bird sanctuary, and over there you got your ramp to launch your Beavertail Stealth."

We parked, all seven of us disembarked, someone lifted the two back hatches, slid open our coolers, and did what we always did when we found a scenic place to pause. We commenced an impromptu party. Bev raised a Jell-O shot, toasting every winged bird according to its kind but especially ducks. The ethereal voice of Stevie Nicks serenaded from Andrea's boom box, and soon several more hunters arrived and launched their boats.

Backing a boat trailer with a boat on it down a ramp toward open water is an acquired skill and on display that afternoon was a wide variety of abilities. Another contradiction: The owners of the oldest, grimiest, crappiest boats were the best at maneuvering them. One driver owned a ridiculously large torpedo-shaped vessel of showroom quality, but when he tried to get it in the water he missed the ramp completely and scraped the glossy hull over some rocks. The sound of ripping fiberglass is not a pleasant one, nor something expunged by the complex rhythms of Fleetwood Mac. Pam—animal lover, nonswimmer, boat avoider—was not someone I ever would have expected to confront a strange man, but something about a large boat, the bad driving, or both must have really irritated her.

"That calls for a citation!" she'd said, strutting a few feet from our group, standing with her feet planted, one hand on her waist and the other jerking open the left side of her bomber jacket.

Low on the horizon now, the sun glinted off something pinned to the lining. I squinted to make sure, but yes, it was a big silver star.

Light reflected off one of the points, and with her short hair, her fit body, and her aviator sunglasses, anyone who didn't know Pam, who didn't know she spent her days behind an elaborate bar serving high-grade liquor and gourmet food to business travelers, would have surely raised their arms in surrender.

To the rest of us, the idea of Pam as the law was hilarious. Pam was silly, Pam was friendly, Pam was fun, but Pam was not going to put anyone in a headlock. Yet it looked like a real sheriff's badge and she'd had it pinned inside her jacket all weekend, just waiting for the right time to flash it.

We all laughed, then crowded around to examine her credential up close. It looked real, but when we asked her where it had come from, she wouldn't tell us. All she'd say was that one of her regular customers at the bar where she worked had given it to her as a gag. We tried to pry more details out of her, but to no avail.

"Nope," she'd said, "not sayin'. I don't want to get anyone in trouble."

The reason it looked real was because it *was* real. If just having it wasn't illegal, flashing it to someone definitely was, and we could tell by her tone that she wasn't going to budge, and we relented. Most of the hunters were out in their boats by then anyway, with just a few stragglers remaining. The boat launch was filled with trucks, empty boat trailers, and us. We'd had our fun, and I thought we'd probably leave then, but before we could, a final vehicle pulled up. It had a gold emblem on the driver's side door and a *real* cop behind the wheel. Pam saw him and blanched.

"Act normal!" she hissed.

Act normal? I thought. *I* am *normal*.

The next sound I heard was Pam's jacket zipper going up in a hurry. What were the odds? Pam was the first one to bed at night, the first one to caution us if we were planning something even slightly dangerous, and she never, *never* did anything risky or illegal. And, Drummond Island supposedly didn't have any cops.

The black-green truck had big side mirrors, a cowcatcher over the front grille (probably for deer), and the gold emblems on both doors identified the driver as an officer with the Department of Natural Resources (DNR).

Although often the subject of ridicule—"Puddle Pirate," "Crick Dick," "Boat Bacon"—in some ways DNR officers actually had more authority than the police. They carried a wider variety of weapons and patrolled much larger jurisdictions. They could write tickets, make arrests, secure crime scenes, and were trained to do it all in hip waders if necessary.

The truck's door opened, a jackboot appeared, and then a park ranger got out. He was short haired, clean-shaven, and all business. While some of the hunters had smiled and waved to us, and one man even happily accepted a Jell-O shot, the ranger acted like we weren't even there and instead headed straight for the few remaining hunters and their boats. Equipped with a sidearm snapped into a holster, along with a radio, binoculars, a small mace dispenser, and a sap, all competing for space on his belt, I heard the squeak of patent leather as he marched past.

He took several minutes checking hunting licenses and counting life jackets. Finding no infractions, he turned his attention to us.

"What exactly are you ladies doing?" he'd asked, obviously annoyed. "Prancing around like you own the place?"

I have searched my brain, yet have found not a single memory of prancing. Yet many others, people we loved and held in high esteem, had asked us a more sincere variation on that same question.

What *were* we doing out there?

What *was* it about Drummond that drew us back, year after year?

Our husbands and boyfriends had asked us and so had our children. Our parents had asked, and George had asked us, too. There was no sandy beach, they'd reminded us. No shopping mall, no casino, no gourmet restaurants, no wineries, no five-star hotels, and certainly no health spa. Drummond Island didn't have one single amenity most people would probably associate with a women's weekend away.

Our island was sometimes called "The Gem of the Huron," usually in tourist brochures and on bumper stickers. It was no diamond, though, and sparkled instead in a way only certain people could see. We were some of those people. When we'd started the trip, not one of us could have afforded to go anyplace fancy. Now that some of us might have been able to, we'd found that wasn't what we wanted at all. Regular vacation spots just seemed too commonplace, too accessible.

Linda had chosen the island because our home lives—our children, our families, our jobs—could really only spare us for a weekend. Even though Drummond wasn't that far away (from Peegeo's parking lot it was only 180 miles), once we were there it seemed like a separate world. The Mackinac Bridge, the coastal highway, the car ferry through DeTour Passage, then the rocks and the thick forest made the place feel both exotic and feral. As once-wild girls, now tamed by marriage, motherhood, or management, we had a longing for the safety of that wilderness. We wanted to reconnect with each other and with our own inner lives, beyond carpools, diapers, tip jars, date nights, or laundry that perpetually needed folding.

We needed to climb on rocks, walk in the woods, get our cars muddy, play pool, and be part of something bigger than our insulated day-to-day lives. And you couldn't do any of that at a mall, a spa, or a five-star hotel. Drummond *was* an actual place. You could point to it on a map, and it had a set latitude and longitude. But by the time that park ranger asked us what we were doing there, the island had become more than a location; it was a feeling. A closeness only we could conjure, and only when we were together.

That had never been an easy thing to explain to our families. I could not imagine how we would explain it to the DNR.

"It's a free country," Linda observed, exhaling a squall of cigarette smoke.

The rest of us nodded in agreement. It was indeed.

Then out of the corner of my eye, I noticed Bev cock her head at Linda and indicate something she had cupped in the palm of her hand. In between her fingers was an object the size and shape of a hard-boiled egg. A pink, rubbery, hard-boiled egg.

"Go for it," Linda mouthed.

Bev held her hand out to the ranger, smiled, and opened her fingers.

"Homemade Jell-O?" she asked.

The ranger stared at the offering in disbelief. Andrea reached into our cooler, pulled out a pressurized can, flipped off the cap, and pressed down on the nozzle. There was a sound like a fart and whipped cream bloomed on top of the cherry glob.

The ranger took it in his thumb and forefinger, held it up to the light.

"Ladies." He sighed. "Is this what I think it is?"

"Try it." Bev giggled, doing a little shimmy. "You might like it."

He narrowed an eye, appraised Bev's wiggle, and then did something that surprised us all. He smiled.

"Ah, what the hell," he said, tipping his head back, opening his mouth, and tossing in the Jell-O shot.

When it hit his tongue he froze, his body stiff as a tree trunk, his only movement the vertical bounce of his Adam's apple. His eyes watered a little, and he finally took a breath.

"What *was* that?" he gasped.

Did Linda say the next word or did I just want her to?

"Decoy" was what I heard.

A coughing fit hit him broadside then and echoed out over the open water. A flock of mallards took flight and banked in the direction of the nature preserve. Without another word, the ranger marched off, climbed into his truck, and drove away.

"He wanted me," Bev said, smoothing her hair. "I could tell."

CHAPTER FOUR   *1998*

*Mary Lynn, Linda, Bev, Susan, and Pam rock hunting
together on Drummond's southern shore.*

We had all passed into adulthood years before, but the eight of us
still did a lot of growing up between 1997 and 1998. Andrea had
given birth to her first child, a daughter. I'd helped start a book
review magazine with two business partners. Linda and Kenny
had discussed getting married, and Bev had bought a house, the
first she'd ever owned with only her name on the deed. Mary Lynn
got a promotion and a raise at the printing company where she
worked, Jill's divorce from Marty was final, and to our great joy,
she'd returned to the island with us.

Perhaps the most visible change impacting us that weekend:
We'd graduated out of Frank's trailers and rented a log cabin on
the other side of the island. It was big enough for all of us to stay
in together and had a name that seemed to reflect the direction our
lives were headed: Fairview.

We had to share bedrooms, and beds, too, but we were used

to that, and when I close my eyes even now I can hear the sounds of us moving in and claiming that rustic little cabin for our own. Stockinged feet scampering up the log stairs, suitcases and duffel bags tossed onto beds, window shades snapped open, and voices all talking excitedly at once. After we were settled, we left to explore our new "neighborhood"—a secluded cove on the island's southern shore, populated with narrow winding two-tracks, aromatic cedar trees, occasional views of the water, and moss so green it seemed lit from within.

We'd been on an afternoon rock-hunting excursion together at Big Shoal Beach when the afternoon sky turned a strange greenish black and Mary Lynn had started shivering. It grew so dark that if there had been any streetlights on that part of the island, they'd have turned themselves on, even at two o'clock in the afternoon.

"Don't you leave on my account," Mary Lynn had tried to command through chattering teeth. "I can't tell the good rocks from a cement block, but I don't want to be blamed for you guys leaving any behind."

Big Shoal was a township park on the southern coast of the island several miles east of Fairview. Part of the shore was sandy, a rarity on the island, so in the summertime it filled up with swimmers and kayakers. In the fall, though, it was often deserted, and in other years we'd had good luck finding fossils there. Dolomite with squiggles of leggy creatures inside, whole rocks that looked like thumb-sized shark's teeth but were actually petrified coral, and composite stones with ancient fan-shaped shells solidified in granite and time.

We'd planned to stay longer, but one look at Mary Lynn had changed our minds. There was no cold like the heavy damp that gripped the Great Lakes in the fall. Linda suggested the only remedy was a greasy cheeseburger fresh from the grill at Chuck's, and back on the road I remember seeing the place appearing up ahead, vibrating at the tree line like a mirage. We'd decided to go there to warm up instead of driving back to Fairview because although both places were about the same distance away, the bar was on a main road and would take only a couple minutes to get to. Our cabin was deep in a cove, on a dirt road, down twists and windings, and would take us a half hour or more. We didn't think Mary Lynn should wait that long.

Just before the trip, Andrea had bought another Ford Bronco, a bigger, shinier, and more luxurious version of the Chuck Truck she'd named Bruno. In front of us, with Mary Lynn wrapped in extra coats in the passenger seat, Linda veered her Explorer into Chuck's parking lot. Andrea followed closely behind and two sets of muddy tires skidded to a hard stop on the gravel. Andrea's curly hair took the bounce like a Slinky, then returned to its pre-skid style.

"All hail the power of a salon-quality mousse," she deadpanned.

"And an object is either at rest or moves at a constant velocity," I added, verbal proof I was no longer able to leave even the most mundane thoughts of my sons behind.

That year, they were three, eight, and ten. My oldest was in the fifth grade and his class was studying Newton's Laws. I have no idea what was going on inside of Linda's car at that moment. In Andrea's, we were talking over Van Halen, fixing our hair, and making sure all laws of physics still applied.

"We're back, Chuck," Jill announced then. "Did you miss us?"

With Jill along, I felt like we girls were whole again. She spoke hardly at all of her missing years, and would only say that after Linda had shared the story of our encounter with the park ranger, she'd returned in order to protect us from ourselves.

Jill had always been the tough one. Still, I'd thought her offer of protection was a joke until I saw the knife. She and Andrea had just picked me up; we hadn't even left Traverse City before she'd reached under Andrea's backseat and grabbed the leather sheath she'd stashed there. Holding it aloft, she'd slid out a ridiculously large bowie knife.

"Girls," she'd said, "you get into any trouble this year and I got your backs."

I couldn't believe what I saw. I trusted Jill, I'd liked working with her at Peegeo's because she was so capable, and she was the kind of person you'd want nearby if something bad happened. But I did not like the idea of having a *weapon* along. It scared me.

Andrea was not a worrier like me, and when she looked in her rearview mirror and saw it gleaming, she seemed both entertained and taken aback.

"Good God, Jill!" she asked. "Where'd you get that thing?"

"Just some guy gave it to me."

What guy, and what it meant when "some guy" gave a newly divorced woman a giant knife, was left to our imaginations. Bev wasn't in the car yet when Jill assured us she really had only brought it along as a joke. She'd heard about Pam's sheriff's badge, and for her return she'd wanted to bring something equally amusing.

A knife didn't seem as funny to me. A knife didn't seem funny, period. When we pulled into Chuck's to warm up Mary Lynn, we'd been on the island for two days and Jill hadn't mentioned it again. I didn't think Bev even knew about it, or if she had, she'd either forgotten it was along or had chosen to ignore it. I was glad. I was a worrier, but about little things. When it came right down to it, not much really frightened me. And that had.

"Hello, all you lucky people!" Bev announced, pausing in the doorway at Chuck's.

She was not being ironic; Bev really believed fortune was shining on whoever happened to be inside that bar because she'd arrived. Along with the rest of us, of course. And that night, the rest of us included Earl II.

At some now-forgotten moment, bachelorette Earl had been lost or wrecked and on Bev's arm that afternoon was a second blow-up doll we'd nicknamed "Son of Earl." The original's replacement had been a gift to us from George, and from the moment we'd received him, Bev had assigned herself to act as his keeper. She'd sit with Earl on the porch swing at Fairview; she'd make sure he was arranged where he could see the pool table at Northwoods when she and I were playing; and she'd pose with him in our group photographs, often grabbing his crotch just as the shutter clicked.

After all the energy I'd put into the original Earl, there was a time when it wouldn't have seemed possible I'd someday forget the details of his demise, but I had. My strange need to impress other people with how much I liked my friends was gone. I supposed it had been born of insecurity, and where the girls were concerned, that was gone, too.

We'd only gone to Chuck's to warm up Mary Lynn and get a quick bite, but it was also an opportunity for Son of Earl to meet People of Chuck's, and I was more than happy to let Bev make the introductions. Her attachment to him was not from any inner turmoil, like mine had been, but from her simple and light-hearted search for fun. For the occasion, she'd dressed him in a beanie hat, a pressed tuxedo shirt, a black vest and bow tie, but no pants.

Bev's enthusiasm for Earl was not contagious, however. The novelty had faded and as Bev held him in the doorway and announced our arrival, several heads did turn our way, and I heard a couple of embarrassed snickers, but then only silence.

"Well, we're here anyway," Bev told the room, "so get over it."

I had to admire her poise. Instead of being embarrassed or standing idly by while strangers made fun of her, or worse, dismissed her and her companion altogether, she'd simply adjusted.

We sat down, Andrea put a quarter in the jukebox, a love song played at full volume—Journey's "Stone in Love"—and at least one group of people did eventually warm to Earl II. It would have been difficult for them not to, after Bev slow danced with him right next to their booth. The song ended on a fadeout, and Bev curtsied, holding Earl's wrist with one hand and the hem of an imaginary skirt with the other. This garnered an enthusiastic round of applause, which she accepted with grace, and she and her dance partner sat down at our table.

"Where's this Chuck person, anyway?" she'd asked.

All out of breath from dancing, Bev was still ready for whatever might be next, and I loved to watch her when she was having that much fun. I told her the bar had probably been named after someone, but then again, "Chuck" could just as easily have meant woodchuck, ground chuck (the place did have amazing cheeseburgers, after all), or God forbid, upchuck.

The bar was the size of a double-wide trailer and contained a wood bar, an L-shaped dining room, a kitchen, and "Does" and "Bucks." The entry door was a white hunk of dented aluminum with a fist-sized hole where the doorknob was supposed to be. Inside, though, was a paradise decorated with beer mirrors, American flags, and the decapitated heads of legendary whitetails. A hard spike of a woman named Garthalene was the owner, and despite the chilly reception for Earl II, she'd always treated us well.

While Bev had been dancing, the rest of us unloaded our purses off our shoulders, removed our jackets, and claimed the big round table. Mary Lynn had stopped shivering and was rubbing her palms together, warming up her hands. Linda took a few minutes to say hello to Garthalene's daughter, Missy, and was the last one of us to get settled.

Anyone appraising our group may have initially slid their eyes right past Linda, obscured as she was inside an oversized coat. Especially with Bev, the human spotlight, in the room. But when Linda's coat came off that night, out she stepped in a lipstick-red, formfitting turtleneck. With her long black hair, dark eyes, and olive skin, in one simple motion she'd gone from Camp Fire Girl to Cleopatra.

Although it was two women who ran the place, the customers at Chuck's were often mostly men. Local rowdies and weekend bear hunters, mixed with pool players, fishermen and the occasional golfer who'd strayed from the island's conference center. If I had been paying attention instead of lining up quarters for the pool table, I might have seen the man in the corner. I might have seen how he looked at Linda when she took off her jacket. But I wasn't paying attention and neither were any of the other girls, not even Jill who'd pledged so solemnly to protect us from ourselves. I'd worked on not being so oblivious, not living so much in my head all the time, but Drummond was the one place where I still felt like I didn't have to pay attention all the time.

"Hey Linda," the man in the corner called out.

Even though he was sitting down, I could tell he was of average height or shorter, but well built. He was in his late twenties or early thirties, with black hair and quick eyes. He was at a table near the door with his back to the wall and with him were a dozen other men all dressed in camo. His voice sounded flat, yet when I think back there was already something challenging in his tone. The two words—*hey Linda*—weren't just a greeting exactly; they'd sounded more like a directive. As if he were used to giving orders and using the fewest words possible to do it.

"How's your mother?" Linda called back.

At first I thought that was an insult, but it turned out to be a real question.

"She's good," the guy said.

By then I'd started a game of pool and was playing someone I didn't know, but because the pool table was situated in between the camo man's table and ours, I couldn't help but hear his back-and-forth with Linda.

She was the only one of the girls who knew him, but that wasn't unusual. She knew a lot of people, and there'd been other times she'd seen men she knew that we didn't. She'd told me bits and pieces of her past, and for someone now so adverse to change, I'd come to learn that she'd sure lived through a lot of it. Getting engaged young, taking Greek lessons so she could speak to her future in-laws, but calling off the wedding. Then traveling around Florida with a new musician boyfriend instead and even living at the Playboy Club. Moving in with another guy when that relationship went sour, a brute who cheated her out of her house and almost everything else she owned.

When I met Linda, she'd just started dating Kenny, and their relationship had grown into a happy and stable one. People from her past still sometimes appeared at random and I'd assumed this guy was just one of those. Within a few minutes, he wasn't safely in her past anymore; he was standing next to our table—*our* table—and smiling like he was expecting to join us. Linda didn't seem opposed to the idea the way I was, but at least she didn't make it easy on him.

"Here's the deal," she told him. "You can sit down, but if you're not entertaining, you're out of here."

Up close he was still good-looking, but younger and fiercer than he'd seemed from my prior vantage point at the pool table. Linda told him we'd only planned to stay long enough to have one drink and finish our sandwiches, but he bought us all a round anyway. As time passed, he must have been entertaining because he and Linda soon had their heads bent, their hair touching, and I could hear their voices chuckling over some private joke.

It wasn't like the other girls were just sitting quietly by, waiting for Linda to finish her conversation. We each had our favorite things to do when we were at one of the island's bars. Bev had Earl, I had pool, Andrea and Jill had the jukebox, and Mary Lynn and Pam liked to play the lottery and were busy working their way through a pile of scratch-off tickets. But even with us all happily occupied, I still thought having a man sit at our table, and stay there, broke protocol.

By 1998, we were six years into our annual trip. If you would have asked any of us why we went every year, we probably all would have said just to be with each other. If you had asked us to elaborate, we would have given you eight different explanations. Linda liked to plan, she liked building a tradition, and during the long months of hard work at Peegeo's, she liked having something to look forward to. Andrea liked to socialize, she liked to drive and party with her girlfriends. Jill and I wanted time away from the stress of our home lives, and I especially enjoyed the chance. With Bev, but with all of the other girls, too. Bev loved all kinds of travel, Susan was up for adventure, and Mary Lynn and Pam just enjoyed our group's happy camaraderie.

So while there were all sorts of reasons we were on Drummond Island, not one of them was to pick up men. It just wasn't done, not ever. It would have gone against everything our sisterhood stood for. Friendship, adventure, emotional connection, and yes, even love.

Just because Linda invited a man to sit at our table, that didn't mean she was planning to pick him up. We knew her well enough to know that probably wasn't what she was planning at all. The guy was good-looking though, in the dangerous and rough way Linda liked, and she obviously knew him. But as the night wore on, I let my worries about him go. She was just talking to him, plain and simple, and in a few hours when we left Chuck's, we were sure that would be the end of it. Still, a few of the girls, especially Mary Lynn, grew increasingly irritated he was spending so much time at our table.

"Who *is* he, anyway?" she'd asked when the guy left for the bathroom.

"Just this cop I know," Linda said.

Although we no longer made a point of drinking and driving, the "no cops on the island" mystique remained, so we liked who he was even less, but Linda said he didn't live on the island and wasn't on duty. He was just visiting for the weekend, like we were, and not interested in writing tickets or making arrests. He'd gotten lucky and won one of two bear tags that specified Drummond Island in the DNR's hunting lottery. He wasn't on the island to pick up women; he was on the island to shoot a black bear. I'd seen the way he looked at her, though, and I wasn't so sure.

I don't think I'd ever seen Linda come on to a man. Before I'd left Peegeo's, Linda and I had worked together for more than three years and not once had I even seen her flirt with anyone.

Linda could be friendly or tough, practical or funny, to both women and men, but her dominant trait was loyalty. If you were lucky enough to be her friend, unless you really screwed it up somehow, you'd be her friend for life. Her boyfriend Kenny enjoyed that same level of devotion. They'd been together by then for seven years and they were a naturally good match. Both tough and people smart, both wry, with a dry sense of humor, and both preferred the woods and the lakes to town.

As a couple, they'd hit a minor snag when first Kenny wanted to get married and Linda didn't; then it switched and she was the one ready to say "I do" and he the holdout, but it hadn't seemed to dull their passion. If anything, I'd thought they were even more devoted to each other, and I couldn't imagine her ever being with anyone else. She wasn't flirting with the interloper overstaying his welcome, but he was definitely flirting, or at least trying to, with her.

Our original plan of staying at Chuck's for a burger and a quick drink faded, and we ordered another round, someone challenged me by putting their quarters on the pool table, and Andrea and Jill pumped five dollars into the jukebox. The other girls were in conversation with each other, and Linda and the guy must have had a lot to talk about because they'd seemed, for the time being anyway, interested in talking only to each other.

I think it was a little before midnight when I saw her push him on the shoulder, hard, her face locked in a frown, and I wondered what had happened. She'd given him the look, and I thought he'd probably leave after that—I would have if someone looked at me that way—but he didn't. By then the place had emptied out some, and so besides him, it looked like we would have Chuck's pretty much to ourselves until close.

Usually, that was just how we liked it, and the rest of our Saturday night might have continued on for longer if Mary Lynn hadn't abruptly decided she'd had enough.

"Time to go," she'd said, to no one in particular.

Mary Lynn was a frequent grumbler, it was just her way, and usually we brushed off her complaints. Her commands were something else. They were rare, but when she gave one it had an edge like a paper cutter and was not up for negotiation. When she'd said it was time to go, she meant right now.

But this wasn't Traverse City, and it wasn't Peegeo's; this was Chuck's Place and we were on island time. No appointments, no deadlines, no watches, and in the morning, no alarm clocks. We all had probably heard Mary Lynn's announcement somewhere in the background, but despite the man at our table we were still having too much fun to take notice of it. Yes, we'd grown up, and yes, we'd curtailed the drinking and driving, but we still had one good night at Chuck's in us and we were right in the middle of it.

Mary Lynn said again that it was time to go, but several minutes went by and still none of us responded. I suppose we hoped if we just ignored it, her desire to call it a night and head back to Fairview would go away.

Mary Lynn might have been short, old ladyish, and persnickety, but that didn't mean she was passive. She had patiently waited for us to respond—twice. When we didn't, she put on her coat, slung her tetherball of a purse over her shoulder, hiked her body up onto her chair, and stood as tall as her short frame allowed, putting both hands on her ample hips.

"Door, bitches!" she hollered.

When Mary Lynn was done, she was done. No negotiations, no whining, no bargaining. Behind her back, people called her Gnomie, but to us her small size made her seem like the bossy relative you were afraid to disappoint, and our reaction that third time was instantaneous. With comical speed we rounded up our purses and coats, I put down the pool cue right in the middle of a game, and Susan paid the bar bill. Even Linda stood up, put on her coat, and turned for the door.

The guy put his hand on Linda's arm and squeezed, but she yanked it away. The red turtleneck had disappeared under her jacket again, and she followed Mary Lynn out the door with Susan and Bev close behind.

I looked at the guy, to see how he'd take her quick exit. His glassy eyes were still on the door.

"I'm coming with," he slurred.

"No, you're not," Jill snapped. "Go back to your own friends."

Pam had stayed back at the cabin that night, so Andrea, Jill, and I were the only ones still inside Chuck's, and without Linda around, Jill must have felt free to talk to him like that. I was glad she had. I felt tired and annoyed. With him, but with Linda, too. No cops on the island had just been something funny for her to say. Not only was one here, but at her invitation he'd spent the whole night sitting at our table.

The guy gripped his chairback, stood in slow motion, weaved for a long second, then steadied himself.

"Can't go back," he'd said, gesturing with his chin toward the table where his friends had been sitting. It was empty.

"Yeah, well, sucks to be you," Jill said, sliding a plastic ashtray across the table so hard it slid off the edge and landed in his lap. Cigarette butts crawled across his legs like worms, and while he brushed them off the three of us pushed out the door.

It was raining by then; long sleeves of water were coming down in icy welts. With our jackets draped over our heads, we jogged across the parking lot toward Andrea's Bronco. We were just in time to see Linda's Explorer peeling out, her happy grin magnified behind rivulets of rain. Andrea hopped in her car, cranked the key, and flipped the heat to max. Jill pulled open the passenger door, lifted the seat, and climbed in the back. I was just about to get into the front when, from behind us, the guy came running.

"Wait!" he barked. "Your friend said I should come with you. Her car's full and I need a ride to my cabin."

"What are you talking about?" I said, angry now.

He didn't have a coat on, just a white T-shirt under camouflage overalls, and he hugged himself in the cold. His wet palms patted his own back like flippers. I climbed into my seat and out of the rain but kept the passenger side door open. I wasn't about to invite him inside, but even in that situation something of the mother in me remained, and I didn't want to slam the door in his face.

There was only one other car left in the parking lot, probably Garthalene's. And the guy just stood there, pitiful and silent, staring into the warmth of the Bronco. The wind was blowing so hard he had to lean into it just to stay upright, although that could have been all the beer I'd seen him drink.

The open door kept the domelight on, and I glanced at Jill and Andrea. Their faces looked skeptical. Music played from the dashboard, and the guitar licks that had been so loud when Andrea had parked Bruno what seemed like a lifetime ago were nearly drowned out by the sleet and the wind.

The guy was so close I could see each smear of rain grease his hair and pill onto his eyelashes. I could see each muscle through his white T-shirt. He wasn't my type, too raw-looking, but he really was handsome. Fit and compact.

"I just need a ride," he said.

I swiveled in my seat and looked over my shoulder at Jill. She shrugged. Andrea looked at Jill, too, said nothing, but leaned out across my lap, her face as close as she could get it to the open door.

"Just so you know," she snarled into the weather, "we're doing drugs in this car."

Her remark had the beat of a punch line but nobody laughed. Andrea's parents divorced when she was young, and her mother and stepfather raised her. Her stepfather was a state trooper, and by cop family osmosis, Andrea believed any self-respecting law enforcement professional, on a weekend off and far from his jurisdiction, would just walk away from a statement like that. Even if it were made by a pretty woman sitting with her friends in a warm car that idled a little fast and even when the law was standing alongside that car, bareheaded and jacketless, in the Upper Peninsula's October sleet. Yes, even then, Andrea knew any good cop would just walk away.

"Yeah?" he said. "So what?"

With those words an unspoken agreement was made.

We'd get this guy safely to his stupid little cabin, wherever it was. We were torqued out about it, and when we got back to Fairview, Linda was going to hear about it, but for her we'd do it. For her, we would have done anything.

It was Drummond after all, a place where the rules didn't apply, at least not to us. Even the most basic ones, like not inviting a strange man into your car, ever.

Andrea exhaled, put two hands on the wheel, and stared straight ahead. Jill moved over and made room, then relaxed against the backseat. The guy took a step toward the Bronco, I hopped out, and he grabbed the lever, lifted the seat, and climbed in the back with Jill. For an instant, time paused. The shutter of a lens in my mind clicked and the side of his face was reflected in the domelight. It had shapeshifted into something sculpted and carved, like a jack-o'-lantern. Then the moment passed, he settled in, I climbed back into my seat, pulled the door closed, and Andrea hit the gas.

"Hoo-whee, it's nice and warm in here!" the guy said when we were under way. "Keep driving, ladies, my cabin is just down the road a bit."

Andrea pulled out of the parking lot and onto Johnswood, a main road, and I glanced over my shoulder and saw the guy close his eyes, put his head against the backseat. A dreamy smile spread from his lips up into those high cheekbones.

Now that he was thinking about it, he said, his cabin was actually up the road quite a ways yet. Quite a *long* ways. But we should just keep going, and he'd be sure and tell us when we were getting close. The suggestion had irritated me then, with an intensity that seemed all out of proportion, and now I know why. *Just keep going* was our motto, not his, and subconsciously I'd known he'd violated a tenet we held sacred.

For what was probably an hour, and maybe even longer, we drove. It was darker than dark, more than half of the island had no electricity, and in 1998, streetlights were spotty or nonexistent on the half that did. We drove down main roads and dirt roads, pulled into driveways, and bounced over two-tracks.

Later, Andrea even drove down some of those roads a second time, but we never seemed to be going the right way.

If we'd just get our shit together, the guy said, maybe we'd be able to find his cabin.

Drummond Island is only thirty-six miles long by eighteen miles wide, and there aren't many main roads. What we learned in that extra-long hour was our passenger's name—I'll call him Dick—that he was a state trooper, that he was single, that he loved to party hearty with *all* the pretty ladies, and that he could not wait to shoot himself a bear. What we did not learn was the location of Dick's rented cabin. He either could not or would not remember where it was.

"This isn't Drummond Island," he'd said delightedly at one point, "this is *Fantasy* Island!"

Jill pulled out a roach and we passed it around, as much to make good on Andrea's warning as to get stoned. Despite the fact that at first it seemed as if Mary Lynn had cut us short, the night was over for us now. We didn't want to party anymore. We just wanted to go back to Fairview, back to the rest of the girls. We wanted to talk to Linda, then put on our pajamas, raid the refrigerator, heat up a sloppy joe, scoop out a big spoonful of Pam's potato salad, and sit at the kitchen table and talk and laugh. That was *our* fantasy.

Someone passed the roach to Dick, but he waved it away in a panic.

"Are you trying to get me fired!" he yelled. "What's wrong with you girls?" He said he had to take random piss tests sensitive enough to pick up THC in his system, even if he hadn't actually smoked any pot.

"You wanted in, remember?" Andrea said. "What part of 'We're doing drugs in this car' didn't you get?"

I watched the end of the soggy brown paper glow, watched Jill's chest inflate, looked out the window, and thought about the bears, the ones Dick said he was on the island to hunt, but I thought about other bears, too.

I thought about the Megabear and wondered if anyone had ever collected that $1,000 bounty on him. I hoped not. I thought about the bears the girls and I, and especially Jill, had wanted to see at the dump. Finally, I thought about the three bears. Not the cuddly ones in the fairy tale, but three real bears I'd read about in a long-ago story in the newspaper.

A decade earlier a man from my town had shot a mother bear, cut off her head and paws for trophies, left the rest of her to rot, and ditched her three cubs in a telephone booth. It wasn't bear season, he didn't have a legal hunting tag, and when someone called in an anonymous tip, he'd been arrested by the DNR.

I'd been a few years out of college then, righteous with my new journalism degree, and closely followed the story. The DNR released the cubs into the wild somewhere on Drummond Island. If they were still alive, those cubs would have been eleven years old in 1998. Full-grown and legal to hunt. It might not make any logical sense, but in my mind, the bear Dick wanted to kill was one of those orphaned cubs.

"What's your deal, man?" Andrea said, glaring at him in her rearview mirror. "Last chance to tell us where you're staying."

Dick crossed his hands behind his head. Well, he said, laughing in the direction of Andrea's neck, since we hadn't been able to find *his* place, we should just take him back to ours. Then we could all get naked.

Our passenger grinned at this obvious solution, then looked around the car at the rest of us. For what, I wondered. Acknowledgment? Affirmation? Since my days at Peegeo's I'd been continually puzzled by how blind some men could be to a woman's facial expression or how deaf they sometimes acted to the acid tone of her voice.

Andrea pulled the Bronco over into a patch of weeds at the side of the road. She put the vehicle in park, the two of us shared a glance, and then we both unbuckled our seat belts and turned around to look at Jill.

She returned our gaze, mouthed *asshole*.

"Somebody's gettin' a blow job tooooo*night!*" our passenger sang out, front teeth extended over his lower lip, fingers pointed at the heavens like a little boy holding pretend six-shooters.

For every action..., I thought to myself, *there's always an equal and opposite reaction.*

I opened the passenger door, hopped off my seat, flipped the back of it forward, and waited next to the car. Jill glared at our passenger but he didn't move. For someone supposedly trained to be aware of his surroundings, he looked completely oblivious. Still just a little boy who, when the carnival ride was over, was still feeling the rush. Dick wore a smile of anticipation on his pumpkin head, and it felt like a full minute passed before he even realized the vehicle he was riding in had stopped.

"Get out," Jill said.

All three of us just looked at him, waiting for the command to register.

"Wait...what?" he said finally, eyes open, cop instinct engaged.

"I said," Jill repeated, jabbing two hard fingers into his shoulder, "get out!"

Jill was small, but when Dick didn't move, she leaned closer, crowding him into the corner.

"It's raining," he said, his voice strangely small. "I mean, just look out there."

"*Get out!!*" we ordered in unison.

Dick tried to sit up, but he couldn't because Jill was still in his way, and for the first time that night, he looked and sounded angry.

"Hey now, wait a sec," he snarled. "You bitches can't do this to me. I'm a *state trooper*, goddammit!"

Andrea laughed and gunned the engine. When she was a girl, her stepfather had been intimidating, but she wasn't afraid of him anymore and he was a lot taller, a lot bigger, and a lot more frightening than Dick. Neither one of my parents were the police, though, they were educators, and my heart was beating so fast and so loud I was pretty sure it wasn't inside my body anymore, but revving under the Bronco's hood. My hands shook so hard I had to steady them on the doorframe.

A cruel smile spread across Jill's face. Sweet, petite Jill. I'd never, ever seen an expression like that on her, but she'd smiled like that before, I could tell, and would probably smile like that again.

Jill actually likes this, I thought.

Then from the backseat came an unmistakable sound.

Andrea heard it, too, and turned on the domelight as if for proof. Had we really heard what we'd thought we heard?

The bowie knife. It was out and laying, glinting and terrible, across Jill's lap.

Dick's ruddy face blanched white in the shadows and he tried to sit up again, but Jill put her face so close to his they could have touched noses.

"I'll *cut* ya," she promised.

And with that, Dick was gone.

He'd launched himself past Jill, out of the backseat, and right by me. He leaped over the weeds at the side of the road and sprinted into the woods. We heard branches snap, his voice yelping "Ow!" then nothing but the wind and the rain.

I climbed back inside the Bronco and pulled the door shut. I was soaked. There was a pause; the three of us just looked at each other, then looked out the window and into the woods, and then looked back at each other again.

"Wow," Andrea said, deadpan, "that boy can really move."

Jill's smile changed back to pretty again and my heartbeat slowed, just a little. We all took a breath, then another. I thought of the other girls and what their reaction was going to be when we told them what happened. I thought of Bev, and how afraid she would have been if she'd been with us, and I was glad she was back at Fairview, safe from harm, still believing the wildest thing you could do with a man on Drummond was dress him in a beanie hat and slow dance with him at Chuck's.

"I wish Linda could've seen that," I said.

At first, a shocked silence surrounded the three of us inside that car, but then we all started talking at once.

Did you see his face? Jill, you were amazing! I bet he never hits on a woman in a bar again. Not at Chuck's anyway. Just look out there—we've got to be ten miles from anything. What do you think the temperature is, forty? I hope there's a bear out there. Yeah, that great big one.

Our voices were young and strong, and I imagine them now swirling and spinning through the glass and metal of the Bronco and following that man beyond the road and the weeds and deep into those primeval woods. Inside Andrea's car, we were warm, we were alive, and we were invincible.

Andrea put the Bronco in drive, we began our dark ride back to Fairview, and I only relaxed when I heard Jill resheath the knife.

"We might have to take that shit back home," she'd said. "But not up here. Up here *nobody* fucks with the Drummond Girls."

The first thing you saw when you pulled into the dirt driveway of Fairview was the rough-hewn wood of the cabin's side porch. When we returned, lights from the sliding glass door shone onto the log railing, so we knew at least some of the girls were still awake. I wondered if one of them was Linda. I was not looking forward to confronting her; she could be formidable. Drummond was supposed to be a time to support each other and have fun, not bail on each other over a guy.

The whole way back, the three of us had been like a highlight reel, reliving the best moments of the previous hours, and we hadn't discussed what we were going to say to Linda. When we finally pulled into the dirt driveway of Fairview, I was about to suggest we stay in the car and talk about it together, when Andrea got out, jogged up onto the porch, opened the door, and disappeared inside the cabin.

A second later, Jill and I heard her loud and unmistakable voice: "What the hell, Linda?" It was the same tone she'd used on me when she thought I'd brought one of my kids to her bachelorette party. Irritated, yet also curious.

Jill had been the brave one in the face of a physical altercation, and it looked like Andrea was willing to tackle an emotional one. What had *I* been doing during both of these? *Thinking* about things. What a rebel.

But Jill and I went inside then, too, and just like the three of us had talked all at once in the Bronco, the girls who'd been with Linda talked all at once when we walked inside. *Where had we been? Did we get lost? What was going on?*

Not one of those questions sounded angry; when I thought about it, not even Andrea's question to Linda had. She'd sounded genuinely perplexed, as if the nighttime ride the three of us had just endured was a mystery to be solved and not an offense to be atoned for.

Later, Andrea would become our group's conscience, our conflict resolver, and her actions that night just the beginning, and showed exactly why she was so good at defusing a conflict. Andrea was fascinated by people, by their motivations, and especially by the *why* of human behavior, making her capable of doing something impossible for the rest of us: keeping her own feelings out and just assessing the situation.

That moment inside Fairview was a harbinger of things to come, when Andrea our friend would develop a reputation as Andrea the Confronter. She was good at it. Fair, compassionate, and willing to get right to the point. She was down-to-earth, too, so that night all her communication skills had come out as simply "What the hell, Linda?"

"What the hell, *what*?" Linda asked.

"Why the hell did you tell that guy we'd give him a ride?"

"*What?*" Linda said, sounding genuinely confused. "I never told him that."

"For real?" Andrea asked.

"Yes, for real. Why the hell would I tell him that? I was trying to get the hell *away* from him. I thought you guys were, too."

Linda had left the parking lot before Dick had come outside.

She didn't know he'd approached our car, let alone been allowed inside, and neither she nor the other girls knew where the three of us had been for the past two hours. It was almost three o'clock in the morning, and they'd thought we were going to follow them straight back to Fairview from Chuck's. That's why they were all still awake. They'd been worried about us.

"*Now*, who's taking the guy's side?" Linda said.

She was right. Dick had lied to us. It was totally out of character for Linda to have dumped him on us like that, and yet we'd believed him, a guy we didn't know, over everything we did know about her.

"We suck," Andrea said, hanging her head. It broke the tension and a few of the girls even laughed.

It must have been all that thinking I'd been doing, but I couldn't resist. I reminded Linda that she'd invited the guy to sit down. We'd all seen that with our own eyes. Yes, she said, that was true, but she just wanted to ask him about his mother, who'd been a good friend, and by the end of the night he'd started to get on her nerves.

That rang true; I remembered seeing her give him a shove and then later yank her arm away when he'd tried to grab it.

Linda said she'd felt relieved when Mary Lynn commanded us all to the door. She'd wanted to get away from him. That was why she'd peeled out of the parking lot so fast, not because she was trying to dump him on us.

"So, like, what?" Linda asked, looking from my face to Andrea's, and then to Jill's. "Did something happen?"

"Yeah," Jill said, poker-faced. "You could say that."

That winter, two months after our trip, Linda was working a day shift at Peegeo's when a woman she hadn't seen in years came in for lunch. She didn't live in Traverse City; she was just visiting from downstate, had taken a chance that Linda still worked at Peegeo's, and come in to say hello. The restaurant wasn't busy, so the woman and Linda had time to talk. They caught each other up on the people they knew in common; then Linda inquired, gingerly I'm sure, about her son. How was he doing?

Great!, the woman had said. He was a state trooper now, stationed in the Upper Peninsula, and she could not have been more proud of how he'd turned out.

CHAPTER FIVE 1999

*Bev, dancing at the Northwoods the night she received
her Drummond nickname.*

I didn't see the point of making all that fuss over the calendar. I thought the Y2K conspiracy theorists were silly, and I didn't join the millennial celebrators, beyond walking out onto my porch at midnight and banging an old pan with a wooden spoon (a family tradition) and then toasting the New Year. If staying clear of all that Year 2000 hoopla made me a know-it-all or a cynic, so be it.

Then again, I'd never been much of a trend follower or joiner, not even when I was a little girl.

I wasn't even a Girl Scout. I wasn't a Camp Fire Girl, a Foxfire Girl, a Girl Guide, or a member of the 4-H, either. I'd never pledged a sorority (unless you counted Alpha Krappy Grammar, the anti-Greek society I'd cofounded in graduate school), and although I actually liked the idea behind the Daughters of the American Revolution, because I was adopted I didn't know whether my biological kin had fought in any war, ever.

When I was about six, I was a Brownie. For about two whole weeks. It's still difficult for me to believe, but it must be true because there is a black-and-white picture in the Link family photo album of me in the uniform. My mother is standing next to me, smiling proudly as she prepares to apply the sash around my neck. If badges could have been earned by having legs that looked like tent poles, I would have been first in line to receive one.

I am smiling in the picture, but I remember feeling uneasy. The word *contrived* hadn't entered my lexicon yet, but that was already my opinion of organized socializing. My family camped, hiked, and spent a lot of time outdoors. Why couldn't I just learn about nature that way, I'd wondered, instead of being forced to go to a meeting with girls I didn't know in someone's basement?

The uniform's socks were unbearably itchy, I told my mother, and I could no longer abide them. In truth, I couldn't abide the uniform, period. Pledges, songs, and candlelit rituals? Even at six, I knew mind control when I saw it. Outside of the Drummond Girls, I've never joined anything.

I didn't know how the other girls felt about such things. It had never come up. Until one night in the new century when Linda took us two-tracking and Andrea was regaling us with a story about a woman she worked with and didn't like. While she talked, an unlit Winston bobbed up and down between her lips and she patted her pockets for her lighter. Finding none, she continued the story anyway, while Linda kept one hand on the wheel and reached around in her purse in the dark with the other. She found it and pulled it out, but before she flicked on the flame she stopped the car and her face became a mask so serious Andrea even paused her story. Linda held up her palm, as if to preface an historic moment.

"Wohelo," she'd said, in a deep voice from the beyond. "I light the light of life. *Wohelo* means life."

The remark was so random that Andrea barked out a laugh,

propelling the cigarette out of her mouth like an arrow. For the rest of that weekend, Linda wasn't Linda anymore, and she wasn't even the Dragon Lady. She was Wohelo.

The word was familiar to me—I had friends who'd been Camp Fire Girls—and I'd just assumed that Linda had been one, too. I could just picture her. A sassy, black-haired hellion bossing a bunch of other little girls in plaid uniforms around. The nickname stuck. Back in Traverse City, and at Peegeo's, she was still the Dragon Lady, but on Drummond Island she was Wohelo.

The thing about nicknames is you can't choose one for yourself. Well, you could choose your own, I suppose, but it probably wouldn't stick. Since Jill had extricated the trooper from Andrea's Bronco, we'd started calling her the Secretary of Defense, and both that label and Wohelo had arisen naturally out of two memorable but unexpected moments we'd shared.

"*I* need a Drummond nickname," Bev declared. "What do you think *mine* should be?"

Bevski, Wojo, the Polish Princess. Bev already had three nicknames, I thought. Why did she need another? Especially when the rest of us didn't have a single one?

"You're not supposed to plan it out like that," Andrea said. "Nicknames just kinda happen."

"I guess." Bev sighed, but she sounded disappointed.

We had liked Fairview so much that we'd rented the cabin again. The nickname conversation had come up when we were all sitting around the kitchen table, recounting Jill's backseat heroics of the previous year.

"I've got a good one for Pam," Linda said. "She's the Sheriff."

"Perfect!" Andrea said.

"You can't have a Sheriff *and* a Secretary of Defense," Pam said.

"Oh yes, you can," Jill said. "We'll each have our own jurisdictions. You handle duck hunters and I'll take the cops."

"Deal," Pam agreed.

Amazing, the conversations the eight of us would sometimes have up there, when maturity was neither required nor expected. Spread out on the table were the colorful cards from Apples to Apples, the game Susan had brought along that year, and she was soon christened Gamer. Jill said Andrea was our very own Jukebox Hero, since she was the one who always brought along her boom box and knew the perfect mix to play at Chuck's and Northwoods. That left Mary Lynn, Bev, and me. Mary Lynn would not have appreciated being reminded of her Gnomie moniker, and I sure didn't want to be called Gloria all the time.

"Y'all just need to do something *crazy*, then," Andrea had told us, rotating her head around in a herky-jerky spiral.

I don't think any one of the three of us took that suggestion literally; Andrea was just being Andrea. Maturity requirements aside, I was almost forty, with Bev and Mary Lynn both more than a decade older. I thought our "doing something crazy" days were behind us, and that weekend I'd made a point of noticing the quirks and idiosyncrasies of the island instead.

We saw more tourists but there were all sorts of endearing things about Drummond that would never be in any travel brochure. The lift of an index finger off the steering wheel that functioned as a roadway greeting for locals. The ubiquity of mounted deer heads inside various businesses, regardless of their decor. Plaid wallpaper and deer head? Check. Wood paneling and deer head? Check. Nautical scenes and deer head? Check.

The women's bathroom at the Northwoods was another of the island's idiosyncrasies, and peeing there could be... challenging. There were three stalls, one sink, one mirror, a paper towel dispenser, and a trash can all packed into a room smaller than my closet. If you opened the door too fast, it'd hit the porcelain bowl of toilet number one. To conserve space, someone had decided mounting shower rods on the walls and hanging three pistachio-green curtains as stall doors was a really good idea. The curtains didn't reach all the way to the floor, though, so if three women were using the facilities at the same time they looked like a six-legged squatting shamrock.

The first year that Bev had joined us, we went to the North-woods straight from the ferry, ordered a round of drinks, then another, intentionally waiting on Bev's bladder. It didn't take long before she stood up, asked us where the bathroom was, and we pointed her in the proper direction.

A few minutes later she'd emerged, a shocked look on her face.

We whooped and gave her a round of applause.

"That's because I'm a Polish princess!" she'd announced to the room, taking a bow.

I'd forgotten all about that moment, but after the nickname conversation, we'd left Fairview for a drive and found ourselves at the Northwoods again. Pam pointed to the bathroom and reminded us of Bev's debut. Not a one of us was what you'd call a girly girl, though if any of us had princess tendencies, it was Bev. After the laughing died down, Pam asked her about the heritage portion of her royal title.

"Are you really one hundred percent Polish?" Pam wanted to know. "Or is it mixed with something else?"

Coming from Linda, Andrea, or even me, the question would have seemed like a joke—a good-natured nudge at Bev's tendency to be a little spacey. Pam did have a good sense of humor, but she wasn't a teaser. She was much too tenderhearted for that. Pam herself was from a big, northern Michigan farm family, knew her own genealogy well, and was honestly curious about Bev's.

"Not all Polish," Bev had answered, unusually serious. "Only ninety-nine percent."

The rest of us frowned. We were all the grandchildren or

great-grandchildren of immigrants, a mix of this heritage and that ancestry, our blood containing European genes randomly scattered in Michigan and the Midwest before the turn of the century. I didn't know any specifics of my own background, just that I was English and Irish. Data I was thankful for, nonetheless, because I thought it might explain my propensity to overthink (English) and sometimes to overdrink (Irish).

Still, it wasn't often, if ever, that the ratio of one bloodline to another could be so minutely computed.

"Well, what's the other one percent, then?" Pam asked.

"Washycocky Indian," Bev said, expressionless.

The name sounded ridiculous. And insulting. I waited for the punch line, but after several seconds there didn't seem to be one. Then again, I'd started to notice that Bev's stories took an increasingly long time to develop. Sometimes the point she was trying to make got lost in an elaborate soup recipe or a distant cousin's overseas travel. Other times, she simply forgot it altogether, changed trajectory midway through, but stoically carried on, regardless.

"Um," Andrea finally asked. "So that's, like, a real thing?"

"When I was nine years old, I thought it was," Bev said, her face collapsing into a giggle.

Nine was how old she'd been when she'd asked a favorite uncle about her family's heritage. Her uncle had told her she was 99 percent Polish, 1 percent Washycocky Indian, and Bev believed him. Which was understandable at nine, but at nineteen? It wasn't until Bev told her husband about her supposed heritage that she'd finally learned the truth.

"I was bragging," she admitted. "I told him that if we ever had children, thanks to me they'd all be one-half percent Washycocky," she said, sheepish at just how absurd that sounded now. "He burst out laughing, then did this…"

Bev stood up, right there inside the Northwoods, and treated us and all the other patrons in that bar to an enthusiastic display of humping.

It might have been just laying there, dormant for almost five decades, but thanks to her uncouth uncle, a green shower curtain, and a sarcastic ex-husband, Bev now had a Drummond Island nickname, whether she still wanted one or not.

It never took much to get us all going once we were inside of Chuck's or the Northwoods, and Bev's new moniker had been more than enough to keep us out late. The next morning, she was already tightening the laces on her hiking boots, though, while I nibbled a bagel, sipped my coffee, and stood at the window, gazing at the cedar trees.

It was the eastern red cedar that was native to Drummond, a tree that wasn't a real cedar at all but rather a species of juniper. The stunted, hardy examples surrounding Fairview looked like senior citizen trees who'd weathered difficult pasts. Their trunks were contorted, their branches shooting out at odd angles, but their flat, scale-like needles were still a lush and waxy green. A late botanical victory after decades of patience and struggle.

All Bev had to do was tip her head toward the door and raise her eyebrows and I ran upstairs to get dressed. I looked forward to our Sunday morning walks. It was good exercise; the scent of pine, fallen leaves, and lake air was always a remedy for what felt like a bottle-stopper of cotton in my morning-after head, but the best part was just her company. Any of the other girls could have joined us, but for this reason or that, they rarely did.

Bev was confident on the trail the same way she'd been confident in the bow of her canoe.

"You must have been a Girl Scout," I said, as she strode in front of me down a rock-studded path.

"Nope," she said. "At Catholic school we never had anything like that."

Bev's childhood had been an urban one of chores, family get-togethers, and daily Mass. While my family went on camping and backpacking vacations, hers drove to Miami. While we had sailed the Great Lakes, canoed the Au Sable River, and waded in Lake Superior until our legs grew numb with cold, she'd fished in city ponds with a safety pin on the end of a string. Yet she loved the woods as much as I did.

"Then how'd you get to be so outdoorsy?"

Bev had hopped over a log blocking our way, her boots finding purchase even over the slick moss.

"My dad," she said.

The same man who'd inspired her to use an early marriage as an escape route had also shared his love of gardening when she was barely old enough to walk. Beyond grapes, Bev couldn't remember everything he'd grown in their city backyard. As newlyweds, she and her husband had moved north, about as far as the knuckle on Michigan's ring finger, and the time she'd spent in that garden with her father had morphed into a love of the woods.

She liked to take walks alone, or with me. Bev had none of my angst over shunning an American-girl tradition, but she wasn't much of a joiner, either.

"I have a new fish tank," she told me, apropos of nothing.

By then I was no longer startled by her abrupt changes of subject, especially when our conversation had ventured close to the roots. I silently congratulated myself for being so present, for not taking it personally, not overthinking it, and instead just accepting the psychology of the moment. This was her coping mechanism, one I did not share but could appreciate and understand.

"I'll have to come over and see it when we get home," I said, past the fallen log and astride her now. "I love watching fish. It's so relaxing."

"Yeah," she said, in a tone almost professorial. "It is supposed to be real good for mentally slow people."

I stopped walking right there in the middle of the trail. She kept going, but glanced over her shoulder and tossed back a victorious smirk. If there had been a merit badge for gullibility, it wouldn't have gone to Washycocky that morning. It would have gone to me. Even the cedar trees seemed to be snickering.

CHAPTER SIX   *2000*

Mary Lynn.

In all her forty-nine years on the planet, Mary Lynn told me, she'd never experienced anything like it before. Finally, some doctor had come up with a diet that really worked! Eat all the bacon, deviled eggs, and pork rinds you wanted, and hey, drink a tub of gin, too, if that turned you on, and still lose weight.

Bev and I had just popped into Peegeo's for a quick beer and to say hello to Linda when we'd also noticed Mary Lynn sitting at the bar. She was with her husband, Jimmy, and the two of them were having dinner together. His plate was covered with a napkin—a signal to the bartender that he was finished—but she was still eating, and I watched her fork up a bite of hamburger, dip it in yellow mustard, and pop it in her mouth.

Perhaps I'd eyed her entrée strangely, because without preamble she'd started in about the diet she'd been on. As long as you replaced the tonic water in your gin with club soda and ate no bread, rice, or potatoes, she said, this eating plan sucked the fat off you like a goddamn vacuum cleaner.

"It's all scientific," she'd explained in her squeaky voice. "Carbs are evil, butter's good, and sugar's like the Antichrist."

Science had been one of my better subjects in high school and that didn't sound like a provable hypothesis to me. But then again, one look at an organic chemistry textbook and I'd switched my major from biology to journalism, so what did I know? Plus, there was no arguing with Mary Lynn's results. Her diet might have sounded crazy, but it was working.

Mary Lynn had never talked about her weight with us, but she'd been sedentary and a little bit round for as long as we'd known her. Short, pinkish, freckled, and unyielding, she dressed in a kind of uniform—ankle-length skinny jeans decades before they were in style and always a pair of flat, pointy-toed Keds on her tiny feet. On top, an oversized sweatshirt, perfectly ironed, and often decorated with a lace collar, embroidered flowers, an inspirational quote, or a basket of teddy bears.

I wanted to ask her for more details, but not in front of Bev. I'd struggled a bit with my weight, too, ever since the birth of my third son, but whenever I'd mentioned it to Bev she would just tell me she couldn't relate to that problem at all. "I eat to live," she'd say. "I don't live to eat."

I didn't live to eat, either, but for some unknown reason, my jeans didn't get that.

As the weeks went by, Mary Lynn stuck to the diet and it continued to work. She still wore the same kind of jeans—just several sizes smaller—and the preppy blue sneakers, but she'd traded the shapeless sweatshirts in for sleeveless blouses with jaunty collars and fitted V-neck sweaters. And she smiled. A lot.

"What's that diet again?" I'd asked the next time I saw her at Peegeo's.

Bev wasn't with me that time; I was alone, so I felt freer to discuss it. I no longer went to Peegeo's to work or to escape a crying baby—my youngest son was four years old. I went there after the boys were in bed to get away from my husband. All we did was bicker; at least at Peegeo's, no one told me I was incompetent, mocked my dream of someday being a writer, clapped their hands and asked me to snap out of it, or suggested I think about washing the windows once a decade.

That night, I'd seen Mary Lynn dine on pizza—after she'd asked for an extra plate, scraped the cheese and toppings onto it, then handed the naked-looking crust back to the waitress.

"Atkins," she'd said. "A heart doctor invented it. Basically, it's meat, cheese, and liquor. Later, you get to have vegetables. If you're good."

Long gone were the days when I could justify my large ass as simply a counterweight to a pregnant belly. I wasn't much for fad diets. I wasn't much for diets, period. Bacon, pizza cheese, and liquor? It was hard to believe anyone could lose weight that way. Yet Mary Lynn definitely had.

I didn't ask her how much, but I would have bet it was forty pounds. Maybe more. On her five-foot frame the results were dramatic.

"I've got the book," she said to me helpfully. "You can borrow it if you want."

There's a book? I thought. *Now she's speaking my language.*

The following day I went to Mary Lynn and Jimmy's house. She answered my knock and I stepped into their foyer. I'd long known where she lived, but I'd never been inside of her house before. Although the Drummond Girls were close as could be on the island, back home our lives were busy; I didn't work at Peegeo's anymore, and so months often passed without me seeing or socializing with some of the girls, her included. Whenever I was with Mary Lynn, it was usually in a big group—either at Peegeo's, at a backyard neighborhood party, or with the girls on Drummond.

She and Jimmy lived in a well-kept 1970s-era bi-level on a hill. It was near George and Susan's house; I'd seen it plenty of times from the road, and their big bay window made the place look cozy and inviting. So I was shocked to see that inside, her house was so devoid of furniture that when I said hello it echoed.

"Are you moving?" I'd asked.

Before me lay an endless expanse of sculpted beige carpeting, broken up by only a couch, an end table, and a lamp. At first she looked puzzled by my question and scanned the space purposefully, as if seeing her own living room for the first time.

"Oh!" she said cheerfully, waving my question away. "No, no. We like it like this. Less to clean."

The place was immaculate. Not a dust speck, cobweb, or window streak anywhere. Would my own house ever be so freshly scrubbed? I thought of the three small pairs of perpetually dirty hands and the pile of my husband's dirty clothes piled on top of the hamper and scattered on the bedroom floor and seriously doubted it.

Mary Lynn didn't invite me to sit down, but put a worn yellow paperback—*Dr. Atkins' New Diet Revolution*—in my hand and wished me good luck. Back home I started reading and pretty quickly realized Mary Lynn had given me her interpretation of the cardiologist's nutritional philosophy. It was not really the bacon-and-liquor diet. Those items were allowed, but liquor especially was to be consumed in moderation and only after the first two weeks. You were supposed to eat lean meats, fish, nuts, and salads and no bread, potatoes, white rice, desserts, or fruit. And by the end of chapter 4, I still hadn't read one single word about pizza.

But here was the more interesting news. According to the doctor it was not my fault that at the age of thirty-nine, my once normal-sized ass looked like two picnic watermelons wrapped in a wrinkled tablecloth. Sugar, as Mary Lynn had already explained, was indeed the Antichrist. To make matters worse, my fat cells were dumb. They couldn't distinguish between sugar from fruit and sugar from a doughnut or a chocolate chip cookie, two items I'd banned from the house in my efforts to slim down. No, all those apples, peaches, bananas, and yes, watermelons I'd been eating for good health were turning my body into a cellulite factory.

I opened my cupboard doors, looked inside, and spied Satan's playground—breakfast cereal (nonsugared), bread (whole wheat), and granola bars (organic)—and made a new kind of grocery list. Ground chuck, rotisserie chicken, jumbo eggs, cheese sticks, salami. I studied Mary Lynn's book, vowed to become a pillar of protein-satiated willpower, and dreamed of a future in which I was five feet eight inches of hard muscle, strong nails, and long glossy hair. Nothing else had worked; maybe *that* would improve my husband's mood swings.

The book did warn about the side effect to following its extreme low-carbohydrate eating plan. Constipation.

Oh, what a small price to pay, I thought. We'd be leaving for Drummond in three months and that seemed like plenty of time for the diet to work. I had saved a pair of my favorite jeans I used to wear on the island but that no longer fit. Mary Lynn's diet might back my system up tighter than a holiday cheese log, but no matter. I *would* be wearing those jeans by the time we drove onto the ferry to Drummond.

"There's something new on this menu I want to try," Linda said after we'd pushed two square tables together at the Northwoods and sat down. "Cheese curds."

"Those are good," Pam said. "I've had them before. Not here, I had 'em somewhere else, but yeah, let's order some."

"They're like these big orange hunks of cottage cheese," Mary Lynn explained. "But dry. Kinda rubbery but still not bad."

I was sitting quietly and just listening. There is a vocabulary to dieting, one that involves certain word choices as well as a particular cadence or tone. It was like a secret language. A secret language that could only be translated into meaning by other dieters. And they were speaking it.

"How many net carbs?" I'd asked, and three heads snapped in my direction.

"Zero," they'd said in unison.

There was an awkward pause before the four of us chuckled a little sheepishly. Supposedly, we shared almost everything important that happened in our lives with each other. Our marriage failures (or near failures), our new careers, our new houses, our planned (or surprise) pregnancies. And yet, diets were apparently off-limits because 50 percent of the Drummond Girl membership roster was on a low-carb one, and besides my brief conversations with Mary Lynn, none of us had spoken a word to each other about it.

I suppose that actually wasn't too surprising. We were not women who dieted; we were women who *lived*. We counted the number of good men we'd loved, the number of children we'd borne, our record tip nights (mine was $185), and our consecutive trips to Drummond Island (eight). We didn't count mistakes, failures, do-overs, or meltdowns, and we didn't count calories, carbs, grams of sugar, points, or portion sizes, either. We were supposed to be perpetual party girls, not a traveling Weight Watchers meeting.

But I *was* wearing those jeans. My husband didn't seem much happier, or for that matter, to have even noticed I'd lost weight, but all the clothes in my closet fit. I'd taken a good look at my low-carbing friends and could see they'd lost weight, too. The island was supposed to be where no rules applied, though I'd never before thought of that in terms of eating. But when it came to successful dieting, hard-fought momentum was difficult to relinquish, even on Drummond.

But I was not so taken with my reappearing hip bones that I didn't recognize something else important had changed, too, and despite feeling good about getting my pre-baby body back, I wasn't sure it was a change for the better.

We'd asked our waitress for menus, we were talking about food and planning out what we were going to eat in great detail, instead of just ordering what we were hungry for, when we were hungry for it. As party girls, that was a bit of an embarrassment. We were thinking about food before we'd ordered a single drink.

So, that's how it happens, I thought. *That's how you get old.*

One minute you were kidnapping an off-duty cop and dumping him in the woods, and the next minute you were sitting in a bar drooling over rubbery cheese.

"Have you tried that cheesecake recipe?" Pam asked. "I took it to a barbecue once. They scarfed it right down. No one even knew it was low-carb."

I recognized the recipe she was talking about—a ground almond and butter crust with a cream cheese, egg, and artificial sweetener filling. It was in the book Mary Lynn had lent me, but I'd never made it. Still, might be a nice addition to my current options of cheese slices wrapped in lunch meat one day, lunch meat wrapped in cheese slices the next.

"Yo!" Jill suddenly called out from the other end of the table. "Are you old biddies going to order some drinks or what?"

"Yeah," Andrea said. "How many carbs in a Michelob? I hope it's a shitload."

Easy for them to talk. Andrea only had one kid, Jill had none; they were still in their thirties and probably wearing the same size jeans as the day they'd graduated high school. But I did take their point. Diets had rules and Drummond was supposed to be our one rule-free zone. If we really were going to start having rules to obey, one of them should have been not talking ad nauseam about your diet within earshot of your younger, skinnier friends.

"I'll have a gin and soda!" Mary Lynn bellowed, turning her face in the direction of the bartender.

"*Zero carbs*," she added to Andrea and Jill.

No one asked Mary Lynn whether that year's trip had been her favorite. Why would we have? There were going to be years of trips yet to come, so there wasn't a need for any of us to single out just one.

But today I know those three days were the most fun she'd ever had on the island. The usual stiffness she'd battled against when getting in and out of Linda's car had diminished. One morning she'd even gone partway with Bev and me on our walk. At Chuck's, she'd ordered shots of something we'd never tasted before called Tequila Rose (*lots* of carbs, but she was splurging) and seemed surrounded by a happy glow from morning to midnight. Her voice had lost some of its shrillness, and she actually posed for our pictures that year instead of hurrying away anytime someone pulled out a camera.

For perhaps the first time since we'd known her, Mary Lynn was proud of how she looked, proud of her new wardrobe, and of how much more active she'd become, and it showed.

In my favorite photograph of her, she's standing sideways but looking right at the camera. Her shoulders are arched, and her head is tilted, almost as if a professional photographer had posed her, and yet she looks relaxed and natural, too. She's got a pair of sunglasses hanging from a strap around her neck and her hair doesn't look quite so sprayed. There are maple leaves on the ground, and they've already changed from green to red and gold. She's happy. You can see a bay of clear water in the background, and whoever pasted the picture into our photo album added a heart sticker on each corner.

After Mary Lynn hollered that drink order from our table all the way across the room to the bar, Beth the bartender came over and the rest of us ordered a round, too. Then another and another. At one point I noted an empty basket of onion rings, an empty basket of deep-fried cauliflower, and the wounded remains of a plate of French fries that had been soaked in melted cheese and a ladle of chili. Off to the side languished the cheese "turds," as we'd taken to calling them. I tried to bounce one off the bar's wood floor to see how high it would go. Pretty high; at least to my knee and once all the way up to my thigh.

According to the trip's log, by the end of the night our bar tab for food and drinks for eight women was $149. And although I would not have known the sum as we left the Northwoods and headed home to Fairview that night, I did know something. The notion I'd had earlier of feeling old was gone. By then we had a reputation on the island as hard partiers and good tippers, and we lived up to it that night.

Both Andrea and Linda were fine drivers, and I never worried about our safety on Drummond Island's unlit and winding roads. There was little traffic; often we wouldn't pass a single car between the bars and Fairview, and neither Linda nor Andrea drove fast. Drummond was the one place where we were never, ever in a hurry. Once, according to the same trip log, on the rocky and sometimes nearly impassable Sheep Ranch Road, it had taken us twenty-three minutes to go five miles.

But on the way to Fairview that night, Andrea missed our turnoff, recognized her mistake right away, and attempted to right it with a quick stop and a three-point turn. It would have worked, too, if Drummond's road builders hadn't made the route to Fairview Cove so darn narrow and if the car builders Ford employed hadn't made Bruno so darn big. Instead, his heavy hind end backed a swift four feet straight down, coming to rest steeply in a ditch.

"I am *not* pushing," I said, which came out, "Eye an *gnat* pushkin'."

Angels can fly, the saying goes, because they take themselves lightly. How many angels can dance on the top of a gas pedal? Just enough apparently, because Bruno's engine revved, his beefy tires grabbed that swampy grass, and we rose from the dark and oozing depths as if by divine intervention.

Back at Fairview, we tumbled out of the car and Jill motioned us to the back, saying she'd brought along some secret snacks. Andrea opened the hatch and Jill rustled around amid the coolers and Bev's extra rolls of toilet paper. After a minute, she pulled a Tupperware container out of a tote bag and eased open the lid. The night was cool and damp, and a perfect amount of humidity was in the air to carry forth the glorious and forbidden smell of chocolate.

"How many carbs in a pot brownie?" Jill asked, giggling.

"Eat one," Andrea said, "and you won't care."

If a woman had ever uttered a more effective diet-destabilizing sentence to me, I couldn't have told you what it was. I couldn't have told you *anything*. My face was numb, my body more relaxed than a vat of mashed potatoes. And for the rest of that night all I did was laugh.

I didn't think about menu planning, getting enough fiber, or the size in the label of my designer jeans. I just stayed up late with Jill and Andrea and laughed.

CHAPTER SEVEN *2001*

Crossing the Mackinac Bridge with Linda in the lead.

Was it only after September 11 that I'd started to truly fear the bridge?

Or had I been feeling increasingly anxious about crossing it even before that?

All I knew for sure was that less than a month after that terrible day, on October 8, 2001, I was sitting in Andrea's passenger seat and preparing for her tires to syncopate over the bridge's grates when an unprecedented attack of vertigo made me nauseated. I tried to tell myself fear was irrational. The terrorist attacks had been horrific—and far from this exposed yet relatively anonymous spot in northern Michigan.

I'd never, ever looked down when we were crossing—who wanted to do that when the view up ahead was so spectacular? Green shores, sandbars, and all that beautiful water. On a clear day if you stared at the horizon long enough, you could just make out the curvature of the earth.

But something had gone wrong inside of me that day because not only couldn't I look down, I could barely stand to glance out the window. In *any* direction. If my pride hadn't stopped me, I would have dissolved in fear and just lay down on the floor of Andrea's Bronco.

"I'm not saying I'm a great driver," Andrea said, turning up the music. "I'm saying I'm a *grate* driver."

She was joking, and I mentally willed her to leave the radio alone and put two hands back on the wheel. For all the miles usually so filled with joy and anticipation, hers was the only moment of levity I remember on that whole trip up. I supposed I should have been thankful. If she was joking, it meant she didn't have any idea how knotted up my insides were.

Every year we crossed the Mackinac Bridge. It was just part of our routine, part of what made the island feel so separate and far away. The only other routes to Drummond from Traverse City were to head southeast by way of Toronto or southwest through Chicago and Wisconsin. That would have been ridiculous—hundreds of miles out of our way, hours wasted, along with several extra tanks of gas.

In 2001, I was closing in on my fortieth birthday. A time when I guessed that it was probably normal for a woman to start worrying. About her looks, about her life, and truth be told, a normal time to start worrying about death. Yet before September 11, the list of things that made me anxious was blank. Now, it had started growing at an alarming rate. Elevators, left-turn lanes, gas grills, odd numbers, stadium crowds, the checkout lane at Kmart, air travel, and crossing the Mackinac Bridge.

The bridge is four lanes across, two each going their separate ways, and as Andrea approached, she had two choices. She could take the right lane closest to the edge, the one with certain death right out the passenger window, but also the one with solid concrete under her tires. Or she could take the left lane, which was a good eight feet in from the edge and usually buffered by another car. The left lane seemed the obvious choice until you realized the devastating trade-off for being away from that edge. The material under your tires wasn't concrete anymore but a series of interconnected metal grates. *Grates!* So transparent, passengers could *see through them* straight to the long screaming plunge of watery nothingness below.

I tried not to think about that Detroit waitress. I tried not to look down. I tried not to look anywhere. Not over the edge, not into the grates, not even at my own toes clenched inside my hiking boots.

This was all just irrational, anxiety-soaked thinking, I told myself. The bridge was safe, meticulously maintained, and certainly after 9/11 being constantly monitored for suspicious anything. But our local paper, the *Traverse City Record-Eagle*, had run an article about one of the hijackers, I remembered that chilling face staring defiantly from the front page, and it felt like we were driving across a mammoth bull's-eye.

I never said any of this out loud, though. Not even to the women who'd long ago become my closest friends. I wasn't going to miss the trip just because five miles of it now scared the shit out of me. I was not a sissy la-la, had never been a sissy la-la, and even a suspension bridge two hundred feet in the air that swayed—yes, *swayed*—in the wind was not going to turn me into one.

There had to be drugs for this kind of malady. Real drugs, prescribed by a real doctor, and not baked by my friend into a box of Duncan Hines. I vowed that next year, I'd be on some.

I took a deep breath. Let it out. Took another. Andrea really was a great driver. She liked cars and had a natural affinity behind the wheel. As the bridge started to slant toward the safety of land and those grates changed into pavement, I heard Led Zeppelin thump from her radio. They were my favorite band, and it'd been a tradition to play something by them when we crossed the bridge ever since I'd first tossed that cassette into my duffel bag. It was CDs now, and their music had probably been playing the whole way over, but I was so deafened by my own blood rushing through my eardrums, I hadn't noticed. "Trampled Under Foot." That was the song and that was exactly how I'd felt.

Since Michigan was a border state, details of increased national security in our area of the country following the attacks had dominated our local news. The day after the Twin Towers went down, all of the Great Lakes shipping lanes came under new scrutiny. Commercial freighters' homeports were from all over the world, including cities in the Middle East. The Coast Guard announced it would be conducting surprise inspections of ships sailing in the St. Marys River, the body of water that made up Drummond Island's northern shore. I pictured armed officers boarding the ships Bev and I used to love to watch, looking for bombs or terrorists. And after that, the attacks didn't seem so far away anymore.

I made it across without either suffering a heart attack or covering Bruno's car mats with my body, and when Andrea drove up to the tollbooth, there was a great big American flag, hanging vertically, affixed to the front of it. It hadn't been there any other year, and I haven't seen it since. Andrea slowed and unrolled her window to hand the operator our three dollars (the fare had increased to $1.50 per axle) but the woman in the booth just smiled and shook her head no.

"The car ahead of you already paid," she told us.

We looked up the road. Pulling away from the tollbooth was a rusty pickup truck with a camper on top. Not a vehicle any of us recognized or that looked as if its driver had money to spare. A complete stranger, yet he or she had still paid our way.

At the Welcome Center, Linda's car was already in the parking lot waiting. When we got out to stretch, we told the others about the stranger's generosity and they were as moved by it as we had been. Then Linda took me aside, her eyes big, her usually tanned face a startling white.

"I don't know what it is," she'd said through clenched teeth. "But my stomach just churns when I have to cross that bridge."

The drive north that year had felt off and out of sorts for another reason, too. Neither Mary Lynn nor Jill was with us. Jill was dating a new man; they were busy building a house, and because all her money and time were going toward those things, she said she wasn't going to be able to go.

Mary Lynn had never missed before, but in the weeks leading up to our departure, she'd made repeated comments about money. Specifically, about not having enough of it. Her job was secure— she worked in quality control at a printing company—but her husband Jimmy was a freelance graphic designer and his workload had fallen off. They were going through some financial difficulties and had to cut back on anything that wasn't a necessity.

The two of them had stopped going to Peegeo's for dinner, and whenever one of us had seen her out somewhere, she'd looked worried. The $275 apiece Linda had budgeted for the kitty that year was a sacrifice for many of us. For Mary Lynn, it was an impossibility, and Linda, Andrea, and I had gotten together to discuss what to do about it.

"I'm worried about her," Linda told us. "She's put a lot of pressure on herself to come up with the money. We need to let her know it's okay if she doesn't go, but I don't want to hurt her feelings."

"Why don't we all just pitch in a little extra and cover her share?" I'd asked.

I wasn't made of money, either, and taking more out of our family budget for Drummond would not make my husband happy, but if it would help Mary Lynn, I'd do it. With seven of us contributing, if we each put in an extra forty dollars, it'd cover her share.

"I already tried that," Linda said. "She wouldn't hear of it. Wouldn't even let me talk to her about it."

We didn't bother suggesting Linda try again; we understood that kind of pride. A Drummond Girl paid her own way. For our trips north, but for the obligations we had in our daily lives back home, too. Financial and otherwise. We would have been willing to cover anyone's share who'd happened to be in a bind, and yet we were also sure we'd never have to. Not one of us would have accepted the money.

"I'll talk to her," Andrea said. "I'll go to her house right now if you think I should."

It wasn't Andrea the Confronter who visited Mary Lynn, it was Andrea the Comforter, and afterward she'd told us Mary Lynn had gotten tears in her eyes when they'd talked, yet quickly wiped them away, she was so overcome with relief. She'd assured Andrea that her financial situation was temporary, and she'd be back with us as soon as she could.

It was only years later that Andrea had the heart to tell us what else she'd seen on that visit. When Mary Lynn came to the door and let Andrea inside, the sight that greeted her seemed too private somehow even to share with the rest of us.

If you needed to make some quick money to pay a utility bill, catch up on an outstanding debt, or get something out of hock, fall in northern Michigan is not the easiest time or place to do it. Our unemployment rate was always several points higher than the rest of the state, partly because our region was fueled by tourism, which plummeted after Labor Day. There were a few short-term jobs to be had picking apples, delivering newspapers, or sealing the roads before winter, but those are not realistic endeavors for a diminutive middle-aged woman with an uneven gait and long fingernails.

What Andrea saw was Mary Lynn and Jimmy sitting on their couch together, TV trays in front of them stacked high with envelopes. They were putting on stamps to make a few extra dollars. They'd sat down with similar stacks from a local direct mail company every night that week, Mary Lynn had told Andrea, and were earning just a couple pennies apiece.

In light of Mary Lynn's troubles, in light of the fear and anxiety over 9/11, that three dollars from the driver of that old pickup truck in front of us at the tollbooth now seems to me an incredible act of generosity. It couldn't have come at a better time. It wasn't the extra money—even without Mary Lynn or Jill, our budget wasn't so tight that a few dollars would make much difference—it was the idea that someone would do something so unselfish. For people they didn't even know, would never know.

I don't have many regrets where our Drummond Island trips are concerned. More than anything else, the annual sojourn has taught me to live in such a way that you don't have regrets. But I do have one. I wish we would have pushed Mary Lynn a little harder to accept our help. I wish we would have told her how much we needed her along. I wish we said she had to go. Or given the money to Jimmy for him to give to her. I don't care how we did it, I just wish she would have been on the island with us for one more year.

As many times as we'd arrived at the line for the car ferry, we never knew what we were going to find when M-134 made its sharp right turn into the town of DeTour Village, population 325. From the bridge, DeTour was a one-hour drive on the coastal highway edging the northern shore of Lake Huron. The view out our windows was of the Les Cheneaux Islands, some thirty pads of land of varying sizes, inhabited mostly by pine trees, moss, and shore birds. It was the quiet part of the drive, with little if any traffic and no scheduled stops. The only time Linda or Andrea took their foot off the gas was to pass through the small towns of Hessel (population 1,264), and Cedarville (population 1,337).

On one of our first trips, back when there'd been only four of us, Linda, Andrea, Jill, and I had stopped at the Cedarville Bar. That was also when Linda had insisted we leave before dawn in order to wring every possible second out of those precious three days off. No one else liked getting up that early, but it was years before we'd be brave enough to challenge her on it. When we finally did, Linda's answer hadn't been to leave later in the morning, but to leave the evening before, which was how we'd started arriving on the first Thursday of October, instead of the first Friday. Our goal had always been to arrive on the island before the sun went down. Usually we made it but some years we didn't and had to dock in the dark.

But when we stopped in Cedarville that year it was a Friday and only eleven o'clock in the morning. At Linda's suggestion, we peeked into the octagon-shaped windows of the Cedarville Bar to see if the place was open. There inside, working a bar rag over the counter was a man with glasses, a collared shirt with a pocket protector, and an expertly arranged comb-over. He waved us inside; we sat at the bar and ordered Bloody Marys. The place was empty except for the four of us, women obviously not from his town, but the bartender nodded approvingly and said we'd chosen our beverages well. He didn't use a premade mix, he explained, but created his special tomato juice, spice, pickle juice, and vodka concoctions by hand, one at a time. We told him they were delicious—we meant it—and he basked in our praise.

"You may find this hard to believe, ladies, but I am not only a bartender," he'd said, assuming an air of mystery. "You can call me Mayor Bob."

I was impressed enough by the position to ask if he'd pose for a photograph, and the following year we told the new girls about the tasty Bloody Marys in Cedarville, that they were not to be missed, and all eight of us had filed into the place and ordered accordingly. But there was an ornery old woman behind the bar instead, and when we asked for Mayor Bob, she looked at us as if we'd gone off our medication.

Cedarville was an unincorporated community, she said. It never had a mayor and probably never would. She knew perfectly well how to make a stinkin' Bloody Mary and she didn't need us to give her any instruction. After a half hour—Susan had gotten so irritated she'd timed her—the woman set a group of skinny glasses containing a bland red liquid in front of us, along with our tab. An obvious cue we were no longer welcome.

Usually, we loved to recount the contrast of those two stops as we zipped past the blinker where M-134 crossed Cedarville's main street, often adding any number of newly recalled details. Such as: Mary Lynn had taken one sip of the crone's version of the drink, made a face, and barked, "These taste like nothing!"

That year, no one brought either of those incidents up, and I know it would have been different if Mary Lynn had been along. I actually missed the sound of her voice, missed her put-on crankiness and comforting negativity. We weren't even to the island yet, and I could already tell the trip wasn't going to be the same without her and Jill.

After 9/11, though, nothing was the same. If life could be erased by a hell descending out of a cloudless sky inside our own jetliners, what good was trying to relive the past? The present was all anyone had anymore, and the thing to do was to live, right now, inside as many new experiences as we could assemble. To pile them up, one right after the other, as fast and as continuously as we could.

The scary-looking hijacker whose face had darkened the front page of our local newspaper had left a long, rambling suicide note. I'd read the English translation and two of his fiendish sentences had stayed with me, no matter how hard I tried to get them out of my brain: "Try to forget something called life. The time of play is over."

*   *   *

M-134 made its turn into DeTour Village at the top of a hill twenty-four miles past Cedarville. It took a name—Elizabeth Street—and aimed itself down the hill through town, became a dotted line on a map when it crossed the water, but then continued on to Drummond, earning it the distinction of being one of only a handful of state highways in the country to traverse an island.

The first thing we looked for from the top of that hill was how long the line for the car ferry was. If there were already several cars waiting, we'd pull up to the back of the line and cross our fingers that we'd arrived in time to get on board the next crossing. If there were just a few cars, it could mean a wait as long as an hour and so we'd often pull into the parking lot of the Fogcutter and go inside for a quick beverage instead.

The Fogcutter was a restaurant and bar sitting on a premium piece of real estate. It had water frontage on DeTour Passage, and its short driveway was at a right angle to the first block of Elizabeth Street, where vehicles lined up for the ferry a dozen times a day, every day, year-round. Its outdoor deck was so close to the dock that even someone with terrible aim could have hit the ferry with an ice cube. The entertainment—freighter watching and ferry line watching—was both free and perpetual, and the chipping paint and plastic tablecloths were welcome signs that the place was affordable for travelers like us on a budget. I'd never in my life had a compulsion to own a bar, but if I did, it would have been the Fogcutter.

When we paused at the top of DeTour hill that day, we saw something strange. There was not a single car in line. When we drove closer we could see the ferry was fully loaded and had just left the dock for Drummond. Which must have meant that the number of cars in line had also been the exact number the ferry could hold, something we'd never seen before or since.

The early afternoon sun sparkled on the water and the lights inside the Fogcutter looked cheery, even from behind its ram-shackle, spiderwebbed windows. We could have been first in line, but even in our subdued state we'd decided to go inside instead. There was a rueful happiness in the twang from the jukebox, people were laughing, and the whole place exuded a welcome sense of normalcy. Not five minutes passed before we met some tourists, strangers to us but also from Traverse City, traveling the Upper Peninsula on an arranged murder mystery tour. Then we talked to some locals, too, and soon the mystery people, the locals, and the six of us were chatting each other up and sharing stories as if we'd been friends for years.

You don't usually just "find room" up at a bar for six women, but that night the people inside the Fogcutter found room for us. Our glasses were filled, then filled again, someone ordered food, and for once it didn't even matter that whoever had pumped the jukebox full of money played only country music, because it seemed right somehow, and not phony, that every song had the word *America* somewhere in it. I looked around at my friends and willed the moment to burn itself into my memory.

I was alive, I was an American, and I was a female in the prime of my life. The weekend I'd looked forward to all year was not only finally here, it had barely started. I wrapped my arms around Bev in an uncharacteristic display of affection. If I was feeling this happy a mile from the island, imagine how great we were all going to feel tomorrow and the next day, too. Mary Lynn would surely have things worked out by this time next year and I hoped Jill would, too.

The time of play was not over. Not for us it wasn't. The only way to ensure that the terrorists hadn't won, that they would never win, was to play as hard as we could, for as long as we could, and with everything we had.

We watched out the Fogcutter's windows as the line of cars grew longer, watched the workers show drivers where to park. We watched them cast off bowlines, heard the horn blow as the ferry left for Drummond, then returned and repeated the process again, but two hours later we were all still at the Fogcutter.

Linda must have realized how long we'd been there about the same time I did.

"Let's wrap it up," she'd said, rodeoing her index finger high in the air. "I wanna make the next crossing."

The fall colors northern Michigan is famous for had peaked early that year, and after several runs to the island, the line of cars for the ferry was still long. Susan had been acting as the kitty's banker, and as soon as she paid our bill, we all trooped back out to our cars.

With chipped concrete under our shoes and in the good-bye glow of the windows, I felt some of my somberness fade. We were so blessed to live in northern Michigan, blessed to live, for this one weekend at least, inside an enveloping fog of happiness. Terrible things happened in our world. But they hadn't happened on Drummond, and God willing, they never would.

Linda and Andrea drove out of the parking lot, windows down, and at the end of the Fogcutter's short driveway, there was a stop sign and both cars paused for it. Linda was in the lead, Andrea right behind, and perpendicular to us in the ferry line, two men in a pickup truck waved.

And I saw our group then as I imagined those men had seen us: two carloads of happy, healthy women. Excited, smiling, and fresh from a bar. Our windows were rolled all the way down, and a few of us were wearing the new and colorful jackets we'd bought just for the trip. A few more had put on fresh lipstick. Our eyes were sparkling and Bev, especially, was grinning at them and waving back with characteristic vigor.

After the anonymous camper driver had paid our bridge toll, and after we'd enjoyed the camaraderie inside the Fogcutter, the wave from those men felt like just more of the same. They were simply two strangers who'd crossed our path, then felt compelled to spread goodwill in our direction. I'd long believed that we were charmed, that our whole trip was charmed, and that happiness was what we naturally attracted. But I'd never felt that more strongly than the evening when we were heading for the island only three weeks after 9/11.

So when those men backed up their truck enough to let both our cars into line, of course Linda and Andrea whipped their SUVs right into that opening.

"Check *us* out!" Andrea had said, returning Linda's thumbs-up with her own.

A couple other drivers in line behind us honked their horns, one was louder and more persistent than the others, but we all joined in with Bev and waved to our new fans. Then the ferry arrived on its return trip from the island, docked smoothly, and the long line of cars waiting to go to the island slowly started to move toward the on-ramp.

We were close enough to the front of the line to see the ferry's back gate swing down, and it was as if a wide metal palm was opening for us and saying, "Come aboard!"

Then a short red-faced man with stormy hair came into view. One by one he pointed at each driver, then pointed to the on-board space they were assigned to occupy. Up a foot, over a tad, stop, next. Just like that, he expertly loaded each vehicle onto the ferry.

Until he came to Linda's.

She was driving a newish Chevy S-10 Blazer she'd recently splurged on. Michigan winters were hard on vehicles, even big SUVs, and her Explorer had started showing its age. It was no longer Drummond worthy, but she wasn't willing to suggest someone else be one of our drivers, so she'd gone car shopping instead. And bought a gold 1998 Blazer with only twenty-one thousand miles on it, all-wheel drive, heated leather seats, and a built-in CD player.

When it came time to drive it onto the ferry, the red-faced man with the stormy hair did not point to her and then point to a space on board. He marched angrily toward her car, held up his hand, scowled, and then pounded with his fist—hard—on her hood.

"Cutter!" he yelled angrily. "Back of the line!"

All the happy energy from our evening evaporated.

Oh, I thought, *of course.*

The men in the pickup truck hadn't been letting us in; they'd been waving us through. Instead of going to the end of the line like we were supposed to, we'd cut.

Did we really think all those other people who'd been waiting their turn behind the pickup truck would happily let us cut in front of them, too? Nope, we didn't think that. We didn't think at all. We'd just been floating along inside our own fog of happiness and what the other people in line thought or didn't think had never even crossed our minds.

The red-faced man had been right. We were cutters.

Through Andrea's windshield I could only see one side of Linda's face, but even viewing half of her expression was enough to realize she was furious. It was as if the red-faced man hadn't just pounded on her car's hood, he'd pounded on *her*. There were men in her past who really had pounded on her, and I knew she'd promised herself that would never, ever happen again.

"You sawed-off little fucker!" I heard her yell.

She made a squealing U-turn out of line. She had both hands tight on her steering wheel and was leaning far forward, as if the angle of her torso might get her away from the red-faced man faster than her V-6.

"Oh, what a shame!" someone in a minivan yelled, as she drove past.

Her response was to give the whole minivan, and every person inside of it, their pets, *and* the yellow Baby On Board! sign, the one-finger salute.

The minivan had probably been the source of that loud horn honk. A noise that had seemed celebratory only a minute ago but was probably just angry. I looked out Andrea's back window. The end of the line was a solid three blocks up the hill, and I wondered if the people inside the Fogcutter, the ones from the mystery tour we'd chatted so easily with, were watching out the bar's windows and being entertained by the fallout.

Here's a clue: The killer was Miss Linda, in the ferry line, with a Chevy S-10.

With Linda banished, the four of us inside Bruno were next in line to board. We braced ourselves for a shaming from Red Face, but he just gave Bruno an easy wave and pointed to a spot on the ferry.

It was split-second decision time. Take the available spot or admit our crime by pulling out of line and following Linda all the way to the back.

Andrea didn't hesitate. She rolled up her window and drove onto the ferry.

"That's Sawed-Off Fucker one," she'd said quietly. "And Drummond Girls one."

If it wasn't loaded down with commercial cargo trucks, motor homes, or pickups trailering their duck-hunting boats, the *Drummond Islander III* could hold twenty-four regular-sized vehicles. Surprisingly, Linda not only got on the same crossing as we did, but because of the way the ferry was loaded, she also got on two rows *before* the horn honkers in the minivan. A perfect opportunity, she told us later, to treat them all to a second look at her middle finger.

By the time Linda's car drove onto the island, Andrea was already parked and waiting for her. "Northwoods," was all Linda had said before driving off in a spray of gravel.

It took at least an hour, and several retellings of the ferry fiasco from every imaginable angle with sound effects, plus a richly detailed analysis of what everyone *else* had done wrong, with some possible minor adjustments on our part, as well as a round of drinks, before she'd started to relax.

About the time she did, movement at the bar's front door caught Pam's eye.

"Uh-oh," she'd said.

There was Red Face, walking in with a couple of the other crewmen from the ferry.

"Whatta we do?" Andrea whispered.

It wasn't an "Oh no, what are we going to do now?" kind of question, but rather an "Oh, good, now's our chance to get this straightened out" kind of question. With Red Face in the house, Andrea the grate driver had instantly became Andrea the Confronter.

She wasn't mean, she didn't get angry, and she didn't usually hold grudges, either, but her sense of right and wrong meant all conflicts had to have a just resolution. Preferably as soon as possible.

But Linda said she'd felt like she'd been personally wronged, and she wasn't about to let anyone else do the confronting. By the time Red Face had walked from the door to the bar, Linda had already pushed back her chair, strode across the room, and was tapping the hood pounder—hard—on his shoulder.

"Uh-oh," Pam said again.

I remembered poor Dan the painter then, and I would not have been surprised if Red Face's earlobe ended up in Linda's fist.

"Look, guy, whatever your name is," we all heard her say, "I don't know where you got your information, but I was not *tryin'* to take cuts. Neither was she. Somebody waved us in."

The ferry guy calmly assured her he had received his information from a reliable source—an eyewitness, in fact. Someone in line had called the ferry captain on a cell phone to report us. Whoever it was had described her gold Chevy in meticulous detail, but had said nothing about a burgundy Bronco. Red Face told Linda that if he'd known we'd both cut, he'd have turned two cars away.

"Score one for you guys," he added, with admiration. "We're usually pretty good at nailing everybody who cuts."

That defused the moment enough for Linda and Red Face to call it good. When she came back to our table, she had some new information to report. While the man's face did seem to be permanently flushed, it wasn't from anger but from spending so much time outside and up on deck. The ferry was his life, he'd told her. Not surprisingly, his real name was not Red Face.

"Everyone calls him 'Worm,'" she'd said. "It's even stitched onto his shirt."

We stayed on the island until Tuesday that year, a first for us. September 11 had made all of us take stock of what really mattered. Drummond mattered, and we'd decided we all needed an extra day of it.

On the Tuesday morning ferry, we'd lined up straight, waited our turn, stopped when we were supposed to, parked where we were supposed to, and exited back onto the mainland when we were supposed to, as well. Maybe Tuesday was Worm's day off, because he was nowhere to be seen; he'd missed our perfect ferry manners, but that was okay.

I thought of how angry we'd been on the trip over, of Linda's fury and Andrea's desire to set things straight. Those were real emotions, not just bluster. I knew that because I'd felt them, too. I think we all had.

But it also made me wonder, when had everyone started getting so mad all the time? When had conflicts—personal, political, religious—all started to escalate so quickly?

Michigan had seemed so far from the War on Terror until we were crossing the bridge. The flag on the tollbooth, the added security in the shipping lanes had brought it surprisingly near. Then we'd crossed over to Drummond and it had seemed far away to me, again. On an island, almost everyone knew each other, and at one point or another, probably needed each other. I was glad that when we left for the year, we weren't plotting anything more devious than how to get Jill and Mary Lynn back with us the next year.

CHAPTER EIGHT   *2002*

*Susan, Linda, Mary Lynn, Jill, me, Pam, and Andrea,
at the Fogcutter in DeTour, Michigan.*

It was George who'd called Linda, and Linda who'd called me, and me who called Bev and the others with the news. Susan, usually so even-keeled and in control, could hardly speak about it. Not even over the phone. Plus, there were arrangements to be made, and someone had to sit with Jimmy and help him make them.

In the early-morning hours of a Sunday in March, Mary Lynn had gotten out of bed and walked down the hall to the bathroom. Maybe she didn't feel good, maybe she was thirsty, felt feverish or, when I thought about it later, probably more like cold and clammy. Her bathroom was closer to her bedroom than the kitchen was, so maybe she was just after a glass of water.

Whatever the reason, getting up that early wasn't part of Mary Lynn's usual pattern. We'd spent all those weekends with her, we'd shared bedrooms and pullout couches, and sometimes, when space was tight, we'd even shared beds, so we knew. Mary Lynn was not an early riser. Back when we'd all complained about Linda's predawn departures, Mary Lynn's voice had been the loudest. She really liked her sleep.

But sometime before dawn that morning, Jimmy had heard a bump loud enough to wake him up. Still groggy, he'd instinctively reached an arm over to Mary Lynn's side of the bed. Empty. It took several minutes of calling and looking before he found her.

"Heart attack," George had said to Linda. "Total, catastrophic heart attack."

Mary Lynn and Jimmy's house on the hill was only a mile from East Bay Township's fire barn, which, although remote, was still equipped with a state-of-the-art ambulance and staffed twenty-four hours a day. Paramedics had arrived within minutes and worked for a long time trying to revive her, but there wasn't anything they could do. What George had called "catastrophic," the paramedics had called "electromechanical dissociation" and "myocardial infarction." For once, knowing the right words for something didn't matter to me at all. Whatever label the living gave it, the mother of Bradley and Christopher, the stepmother of Bridget, the wife of Jimmy, and the Drummond Girls' funny, sarcastic, naysaying, redheaded lady was gone.

"Mary Lynn was a graduate of Bangor High School and the Cosmetology School in Kalamazoo, where she maintained her license to date," her obituary read. "Mary Lynn enjoyed the company of her many friends and neighbors and especially the neighborhood haunt at Peegeo's. She will be greatly missed by all who knew her."

Mary Lynn Dewart died Sunday, March 24, 2002, at 6:18 a.m. She was fifty-one.

Why is it that the only way for small towns like ours to preserve their Victorian mansions is by turning them into funeral homes?

I was so angry over Mary Lynn's death, even historic architecture pissed me off.

Built in the 1890s, the Perry Hannah House, named for Traverse City's founding lumber baron, was a mix of Queen Anne and French Chateau styles with four floors, forty rooms, ten fireplaces, an endlessly swirling front porch, and a grand staircase fit for Scarlett O'Hara. When Hannah's descendants could no longer afford its upkeep, they donated it to the American Legion, which then sold it off for a funeral home.

It was on that elaborate front porch, wearing black tights and somber dresses yanked from the backs of our closets, that most of the Drummond Girls gathered together before Mary Lynn's funeral. Susan would come later with George, Pam with her husband, and I didn't know if anyone had thought to call Jill, but the rest of us stood outside, huddling together and stamping our feet against the spring cold.

For a group of women who never seemed to stop talking, nothing we could have said seemed sufficient, so at first we didn't say anything. I found it difficult to so much as look at these women's faces, my best friends in the world for God's sake. It made me mad at Mary Lynn for putting us through it, and I looked up at the ceiling of that porch instead. It was delicate beadboard some long-dead carpenter had bent to his will. I didn't feel awe at his craftsmanship, though, just a dizzy emptiness.

Jimmy had opted for cremation but decided for her actual funeral, the service would be open casket. We knew that and were both preparing ourselves to go inside yet also pretending we were somewhere else.

I'd only ever seen three people in caskets—my paternal grandfather, my maternal grandmother, and a friend who'd horseshoed his wife's car around a tree. The experiences had forced me to accept the people I'd loved were really dead and I felt both nervous and afraid of seeing Mary Lynn in one. What if she didn't look like herself? What if she *did*?

"Is it usually this warm in March?" Andrea asked, fanning herself with a copy of the order of service. It was only twenty degrees outside, yet her green suede coat, the one with the fake fur collar, was unbuttoned all the way and her face was flushed.

"What the hell, Mary Lynn?" Linda said to the air, her arms flung uselessly out from her sides. "I mean it. What the hell?"

She walked away from us and lit a cigarette, waving her hand through the smoke before it could float toward Bev or me. I'd never smoked a whole cigarette in my life and Bev, a smoker for years, had recently quit.

"Do you think Jimmy got our flowers?" Bev asked, rummaging around inside of her purse. "We did the green arrangement, right? The one with the pinecones and the driftwood?" She waved a ten-dollar bill in the air. "Who am I supposed to give this to?"

Linda leaned on the porch railing, staring out at the snow-covered lawn. March was a hard month in northern Michigan. Still so cold, still a good three weeks left of snow, an insult when all you wanted was spring. Linda said nothing, but stuck out a hand for the money. Bev gave her the ten, then pulled a wrinkled piece of newsprint out of her purse. It was Mary Lynn's obituary. Bev had cut it out of the paper and brought it along in case any of us had wanted to read it.

No one did, but it struck me right then how good Bev was at difficult occasions like this one. She'd suggested we all pitch in for the flowers and had gotten us a deal at one of the nicer florists in town because she knew the manager. She didn't subscribe to the newspaper but she'd taken the time to buy a copy on the right day and had gone to the trouble of cutting out the obituary. She'd suggested where to meet—the porch was out of people's way but close to the entry door. And, she was the only one who didn't seem angry. Sad, sure, but not mad like the rest of us were.

Bev had lived longer than we had, which also meant she'd had more people she knew and cared about die. She didn't avoid funerals the way some of us were tempted to do, because she knew how much having people show up comforted the grieving.

I watched the sidewalk and saw many of the people I'd often waited on when I worked at Peegeo's walk up and then into the funeral home. I pictured Mary Lynn, but not Mary Lynn, lying inside a dolled-up wooden box displayed on a stand somewhere inside. It was cavernous in there, and she'd become so small after losing all that weight. I hoped they hadn't lost her. Or put her in the wrong room.

I hoped *I* didn't get lost somewhere in there, and a dreadful image of what I might see if I did, if I walked down the wrong hallway or opened the wrong door, filled my brain. Cold people. Tubes. Strange fluid.

Just then, another woman walked up those ridiculously grand steps. She was alone, and I was sure she was probably the only person in the whole world who could have made us all smile on that awful day just by showing up.

Jill.

She had on a gray dress and a new wool coat and was walking slowly up those stairs in a beam of pure sunshine. She made it onto the porch, and we enveloped her in a hug.

"I can't believe it," she'd said, looking stricken. "I just can't believe it."

The rest of us had repeated that sentence a hundred times or more. Even Bev, who'd seemed to be handling Mary Lynn's death better than the rest of us, had said it. We couldn't believe Mary Lynn was gone. We couldn't believe we were all together and not in a car, or in a bar, or inside Fairview, or even at Peegeo's, but at a funeral home. We couldn't believe Jill had been gone for so long or that she'd suddenly appeared to us again. Most of all, we just couldn't believe a Drummond Girl had died.

We were just girls; girls didn't *die*.

We'd planned everything about our friendship so well, too. We'd reserved our rented log house a year in advance, we'd all made our particular food just the right way, brought along particular games, and we'd even packed carefully, bringing just the right clothes for any kind of weather. We'd just never planned for this.

Andrea put her hands on Jill's apple-shaped face and squeezed. It'd been two years since I'd seen Jill, and she'd divorced, moved, remarried, moved again, and acquired a stepson since then. I didn't say it out loud—it wasn't the time—but when she walked up those stairs, a sense of renewal came up them along with her. We'd lost Mary Lynn and gained back Jill on the very same day. It felt like a miracle. Except that I didn't believe in miracles.

"Well," Linda said, as if she'd read my mind, "if this isn't just a miracle."

"Yes," Jill agreed without a trace of irony. "Yes, I am."

Bev opened her arms and gave Jill a hug.

"Here's the obituary if you want to read it," she told her. "It mentions Peegeo's."

Jill took the clipping but only glanced at it. She was back in our circle for a moment or for good, I wasn't sure which, and the surprise of seeing her again took away some of the awkwardness of death. Someone asked if Mary Lynn had known about her heart problems and just not told us; someone else wondered if the diet was to blame. Since when did women get heart attacks? Since when was fifty-one years long enough for our friend to be with us on this earth?

"It's really good to see you, Jillsy," Linda said, the sarcasm gone. "How you been?"

"I'm all right," Jill said, but her voice held not a trace of conviction that was true.

Her reappearance was because of Andrea. She'd called Jill, broke the news about Mary Lynn's death, and explained that some of us were going to the service together. Andrea hadn't mentioned the call to the rest of us in case Jill didn't show.

When we asked her where she'd been, why it had been so long since we'd heard from her, Jill explained that her new husband was dealing with grief of his own and didn't like the idea she had friends from before they'd met that he didn't know.

I thought he sounded like a jerk, but my opinion on men back then, any man, actually, wasn't particularly objective, so I kept that one to myself. Andrea was a capable person, and maybe she had talked Jill into coming, but there was still something miraculous in her presence on that porch. Andrea could not have ordered that startling bit of sunshine that followed our lost friend like a spotlight when she'd walked up those stairs.

March is a dark month in northern Michigan. Winter isn't quite over yet, and from February to May, almost every day is cloudy and dreary. It was the time of year when it seemed like the sun had forgotten we even existed, all huddled and waiting for spring there on the 45th parallel.

Before we went in, I decided that where miracles were concerned, I could adjust my thinking.

We waited until the last possible moment before we went in that funeral home. Depressing music had already started playing. Getting lost turned out to be impossible. The room assigned to Mary Lynn's service was obvious because it was so full. We found seats together, though, and saw Jimmy slumped in a chair up at the front. He was sitting next to Bradley, one of Mary Lynn's sons. Even with all the people crowded into that room and talking softly, even with the organ music playing, Jimmy still must have heard us come in, or felt our presence, because he turned around and gave us a tired wave.

We waved back and tried to give him a smile. I'd never seen him in a suit before. It was nice, but it was too big for him. Mary Lynn had been the couple's planner, fixer, and problem solver and he looked lost. Lost and scared.

The room was elaborately decorated with wallpaper and light sconces and swirly wood trim. It was supposed to make you forget how terrified you were, I supposed.

I remember nothing about the actual service, but afterward the five of us with Bev in the lead walked down the center aisle and up to Mary Lynn's casket. It was pretty, if you can say that about a casket. Dark wood lined with white satin ruffles.

Her face was okay; I could look at her face, even though her head was lying on a lacy pillow I'm sure she never would have chosen for herself. You know how sometimes people leave funerals and say the dead person looked like they were sleeping? She didn't look like that. But staring at her face wasn't terrible. Her makeup wasn't garish and her strawberry blond hair was perfect.

What got me were her hands. They looked like someone else's. Too small, too pale, and way too still. Bev wasn't at all put off and clasped Mary Lynn's hands with her own, but I couldn't bring myself to do it. The worst part were Mary Lynn's fingernails. They were bare. Thinking of how perfectly she'd always kept her nails; how she'd favored tropical pinks and oranges, even in winter; how pretty her hands looked whenever she was holding a euchre hand; and how uncared for they looked now, I started to cry. Then Bev did a little bit, too. Jill wiggled in between us and put her arms around our shoulders.

I thought about that night at Peegeo's, rolling silverware with Linda. The night she'd told me that Mary Lynn was going to be one of the new Drummond Girls. How I'd doubted she'd be able to keep up with us. How I'd thought she'd seemed so old.

Now I couldn't understand how someone so young could just

up and die. How someone just fifty-one years old could go to bed on a Saturday night and be inside an oak casket by Thursday afternoon. That wasn't possible. Until it was.

Did it hurt to have a heart attack? I wondered. *Had the last thing she'd ever felt been pain?*

Linda wiped her eyes; Andrea rested her purse on the edge of the casket and pulled out a deck of cards, and the surprise of the gesture was enough to make my chest stop heaving.

Andrea handed us each an ace or a face card and then passed around a black permanent marker. We signed our names, Andrea put the cards back in the deck, wrapped a rubber band around them, and slipped the bundle under Mary Lynn's hands. Her nails weren't polished, but at least she could still play euchre.

"Okay," Andrea said, her voice husky and thick. "Now she's ready. Now our Drummond sister can go on her next trip."

After Mary Lynn's funeral, Andrea made it her mission to get Jill back to being an active Drummond Girl. Her plan was a good one, and it should have worked, too. If we would have foisted it upon any normal man with half a personality, I'm sure it would have worked. But no, we'd foisted it on Tony.

The only reason any of us could think of for Jill's new husband to forbid her—*forbid? What the hell?*—from going with us to Drummond was that he didn't know us.

"Once he meets us, and we meet him, it'll all be good," Andrea said.

"I don't know…," Jill said. "Tony's not a real people type of person."

Immediately after the funeral, we'd convinced her to come with us to Peegeo's for Mary Lynn's wake, and right away we could tell something was wrong. Jill shared just as many Mary Lynn stories as the rest of us did, but when the conversation shifted to her, she shut down. How's your job? *Fine.* How's the house coming? *Fine.* How's everything with Tony? *Fine.*

Jill, usually so animated and outgoing, had gone suddenly flat when the subject of her homelife came up, like a can of pop after all the bubbles had gone out of it.

"Look," Andrea said. "As soon as we get a nice day, I'll have a cookout. Not just for Tony, but so all the guys can meet each other. Kids, too. We should have done it a long time ago."

The cookout didn't happen until September, but it did happen, and it really was just for Tony. Our husbands already knew each other, or at least knew of each other, and besides a friendly hello at Peegeo's, they didn't socialize much. And our kids were so far apart in age, they had nothing in common, either. Linda and Pam didn't have kids. Bev had a son and a daughter, but they were both grown and in their late twenties. Susan's sons were in high school, I had three sons in elementary and middle school, and Andrea's daughter was still a toddler.

But on an early Saturday evening in September, we'd assembled at Andrea and Steve's, ostensibly for hot dogs and hamburgers, but actually so that we could meet Tony, and he, us.

He was tall, well built with short sandy-blond hair, and might have been handsome if he didn't look so uncomfortable. His jaw was so square, he looked like a manly cartoon character. He ignored all of us, shook the men's hands, poked a boot in the campfire, moved the logs around, and scowled.

"What's that for?" he'd asked Andrea's husband, pointing toward the building with an adjacent parking lot that sat at the front of their property.

"That's Roots and Wings," Steve said proudly. "My wife's preschool. We had it built and then furnished the whole inside just how she wanted it. During the week there's two dozen kids in there every day."

Jill had never seen Roots and Wings and neither had some of

the other men, so Andrea offered to give everyone a tour. My two younger sons had both been her students, so I knew exactly what it looked like inside. Colorful, busy, and fun, just like she was. But I went on the tour anyway. I missed seeing all those creative little bodies, careening around the room from dress-up to finger painting to the book corner.

Andrea went to get her keys, then unlocked the door and turned on the lights. They flickered at first, then caught, and shone down on great big paintings taped to the wall, a rectangular tub of water at waist level, and two furry beanbag chairs. One corner had cots and blankets, another bulging bookshelves.

The place was her creation and Andrea just beamed. I had my writing; Bev, Susan, and Linda each had elaborate flower gardens; Pam liked to cook; but Roots and Wings was Andrea's work of art. It was her creative outlet but also her job, and I thought how lucky her young daughter was to have a mom who owned a preschool.

Everyone but Tony had gone inside, walked around, and touched everything, just like I'd seen the three- and four-year-old kids do. Jill gravitated to the art supplies. Up close, the big paintings on the wall were actually bright outlines of children. I knew they'd lain down on the long sheets of paper, had someone else paint their outline, then colored it in themselves.

"That looks like it was really fun," Jill said, looking up at them.

After a few minutes, something must have changed Tony's mind about coming inside because I saw him take two manly strides past the threshold and look around. He slouched, put his hands on his waist, threw his shoulders back, and scrunched up his face.

"Smells like kids," he'd said, then lumbered back toward the door and left.

Jill gave me an apologetic look, put down the jar of poster paint she'd been holding, and followed him out.

*   *   *

There was no other way to say it. Sometimes, Cupid was just an asshole.

How else to explain Jill's marriage to that man?

We wanted to talk to her alone, to find out what she saw in him and how she was really doing, without him around to intimidate her. She'd given us her new address, but we didn't visit her because we couldn't be sure Tony wouldn't be there when we showed up. But a few days after the cookout, Linda and I went to the Hoffbrau, the bar where Jill worked.

"What are you two doing here?" Jill had asked.

Our friend was smiling, but I could tell she was also surprised to see us. Before Mary Lynn's funeral, we hadn't seen Jill in two years. Then there'd been the wake at Peegeo's, the cookout at Andrea's, and here the two of us were again, popping up at her job.

"We heard you added a deep-fried pickle to your menu," Linda said. "Thought we'd come by and try one."

Jill raised an eyebrow, but I had to give Linda some credit. As cover stories went, the pickle wasn't bad. The Hoffbrau was twenty minutes from Peegeo's, but the two places shared some of the same customers. If a whole dill wrapped in Swiss cheese and ham, then battered and deep-fried was popular at the Hoffbrau, it'd be popular at Peegeo's, too.

Jill called our order in to the cook, waited on a couple people at the bar, then circled back to our table. The rest of her section was empty, no one was waiting to be seated, and she pulled out a chair and sat down.

Linda and I looked at each other—George would've had our heads on a skewer if we'd ever done that, no matter how quiet things were. His motto: If you could lean, you could clean.

"It's fine," Jill said, waving away our concerns. "The owner's cool."

I wondered how the two of us were going to work her husband

into the conversation and make it look natural, but as it turned out, we didn't have to. Jill did it for us.

"That's where I met Tony," she said, pointing across the restaurant at an empty barstool. "After his wife died, he came in here a lot and always sat right there."

Tony's first wife and the mother of his young son had died of cancer. He'd needed someone to talk to and that someone had turned out to be Jill. Before she knew it, she was dating him, then giving him advice on his son, moving in with him, and finally marrying him.

"Any chance of you coming back to Drummond?" Linda asked.

"I'd like to...," Jill said.

But she said it the way someone might say they wanted to sail to Hawaii or spend Christmas in Paris. As something to dream about, but not something they believed they'd actually do.

"We miss you," I told her.

Tears welled up in her eyes, but she wiped them away before they spilled over. Jill had enough maternal instinct for a dozen kids, so it didn't surprise me that she'd married someone who already had one. Jill had been our muscle that night at the edge of the road, and I knew her as someone who wouldn't hesitate to throw a punch at a bully or step in front of one, either. But our Secretary of Defense couldn't ignore real suffering. Baby birds, lost dogs, motherless children, and now, grief-stricken men. There was room for all those wounded creatures in Jill's compassionate heart.

"I miss you guys, too," she'd said. "Just terrible."

Tony was still mourning, she explained, and he didn't even like it when she went to her parents' house for dinner. That sounded more like control than grief to me, but my own relationship wasn't one to emulate, so who was I to give her advice? Jill and Tony were building a house together, and every penny she made was going to buy materials. There was no way he'd agree to her leaving for a whole weekend with her friends. Even now that he'd met us.

Linda pulled enough cash out of her purse to pay for the pickle, our two glasses of pop, and a ten-dollar tip.

"Door's always open, honey," she said.

I'd been so disappointed when we'd left the Hoffbrau. It was good to see Jill again but we hadn't accomplished anything. Then on departure day, when we were all still in Peegeo's parking lot getting organized, icing the coolers and loading our bags into Linda's Blazer and Andrea's Bronco, a little black car with a loud muffler pulled into the parking lot. Operation deep-fried pickle had not been a bust, after all.

"My mom told me that if I didn't start going with you guys again, I would regret it for the rest of my life," Jill said, putting a stack of twenties in Susan's hand. "If Tony doesn't like it, well, tough titty."

Advice wasn't the only thing she'd received from her mother. The money had come from her, too. Jill told us she had mixed feelings about accepting it—she'd been paying her own way since she was fifteen. But all her earnings went to Tony now, to their house, and to provide for her stepson. The cash was a gift to Jill, but knowing she'd be back with her girlfriends was a gift Jill's mom wanted to give to herself, too. When she put it that way, Jill said she'd decided to come.

I didn't know Jill's mother, but I loved her just the same. The idea that a woman from a different generation understood what Drummond meant to her daughter filled me with gratitude. For my Drummond sisters, for my gender, for mothers in general, mine included. It was my mother, and my father, who'd stayed with my husband the year our son was still a baby so I could go.

Without Mary Lynn, having Jill back seemed all that much more important. We couldn't lose another girl. We just couldn't.

*   *   *

As we drove north on US 31, I looked up ahead at Linda's car and couldn't help but think about the empty seat. I had planned for us to observe Mary Lynn's death up on the island, but in the excitement of Jill's return I hadn't yet mentioned it. Our departure and the ride up was for anticipation, not reflection, and when we arrived at the Fogcutter, Linda ordered seven shots of Tequila Rose.

"To Mary Lynn," she said, and we raised them up high.

Even with Jill along, the ride had been somber. It was as if we thought it'd be disrespectful to laugh too loud or have too much fun. We'd skipped the Jell-O shots at the Welcome Center, ignored the walkie-talkies, and hadn't even played any Led Zeppelin. When Linda made the toast, we all held that pink liquid in our hands as if it was something pretty to look at, but not to actually drink.

It was Bev who broke the spell.

"If I miss my mouth," she'd said, pointing to her pants, "it won't matter."

I looked down. Bev was wearing a pair of corduroy jeans the color of Pepto-Bismol.

That strawberry-flavored tequila slid down easy then, and we gave ourselves permission to laugh. Bev had been the one to lead us through Mary Lynn's funeral, and now she was the one who let us know, just by being herself, that it was okay to have fun again. Not in spite of Mary Lynn's death, but perhaps because of it.

Time was short, Mary Lynn was gone, we missed her terribly and always would, but that didn't make Bev stop being funny.

That night we splurged on dinner at Bayside Dining, the only upscale restaurant on the island, but instead of going out to hear the band at Northwoods or to play pool at Chuck's, we all went back to Fairview and played a few rounds of euchre, then ate everything in the refrigerator instead. Being out at a bar among people we didn't know, where it was loud and everyone would be drinking and laughing, didn't hold the attraction for us it usually did, and we went to bed early.

At Fairview, Bev and I shared a bedroom. Down the hall, Susan had shared hers with Mary Lynn, and although some nights Bev and I talked and giggled like teenagers, until we were both too tired to speak and were forced into sleep, that night I'm pretty sure we both just lay there, silent, listening to each other breathe.

I really felt for Susan. She was the closest of us to Mary Lynn and I didn't even want to imagine the loneliness I'd feel inside if something were to happen to Bev. I wondered if Bev was thinking the same thing about me, but it seemed too morbid to ask.

Saturday morning arrived, bright and clear. Because Drummond is surrounded not just by water but by *big* water, when the sun was out, yellow light sparkled and bounced everywhere, reflecting random beams of glare in odd places. On a tree branch but not on any of the others next to it; sideways on the waves close to shore but not out deep; on your right leg as you took a walk with your friend, yet no matter which way you went, your left one stayed strangely in shadow. It wasn't anything I'd ever noticed before, but since we'd lost Mary Lynn I'd started trying to be more aware.

Bev was already up and dressed when I came downstairs to get a cup of coffee. She drank only decaf, yet after my obligatory two cups of regular she was still more awake than I was.

"Walk?" she asked me.

It was one of those exceptional October mornings that felt like a gift; there were always a few, but you never knew how many more of them you'd have before winter. Sunny, no wind, and a little warmer than the forecast called for. Morning walks were our Drummond tradition, hers and mine. Sometimes, one or more of the other girls would go along, too, but often, it was just the two of us.

That morning was like that; the rest of the girls slept, cooked a late breakfast, or worked with Linda on the puzzle she'd brought along and now had spread out over the dining room table.

"How's everything at home?" Bev asked me when we were well past the cabin and a fair ways down the two-track angling off the main road.

"The same," I told her. "How's everything at work?"

"The same," she'd said, and we looked each other in the eye and made synchronized crazy faces. Eyes crossed, tongues sticking out, heads cocked goofily to the side.

Mine was meant to depict my marriage; hers her stressful job at a law office. I'm not sure if it was the facial muscle workout, the belly laugh afterward, or breathing the fresh air, but something about those walks with her made the troubles of home seem less important.

"When I retire, I'm going to travel," Bev said. "I'm going to get myself a little keyboard and learn to play the piano, and I'm going to find somewhere fun to volunteer. Forgetting some appointment or losing some stupid paperwork won't even be in my world."

The year Mary Lynn died, Bev was fifty-eight, and although she'd said she planned to work until she was at least sixty-three, I'd noticed she'd been beginning a lot of her sentences the same way: "When I retire…"

Retire? The word made me think of blue hair rinse, crocheted afghans, and facial moles. Not one of which had any relation at all to Bev.

That night at the Northwoods there wasn't a band, so Bev and I played pool. We enjoyed the game enough to have joined a weekly eight ball league back home and we played together on the same

team. The league met every Tuesday night at a pool hall connected
to a bowling alley. It cost eight dollars an hour to play unless you
were on the league; then, during the day at least, you could play
for free. A perk I often took advantage of when my sons were at
school; sometimes, I'd even take my youngest to the pool hall with
me on the days he didn't have kindergarten.

My other friends were aghast, but not Bev. "It's good for him,"
she'd said. "Balances out the other boring half of his parents."

After hours and hours of practicing eight ball, I'd occasionally
want to play something else. Bev knew how to play nine ball—you
use balls one through nine, the cue ball has to strike the lowest
numbered ball first, and whoever sinks the nine wins—and sometimes she'd meet me at the pool hall after work and we'd play a
few games just for fun. The rules called for the balls to be racked
a particular way, with the one up front and the nine in the center.
No matter how many times I showed her how to do it, though,
she'd never remember.

She didn't forget how to shoot, ever, and would gleefully kick
my ass. Nine ball was definitely Bev's game. Whenever she knew
she wasn't going to make her next shot, she had an uncanny ability to slow roll the cue ball into a confusing cluster so that you
couldn't make your shot, either.

At the Northwoods I was just explaining to her again how
to rack the balls when a man and his friend approached, asking
if we'd like to play partners. I'd been in this exact circumstance
with her before on Drummond, so I knew it wasn't me, or my pool
skills, that had attracted their attention. It was Bev, the human
testosterone magnet, who had.

When *I* asked a man where he was from, I was asking him
where he was from. When Bev asked the same man the same
thing, her happy tone, casual hip placement, and winning smile
conveyed all the promise and fizz of a beer commercial. Complete
with cheerleaders, acceleration, and hearty toasts to winning sports

teams. Of course we wanted to play partners, she told them, and the two challengers were soon vying for Bev's attention, obviously in her thrall, and completely unaware of the three ESPN-highlight-quality shots I'd just made.

"How do you *do* that?" I asked, when the game was over and the men had raced each other to the bar to buy her a drink.

"Do what?" she'd asked, genuinely unaware.

Was it possible to be jealous of something you didn't even want? Perhaps, because that was how I felt about Bev's ability to attract the opposite sex.

While we played, the rest of the girls were scattered around the bar. Susan was holding the orange plastic gun of a turkey-shooting video game; Linda, Jill, and Pam were sitting at a table, talking; and Andrea had gone to the bar to order another beer. I saw a man approach her, they chatted a bit, and then I overheard him ask, "So, where do you ladies stay then?"

Andrea didn't answer. Since our run-in with Dick the off-duty cop, we'd kept that information to ourselves. We were friendly and didn't mind volunteering certain details—that we were from Traverse City, that Peegeo's was our home base, that most of us were married, that we didn't hunt or fish, just hiked, rock picked, and enjoyed each other's company. But we never told anyone where we stayed.

"I'm not trying to find out any state secrets here," he'd said, holding up both hands in surrender. "It's just that I have a new house I'd like to rent out. It's on the water. Sleeps ten. And," he added, gesturing toward Bev and me, "it's got a pool table."

His name was Dave; he lived in Whitehall, a coastal town on the west side of the Lower Peninsula. He was a builder, the house he had for rent had a name—Mariner's Passage—and someday it would be his retirement home. He needed to work a few more years before he could afford to move to the island permanently, and while he did, he'd be renting the place out. It was right on the

St. Marys River, had a big deck, a hot tub, and other luxuries he was sure we'd like.

"How much?" Andrea asked him.

"Eight hundred and fifty dollars for three nights," he said. Which was way beyond our budget. We were paying $630 for Fairview, and even that seemed like a fortune. Andrea asked if he'd take $800.

"Nope, but believe me," he said, "it's worth the eight fifty."

Linda and Susan overheard the conversation, drifted over, and peppered him with questions. *Where was the house? What was it like inside? How close were the neighbors? How many bedrooms?*

Dave explained how to get there. Back toward the ferry dock on East Channel Road (M-134), then a right turn on Dix Point (no, he wasn't making that name up), and the driveway was two miles down on the left. Tonight he was headed to DeTour to pick up a new washer-dryer set, but would be happy to give us the full tour the following day.

Linda was just about to arrange a time when, from across the room, Jill selected that moment to remind us she'd returned.

"I've got too much blood in my alcohol system!" she hollered.

Dave looked at Jill, watched her dance happily in place for a minute, and then looked back at Andrea.

"She with you?" he asked

Andrea nodded.

"Yeah," Dave said. "Definitely eight fifty."

After he left, Bev and I played a few more games of pool, Andrea chatted up some other people at the bar, and by the time the three of us returned to the table where the other girls had been sitting, only Susan and Jill remained. Linda and Pam had left to see if they could find Mariner's Passage and, if the door was unlocked, look around. In the dark and without permission from Dave.

When they returned an hour later, they were both excited.

"You have *got* to see that place!" Linda said.

"It is pretty nice," Pam agreed.

We paid the bill and drove to Dix Point to see what $850 could buy. The answer was a lot. Mariner's Passage was spectacular. Back in Traverse City, we were seven grown women and, for the most part, acted like it. Inside that beautiful house, we ran around like little kids who'd been left at home alone for the first time. Feet pounded up carpeted stairs, water splashed from the gold faucet into the whirlpool tub, canned lights flashed off and on. Whenever someone made a new discovery, they called it out. *Did you see the hot tub? The pool cues are good. Not like the crappy ones at the bars. Check it out, there's a dishwasher nicer than the one I've got in my house. Look at the size of those windows. I bet you can see the freighters go by. Well, duh! That's what the telescope is for.*

Mariner's Passage was a log A-frame made of huge timbers, with a two-car garage, second-story balconies, and an extensive deck. On the first floor was a tiled kitchen with an island, a dining room, two bedrooms, a great room with views of the water and a stone fireplace, a big screen TV, leather couches, and an open staircase along one wall to the upstairs. On the second floor were more bedrooms; the top area of the A-frame was open, with huge exposed logs, a foosball table, an electronic dartboard, and something else.

"Come upstairs, come upstairs!" Bev said, grabbing my wrist and pulling me toward the second floor. "Look at that!"

If there were any angels around with a hankering to sing the "Hallelujah" chorus, that would have been a good time for them to let it rip. Sitting in the center of the open room was a nine-foot hand-carved Brunswick. A rack on the wall held two dozen brand-new cues. Unlimited pool, for free, with no men to mess it up. After a weekend in this house, I could die happy.

I heard the sound of the girls' feet pounding up the stairs, they took a look around, then pounded back down. After we'd all seen every inch, we ended up back in the kitchen together, standing around the rectangular island, our elbows on the cream ceramic tile, almost afraid to speak. As if talking about us actually getting to *stay* there would jinx it. As if the house was a mirage our voices would make disappear.

"It's a long way from the trailers, huh, girls?" Linda whispered. The house must have been real because even after she spoke, Mariner's Passage stayed standing.

It's light years away from the trailers, I thought.

That beautiful house with the magazine view and the rich-people vibe was one happy marriage (Andrea and Steve's), one divorce (Jill and Marty's), a second marriage (Jill and Tony's), two healthy babies (a daughter for Andrea and a son for me), and one forever-departed sister away from the trailers.

"I say we do it," Linda said. "It's going to mean another thirty dollars each, but I think it's worth it. Who's in?"

I believe all of us would have been, if given the chance to say so. We weren't. The rumbling of a diesel engine outside interrupted any thought of housing we might have been entertaining and replaced it with a more primal one: escape.

The door to the garage was the nearest exit and we all ran toward it.

Linda put her hand on the knob and yanked it open.

"Dave!" she said, as the rest of us dominoed against her back.

"Ladies?" he said.

Parked in the garage was a big black pickup truck with a front-loading washer and dryer wrapped in plastic and sitting in the bed.

"Hi!" Bev said.

"Nice place," Linda said, giving Bev the look. "We'll take it."

Dave's face broke into a smile, and he said nothing about the breaking and entering. Though technically, since the place wasn't locked, it had really only been entering and giddily roaming around.

"I thought you'd like it," he said.

While the rest of us jumped up and down like lunatics, Susan was the one with enough presence of mind to take care of the details. She wrote down Dave's mainland address and arranged to mail him a check for $425. The deposit for next year's trip.

Sunday afternoon it rained and we all lounged at Fairview. Some girls took naps and I tried, with mixed results, to find the Michigan State Spartans football game on the little TV's foil-wrapped antennas. When everyone was awake again, I decided it was a good time for the reflection I'd planned for Mary Lynn. I'd told Linda about it, she called the girls to the kitchen table, and I set something down in the middle of it.

"It's for Mary Lynn," I explained.

There was a pause while everyone stared at the heart-sized metal orb.

"I don't get it," Andrea said.

It was a small brass doorknob polished to a high sheen from years of use. I'd found it at a store south of Traverse City that sold hardware salvaged from old buildings. I didn't know what Jimmy had done with Mary Lynn's ashes—and I hadn't felt like it was my place to ask—but I still wanted to leave something of her on the island. My fondest memory of Mary Lynn was the night she'd stood on that chair at Chuck's and yelled out, "Door! Bitches!" and so that's why I'd bought the doorknob. When I made the plan, I hadn't known we'd be moving houses; now that it was going to be our last year at Fairview, a place Mary Lynn had loved, the gesture seemed even more important.

The hard rain of earlier in the day had drained to a light sprinkle. We put on our jackets and went outside. Most of the houses and cabins on Drummond Island had only tiny yards or none at all. The woods were vigorous and could reclaim a yard in a single summer if it wasn't constantly mowed. There was a thin strip of grass around Fairview, then a rocky, mossy cedar forest. I hadn't thought to bring a shovel so we grabbed a few dinner knives from the kitchen, stood in a circle, and started digging. When we had a little hole a foot or so deep, I dropped the doorknob in, we refilled the dirt, and Jill arranged a thick piece of moss on top. We found some flat rocks and built a small cairn for a marker.

Sunday night we had dinner at Pins, Drummond Island's bowling alley, and made cursory stops at Northwoods and Chuck's, and everyone but Andrea and Jill said they wanted to head back to Fairview early. It would be our last night in the little cabin in the woods we'd stayed in since 1998—five whole years, and it felt like the end of an era. It would also be our last night in the cabin where we'd stayed with Mary Lynn. We were excited about moving to a newer, more lavish home next year, but I was feeling a little melancholy about it, too. As if we were officially leaving Mary Lynn behind.

Andrea and Jill tried to settle in that night but were acting jumpy and still full of energy—from the excitement of the new house, from Jill's return, from reckoning with their own mortality, or perhaps from all three. They didn't want to play euchre, they didn't want to play Pictionary, they didn't want to make a snack, and they certainly didn't want to work on the intricate puzzle of the United States Linda had spread out on the dining room table.

"We're headed back to Chuck's," Andrea said, jacket on, car keys swinging from her finger. "Anyone else?"

Until Linda and Pam's scouting of Dave's house the night before, we didn't split up when we were on the island. If one car was going somewhere, the other car was going there, too, sometimes whether the occupants wanted to or not. Whether for safety, unity, loyalty, or tradition, that's just the way it had been ever since two cars of girls had traveled to the island.

But that year, we'd felt surrounded by changes. We'd lost Mary Lynn and gained back Jill. We were staying an extra day again and had made arrangements to move to a new house. We'd always be together in our hearts, but that didn't mean we always needed to be within a few feet of each other, too.

Linda must have approved because when Andrea announced she and Jill were going back out, she gave Andrea forty dollars from the kitty and then returned to her puzzle.

"Anybody else?" Andrea asked.

"Me," I said, grabbing my purse and a flannel shirt and looking over at Bev. "Wanna go?"

"I'm tired," she said.

I was tired, too; I needed a shower; there were tangles the size of wolverines in the back of my long hair; I had sloppy joe grease on my jeans, and I was going.

The drive from Fairview to Chuck's was about ten miles and involved a complex series of two-tracks, dirt roads, familiar objects (turn left at the old bulldozer stuck in the clay), and guess-work. It was weird, the way you could get lost on an island you'd been on every year for a decade, but that was Drummond. After a few minor turnarounds and an attack of forest vertigo (*didn't we already go by that tree?*), Andrea finally navigated us to our destination.

"Where is everyone?" she'd said, disappointed by the nearly empty parking lot.

"This island is obviously uninformed," Jill said. "Because if they knew we were coming, I'm sure they would have been here."

By "everyone," Andrea didn't mean people we actually knew. We did have acquaintances on the island—Frank, Garthalene and Missy, bartender Beth, a friendly pool-playing guy named Duane, Worm, and now Dave, our future landlord—but it wasn't like we ever made plans to meet up with them. By "everyone," Andrea had just meant a collective everyone, the people of Drummond, the tourists, the locals, and random travelers.

What we'd forgotten was that we'd arrived on the island on Thursday. By the time the three of us broke ranks and drove to Chuck's, it was Monday night. We were still on vacation, so we still felt like whooping it up, but Monday was just Monday for the people who lived on Drummond. The start of another workweek and the last day most of them would even think of looking for some late-night fun.

If we'd realized that, the mood inside Chuck's wouldn't have been such a surprise. But we didn't. For us, Monday might as well have been a Saturday, and a Saturday-night feel for us meant a Saturday-night feel for the whole world. Obviously, no one had informed Chuck's of that, because there was just one table of two couples, and then two men at the bar, and all six were slumped down and tired looking.

"What the hell happened?" Andrea asked the bartender.

"We had a very bad night," she said. "Someone didn't like their soup and all hell broke loose."

The three of us laughed, sure it was a joke. The place was empty enough that everyone had to have heard what she said, but the other customers only glared.

"I know you," a beefy, fair-skinned blond man at the end of the bar said, pointing a hefty finger our way. "You girls are from Hessel. You were at the football game."

If it got a little levity into that somber room, then sure, we'd be from Hessel. We'd have been from Kalamazoo, Timbuktu, or bippity-boppity-boo.

"Yeah! Hessel!" Jill said, hoisting her beer in salute. "Whoo-hoo!"

More glares.

Andrea tried a new tack. She had the forty dollars from the kitty in her pocket and told the bartender to get the big guy a beer on us.

"What about my *wife*?" he'd said, in lieu of a thank-you.

"Take it easy, Hamberg," the bartender said, but there wasn't any authority in her voice. She wasn't Garthalene; she wasn't even Missy; she was someone new, someone we'd never seen before.

The big blond looked like the Skipper from *Gilligan's Island*. And the Skipper was in a very bad mood. I wondered if even Bev could have softened him up. But Bev wasn't there, and it was actually the person sitting next to the Skipper who had concerned me. He wasn't just irked, but rather doing a slow, infuriated burn. That person was built like a mini Hulk Hogan. A zombified mini Hulk Hogan. When we looked closer, though, we saw that there was a purse hanging off the back of the barstool. Yup, a woman.

"And a beer for the little lady," Andrea said, with false cheer and a paralyzed smile on her face. She leaned in to us and whispered, "Drummond Girls order beer, then torn limb from limb."

"I can take him," Jill whispered back, smiling and trying hard not to move her lips. "But I'm not going anywhere near her."

"You're a bunch of cheaters!" the Skipper yelled. He'd cracked open his free Budweiser and had slopped some into his mouth. Ms. Hogan stared straight ahead, not touching her beer, not even looking at it.

What we did not know then was that because there was no high school on the island, Drummond children went to DeTour for tenth through twelfth grades. And for decades, the towns of DeTour and Hessel had been locked in a vicious high school football rivalry. Three nights before, Hessel had defeated DeTour in an important game. The Hessel boys were going on to the play-offs; the Drummond boys were going nowhere.

"These colors don't cheat!" Jill said, smacking herself hard in the breastbone.

Maybe his insult had taken her back to her own high school days when she was a cheerleader and ran track. But she wasn't wearing Traverse City Central's black and gold, and it wasn't 1985. It was 2002 and she had on a plain gray sweatshirt.

The Skipper eyed her chest and looked confused.

"We're from *Traverse City*," Andrea explained, as if he were a boy at her preschool in the grips of a tantrum. "Not Hessel. We thought *you* were from Hessel."

Wrong assumption. Skipper's wife turned her jaw four clicks to one side, then four clicks to the other, and we heard the bones in her neck crack. She looked right at us then, as if finally noticing we were even in the bar. Three powder puffs about to be slammed by a folding chair.

"You Traverse City girls are a different *breed*," the Skipper said.

"You *rich* girls from Traverse City," his wife corrected.

"Time to bail," Jill said, not even bothering to whisper it.

Andrea threw a twenty on the bar and we left.

Once safely inside Bruno, I thought of the glee we'd felt the night before, secretly running through that beautiful log mansion, trespassers in a wealthy person's home. I thought of my own house, with its bad insulation, single-pane windows, ancient furnace, and chipping plaster. And finally, I thought of Mary Lynn. How she'd missed what would have been her last year because she couldn't afford it. And I thought of her immaculate bi-level. The one with hardly any furniture. The one that Jimmy lived in all alone now.

At breakfast the next morning, we told the rest of the girls about our encounter. They were as surprised by what had happened as we had been. We loved Chuck's and had never felt anything but welcome there.

"It was really weird," Andrea said. "It was like that Hamburger guy *hated* us."

What I thought was strange was that we'd never seen that big blond guy or his wife before. But the bartender had called him by name, so they must have been regulars. For reasons we didn't know, they'd despised us.

"Oh, well," Bev said cheerfully. "They're probably just unhappy and taking it out on you."

"You weren't there," I told her.

Bev always tried to see the good in people. Always tried to give everyone the benefit of the doubt. Even belligerent, angry people who drank their bitter feelings about a high school football game and radiated what I could only describe as hate. I couldn't imagine being as serene as Bev was, but I did admire the quality in her. Even at fifty-eight, she had remained amazingly innocent.

Bev's assessment of Hulk and the Skipper was in the minority, though, and we decided to stay clear of the bars and town, at least for the afternoon. It'd been a few years since we'd spent much time two-tracking, and when Linda suggested we do that instead of staying at the house, we realized how much we'd all missed just driving slowly and randomly through the woods.

There was something inexplicably transporting about sitting in the passenger seat as one of your best friends drove her SUV down a rugged dirt path deep into uninhabited woods at five miles an hour. After only a few minutes, you'd forget the impossibility of your work deadlines, forget your shrinking bank account, and even forget the alarming fissures in your marriage.

You could just sit in that seat instead, without a single care, without even your purse, lean your head back, and turn your face toward the open window. Your mind would fill up with the smell of pine needles and moss, and your friends would be so overcome by the beauty of it they'd stop talking and turn off the music. You'd all just listen as the median of switchgrass polished the undercarriage and even finally feel that one stubborn muscle in the back of your neck relax.

And it was right there, in the backseat of Bruno with Andrea at the wheel, that I felt truly *present*.

"I have to pee."

And I watched the chickadees flit, so delicate they could perch on a fern frond, and breathed in so deep I could've almost OD'd on all that chlorophyll, and the very best part was that—

"I have to pee," Bev said again, "like *right now.*"

We were far back in the woods when Andrea flashed her headlights at Linda and hit the brakes. Linda stopped, too, and all seven of us got out to stretch.

"I gotta go so bad I don't think I can even make it to the woods," Bev said, struggling with the button on her pink pants.

"Well, my bumper's right there," Andrea said, pointing.

Before we'd stopped, we'd been looking for the stone chimneys that were supposed to be all that was left of the original Fort Drummond. We'd driven far back into the center of the island, and it had been at least an hour since we'd seen another vehicle. There were no power poles, no tire tracks in the road but ours, no sign of human life anywhere except for the two-track itself.

The forest was so dense, civilization so far away, that if I'd have been alone, even there in the bright afternoon sunshine, I might actually have been a little frightened. Sixty bears on the island. Wolves and cougars. Megabear still perhaps at large.

Bev got her pants unbuttoned, and the rest of us moved off and stood in a little group between the two vehicles, just talking about our day, the trip, and what we might want to do that evening. For the first few seconds, all we heard was the unmistakable sound of liquid under pressure meeting hard-packed dirt. Bev's relief even quieted the birds and the cicadas. But then it was joined by another sound: truck tires and a chugging engine. *Big* truck tires and a *big*-sounding engine. It wasn't like the diesel of Dave's pickup truck; it was more like the rumble of a semi. And it was getting louder.

"Bev?" I said. "Someone's coming."

"I know that!" she'd said.

But she didn't stop making her sound. Judging by the intensity of it, I didn't think she could.

From around the corner came a rusty black dump truck, with thick smoke chugging from two dirty exhaust pipes attached to either side of the cab.

It steamed closer, but Bev was still perched on Andrea's bumper, her underwear and folds of pink corduroy bunched around her knees. She had no choice but to hold her position, and we all knew that feeling. Every woman knows that feeling. Sometimes, you just have to see your pee all the way through.

"Oh, well," Bev said, fully accepting her situation.

The truck churned closer, though, so we gave her the only support we could. We stood in a half circle in front of her. We couldn't see the driver very well, but we could at least tell that it was a man. If he wanted to see Bev's lady parts, he was going to have to run us over in order to do it.

The truck finally stopped twenty feet away. More black smoke choked from the exhaust pipes, and to our shock a man's blond head popped out of the driver's side window. He pulled on a cord and a horn blew. Loud.

"That's him!" Andrea hissed. "That's the asshole from the bar!"

"*What?*" Linda said, just as Bev pulled up her pants.

"Oh yeah, that's him all right," Jill said.

Our Secretary of Defense kept her eyes on the Skipper, but she bent down, felt around in the dirt, and closed her fingers around a grenade-sized rock.

The Skipper was alone, unprotected by his fierce wife, and when he saw what Jill had in her hand, his expression changed from glee to alarm. He pulled his head back in the window, and the truck engine revved.

Somehow, the Skipper managed a speedy three-point turn. A marvel, because the road was so narrow it would have been a difficult maneuver for a car.

The dump truck rumbled away then, leaving waves of heavy dust in its wake.

"He wanted me," Bev said, fluffing her hair.

Next to her, Jill's hand relaxed and the rock she'd been holding rolled out of her palm, landing on the ground with a soft thump.

CHAPTER NINE   *2003*

Andrea (with me about to join her) on top of the Northwoods bar, celebrating The Pledge.

Who was in and who was out?

It was a question I didn't want to ask out loud, but one I was also sure had to be on everyone else's mind, too. We'd been going to the island together for ten years. Drummond was supposed to be an automatic on our annual calendars. You made a New Year's resolution, you celebrated Christmas and the Fourth of July, you took your husband out for dinner on his birthday, you shopped for the kids' back-to-school clothes in August, and on the first weekend of October, you gave it the gas to Drummond.

But with Jill's repeated absences and returns and Mary Lynn's death, it felt like our once-sacred pact was starting to erode. It had been a decade since Linda, Andrea, Jill, and I had sworn our oath. When Bev, Susan, Pam, and Mary Lynn joined us, they'd promised to keep coming back, too. Over time, things had changed, and the "pregnant or dead" clause wasn't funny anymore.

"We have to face the fact that Mary Lynn is gone," Andrea said. "Are we going to add a girl or what?"

There had been years when substitutes were invited to take the place of someone's unavoidable absence. During my pregnancy and Andrea's, while Jill struggled with her homelife difficulties and Mary Lynn battled her financial ones. Often it was Andrea who'd suggest this friend or that one, assuring us they were the perfect new person to bring along. Sometimes we'd agree with her and other times we didn't, but whether a substitute was along or not, on any given year we remained optimistic that any true Drummond Girl's absence was only temporary.

Then Mary Lynn died. We discussed inviting someone new to join us permanently, but the talk didn't get very far. Mary Lynn was irreplaceable. All eight of us were. Except that now, we were seven.

That ended the topic for the rest of us, but not Andrea. She said later she felt like we needed to renew our commitment. To the trip, to each other, and also to our friendship. She'd always been the one to set a lot of stock in our rituals, even the seemingly trivial ones like playing Led Zeppelin while we crossed the bridge, sharing a Jell-O shot in the parking lot, and then calling our husbands and boyfriends from the pay phone in the Northwoods parking lot as soon as we arrived. These small gestures, re-created year after year, held meaning for her. She wanted a new ritual that would solidify our pact for another ten years and beyond.

And so on an old computer she kept in her basement, she started the work of drafting an official Drummond Girls' pledge. She looked up pledges that other groups used and tried fashioning one for us based on those, but she wasn't too happy with the result. They succeeded in the loyalty department, but sounded formal and serious, and not like us at all, so she threw them out and started over.

"I wanted ours to have a rhythm to it," she said. "And I decided the only way it could be just for us was by including as many Drummond-isms as I could think of."

Andrea's basement computer didn't have a very good printer, so when she'd finally written something she was satisfied with, she e-mailed it to Susan, and then swore her to secrecy. The Pledge was going to be a surprise. She'd unveil it to us all sometime on the trip, but even Susan didn't know when that would be.

Susan had a brand-new printer, bought some nice card stock, printed out seven copies, decorated them with stickers of fall leaves, had them laminated, and gave them back to Andrea for safekeeping.

"This is for us and for the car behind us," Andrea said, handing the tollbooth operator six dollars. "Tell whoever's back there that the money is from a woman named Mary Lynn."

When we parked at the Michigan Welcome Center, Andrea said she had an announcement. "Okay, my sisters," she announced in an uncharacteristically solemn tone, "get a Jell-O shot and gather round."

We looked at each other—she'd sounded so serious!—and while Susan must have known what was coming, she didn't say a word. The rest of us were mystified. Was Andrea mad that we hadn't added anyone to the trip? Was she going to give us an ultimatum, or worse, was Andrea the Confronter about to appear?

We didn't know, but followed her direction anyway. I opened the cooler and pulled out a plastic bag of Black Raspberry, Berry Blue, and Strawberry Jell-O shots and passed them out. Andrea's face stayed serious as she moved among us, squirting a floret of whipped cream on top of our shots. When everyone was taken care of, she put the whipped cream away, reached into her back pocket, pulled out what looked like a stack of bookmarks, and handed one to each of us.

"This is a sacred time in our history," she said. "We've lost one member and another has returned. It's time for us all to recommit to this trip. If you're ready to take the Drummond Girl Pledge, repeat after me..."

By then we'd started reading what she'd written and were already giggling at some of her words, laughing out loud at others, and then I felt tears unexpectedly sting my eyes. Perhaps she had become the Confronter, but it was about something we all needed to hear, whether we knew it or not.

Andrea seemed to ignore all our varying emotions and remained standing military-straight in front of us, and then she even raised her right hand. When we didn't react, she said nothing more but jerked her chin at us until we, too, held our hands up and stood at attention.

"I, state your name...," she said. Her voice was so loud that several people—strangers—standing outside their cars looked over.

"I, state your name...," the rest of us responded.

It was too much, and Andrea dropped her guard and burst out laughing. We were supposed to say our own names but we'd been so caught up in the moment that we'd followed her, word for word, instead.

That was typical. While we had shared a few serious moments on our way to the island, they'd only felt that way in retrospect. In the present, whether we were twenty-one or fifty-one, the trip up had always been giggles and glee, just two cars full of warm clothes, rock-and-roll, and us, high on a drug called anticipation. The serious things—the health problems, the life problems, and even the absence we surely felt that day without Mary Lynn, would only be acknowledged late at night, or not until the drive home.

When Andrea regained her composure, she tried again. And we all raised our right hands, remembered our own names, and said the pledge together.

DRUMMOND GIRLS PLEDGE

I, <u>state your name</u>, pledge upon a Jell-O shot
A Drummond Island Girl I'll be
Beginning from this spot.

If I choose to vow upon a shot of any Pucker
I know I may be called
A "Sawed-Off Little Fucker."

I also pledge to thee
A "Cutter" I may be
And when that cutting does take place
I'll keep a smile upon my face.

I pledge that what goes on
Beyond the bridge above
Stays above the bridge
And it's all about the LOVE.
I pledge that as a Drummond Girl
One thing will come to fruition.
I promise to each one of you
There will be too much blood in my alcohol system.

As it was in the beginning
I pledge with all my might
To remember the Drummond Island phrase
"Wohelo, let there be light."

I pledge that when each evening's through
To each of my sister witches
A loving phrase of a sister gone,
"DOOR, BITCHES!"

CHAPTER TEN 2004

Me vs. Tennessee, Chuck's Place, October 2004.

I wanna play her," the skinny man leaning up against the pool table said.

We were all at Chuck's and the stranger had already dispatched his third or fourth opponent but then pointed his cue stick directly at me.

I was sitting with the girls, admittedly only half listening to their conversation because I'd been so intent on watching him instead. It wasn't his good looks that had attracted my attention—he was squirrelly and strange—it was his ability on the pool table. He was an accomplished if spastic player, and he'd had plenty to drink, I could tell, but even cheap liquor poured into that fence post of a body couldn't erase the hours he'd spent at a pool table. Probably at many pool tables.

The drink hadn't affected his break any, and he could bank the ball really well, too. A skill that, despite my success in our home league, I was still vexingly deficient in. I just couldn't visualize the angles, though it wasn't from a lack of trying. The only reason I knew this guy had spent long hours practicing was that I'd put in so many of my own. Like recognizes like, and again he pointed the tip of his cue my way.

"You been watchin' me," he said in a Southern drawl that sounded out of place at Chuck's. "Now it's your turn."

Our brief exchange caught Bev's attention, and she called out a flirty hello to him. She said she liked his accent, and asked him where he was from, but he ignored her.

"Get some quarters, girlie," he said to me instead.

"Rack 'em," I said, holding out four shiny ones I peeled from the ten-dollar roll in my pocket.

"Here it's winner breaks," he said, as if educating me. As if Chuck's was somehow his bar and not ours, as if his soprano twang and toothpick Wranglers and tucked-in shirt belonged anywhere north of the Mason-Dixon Line.

"You can break your own rack," I said, staying in my seat. "I'm okay with that."

His face brightened—breaking your own rack gave a player the advantage because they knew exactly what to expect—and out of the corner of my eye, I saw Linda and Susan exchange a look.

"Here she goes," Linda said with what sounded like a mixture of pride and resignation.

There's almost zero strategy to bar pool. The tables are too small to maneuver the cue ball much—not at all like the nine footer I'd learned to play on. Winning in bar pool was a matter of breaking well, making the obvious shots, and keeping the cue ball out of the pockets and on the table. Against a good player, a scratch would kill you. Banking was helpful because it gave you more options, but you could win without it.

Skinny, as I'd come to think of him, had a short length of string attached to one of his belt loops and a hollowed-out square of blue hung from the end of it. He chalked his cue stick with it, racked the balls, then took his stance and aimed.

His break was a gun. Besides the moment earlier in the day when we'd all taken the pledge for a second time, I'd been in a fog that entire weekend. My husband and I had argued only minutes before I'd left home, and the tension still hadn't left my body even two days later. But when I heard those balls explode, my mind immediately cleared. I loved that sound. It was what had kept me in my basement late at night, what had inspired me to sign up with Bev for that coed pool league, what had led me to check books about pool out of the library, and to start paying part of my money to Drummond's kitty in quarter rolls. That way, I wouldn't have to ask the bartender for change.

There's no ladies' tee in pool. It might have been played in a bar, and not on a court or a field, but it was the only sport I knew of where women competed equally with men. And won.

"You ain't gonna be able to cut that," Skinny said, regarding a shot I'd been considering.

He'd made a ball in on the break, then made several successive shots, but hadn't run the table—all my balls and the eight ball were still in play. In my first turn I'd sunk several shots and that plus his constant chattering had attracted attention. The girls were all watching us play, but the people sitting at nearby tables and up at the bar had turned in our direction, too.

"C'mon, Mardi," Bev urged. "*Beat* this guy."

I had one ball still on the table before I could shoot the eight, and it was wedged tight against the rail at a terrible angle. Skinny would have banked it and probably made it, too, but that wasn't an option for me.

Like banks, there's a science to rail shots, too, even the seemingly impossible ones. You can run an object ball all the way down the rail, from one end of the table into the corner pocket, if the cue ball strikes the object ball and the rail at exactly the same time and with just enough force. Too hard and the object ball will either pop into the middle of the table, or bounce off the felted point near the pocket, instead of going in. Too soft and it wouldn't have enough energy to go the distance.

I'd played a lot of pool against both men and women, and in my experience, when faced with a tough shot, men were bankers and women were cutters. Men tried to force things while women finessed them. Perhaps that's actually true, or perhaps my thoughts on pool back then reflected my thoughts on relationships.

I took the shot, and it felt like the whole room watched that ball amble down the table and drop into the pocket. It hit bottom with a satisfying thud.

"She's a cutter! She's a cutter!" Bev cheered.

The eight ball was next, an easy straight-in shot, and Skinny had his quarters out and resting on the table's edge even before I sank it. Some places money breaks, some places winner breaks, but in every place I've ever played, losers pay for the next game.

"I'm Tennessee," the guy said, giving me a fist bump. "And I ain't lettin' you break your own rack."

As the night progressed, Tennessee and I traded victories. But despite the outcome of our first match, his wins soon outnumbered mine, and while at first the girls had all cheered me on, after several games only Bev was still watching. Beyond a few moments of high drama, pool is not much of a spectator sport. But for people actually playing the game, time is absorbed into that rectangle of green felt as if hours were minutes. My enthusiasm for beating men (and it was always men who played in bars back then) was boundless. It was the one place where I felt I was in control of my life.

"Okay," Linda called to me. "Last game. Beat him, and then let's go."

She'd said it as if a final victory was a foregone conclusion, as automatic as paying the bill or getting out the car keys. I did have a reputation for making sure a night of pool ended for me on a high note, but Tennessee wasn't just any player. He had an abrupt style that was deceiving and he was superior to anyone I'd played on the island, better even than most of the men in the Tuesday night league back home.

"She can't beat me," he bragged to Linda. "She ain't got the stuff no more."

Mostly I was a quiet player, and in contrast to Tennessee's flamboyant chatter, I tended to be a lot more reserved during a game. If I had a winning streak, I might swagger a little when I walked around the table sizing up shots, but the energy some players put into talking, I put into thinking. "Overthinking," my husband would have said. I'd talked him into playing in the league for a while, but he'd quit after getting into arguments about the rules with several of the other men.

Linda's faith in my ability, Tennessee's cockiness, vodka, and thinking about my husband must have combined that night to embolden me. That's my only explanation for what happened next.

"Not only can I beat you," I said, grabbing the handle of something I'd seen leaning against the wall. "I can do it with this!"

In my hand was a bristle-headed push broom. When the girls saw what I was holding, they whooped out their encouragement and some of them even stood on their chairs.

"She's a sweeper! She's a sweeper!" Bev called with glee.

The jukebox at Chuck's is all computerized now, but back then it was dominated by Detroit rock and roll—Bob Seger, Mitch Ryder, Grand Funk, Alice Cooper, and Ted Nugent. Andrea found the button on the back that controlled the volume and turned it up as loud as it would go. When Tennessee saw my new cue stick, he danced a jig, but I didn't care. I started to unscrew the bristled head from the handle, but Tennessee waggled his finger.

"Oh no. You said you'd whup me with *that*. No changing it around now. You gotta use it just like it is."

My break sucked. It's impossible to get any power behind the cue ball by poking at it with a back-weighted broom handle. But Tennessee's victory dance had been premature. After he missed his first shot, I sunk balls one after the other and then even banked in the eight.

Since that night, I've won local tournaments, won bets on games, and even placed in the Michigan Women's Eight Ball Championship one year. But not one of those victories was as sweet as the night on Drummond when the North defeated the South once more.

In the car on the way back to the house, I picked slivers from that broom handle out of my palm. Some were big and deep and my hand was sticky with blood, but I'd been so focused on the game I hadn't even noticed them. Andrea and Jill narrated the night's highlights, and I basked in their enthusiastic replay.

"He was all 'I can kick your ass.'" Jill said. "But did you see the look on his face when you *won*?"

"Dude, Dixie is goin' down!" Andrea said. "Our girl will take you down with a broom!"

Back at the house, the girls all congregated in the kitchen for drinks and snacks while Andrea and I relaxed in the living room, reliving the night.

"Mardi and Andrea, get in here," Linda said.

Her voice was stern, and I hadn't heard that tone since I'd worked at Peegeo's. The other girls were gathered around the kitchen table and Linda was standing up with her hands behind her back.

"That display of yours tonight? I have no words," she'd said, her hands clasped behind her back and her face in an angry scowl.

I didn't know what to say to that. Maybe the night had gone a little long, but not to the point that she should have been angry with me. She let my anxiety build, but then her face lit up in a grin, and she pulled something out from behind her back. It was shining and heavy and huge. The pool trophy from the shelf on the wall at Chuck's.

While I was beating Tennessee, and Andrea was cranking up the volume on the jukebox, making sure I had the perfect soundtrack for victory, Linda had swiped a three-foot-tall marble-and-brass pool trophy from Chuck's, loaded it into her car, and brought it inside Mariner's Passage. All without being detected.

They heated up sloppy joes and scooped out potato salad then, and I wanted so badly to hold on to the glow of the night, but it took everything I had not to go up to my room and brood. I'd felt powerful around that pool table in a way I'd never felt at home, and I didn't want to let that feeling go.

It wasn't just winning some game in some bar against some guy. It was feeling so in control when I did it. The cue stick was an extension of me, and I was the one who decided not only where those balls were supposed to go, but in what order and how fast.

For a few months, my husband had been in that Traverse City pool league with Bev and me, but then he'd quit. He didn't like the people, the pool hall inside the bowling alley where the games were played was too smoky, and since the game didn't require any physical exertion, he'd objected to the activity even being called a sport.

He was right about all of that. But I didn't disagree with his complaints, I just saw things differently. I worked especially hard to beat the people I didn't like, washed the cigarette smell out of my hair as soon as I got home, and for once didn't get hung up on the literal meaning of a word. Pool was my sport, and I planned to keep right on playing it.

When everyone else went to bed and only Linda and I were still up, I told her something that I hadn't told anyone else but Bev. I thought my marriage was probably over. And if I was going to be single again, with three sons to raise, I needed a job with a regular paycheck. Something more stable than the occasional freelance writing and editing assignments I had now.

"So," I asked her, "does Peegeo's need any waitresses?"

CHAPTER ELEVEN *2005*

*A sign on Drummond that seemed to have been
erected just for us.*

My only stipulation for returning to work at Peegeo's had been
to ask Linda not to schedule me for Tuesdays. Make me hostess
on Friday night, give me the Harley motorcycle club on Saturday
afternoons, stick me on the Monday day shift; I didn't care, money
was money. Just keep me off the floor on Tuesdays. That was pool
league night, the team Bev and I were on was giving third place
a run for its money, and I *had* to be there; I didn't want to miss a
single week.

Linda obliged, which was why I was home that January night
after pool, and had barely stamped all the snow off my boots, when
the hospital called.

Did I know a Beverly Whoa-ja-hof...? A Beverly Whoa-ja-
see...? Did I know someone named Beverly?

What I remember most from that night was how fragile she
looked, lying on that gurney.

What she remembers most was how kind the people who'd helped her out of her car had been and how when she arrived at the hospital a doctor had told her to take off all her jewelry, and after she was sedated someone stole her favorite necklace.

"Oh, Bevvy, what *happened*?" I said, arriving when she was still in the emergency room.

"You'll have to get a sub for me next week," she'd said, gritting her teeth.

You are amazing, I remember thinking. *You just almost died and your biggest worry is pool league?*

She'd been stripped down to her bra, could barely talk, and was trying to arch her back in pain. She couldn't because a doctor—a woman—was kneeling on top of the gurney, straddling Bev and manhandling her collarbone. It was broken; anyone with two visual organs could see that.

"Do you have to hurt her like that?" I'd asked.

Do they teach Condescending Look 101 in medical school, or is that something doctors pick up during their residencies?

After the X-rays, after the orthopedic consult and the pain pills, I learned what had happened. On the way home from pool league that night, the weather turned bad—snow flurries, the kind that look like they're coming right at you—and Bev had gotten disoriented. She lived several miles farther from the pool hall than I did, so when I was home, safe and warm, she was still gripping her steering wheel, traveling a dark road that serpentined between several lakes before it finally led to her house. She'd had a hard time seeing the pavement, and before she could slow down, her car had slid on a patch of black ice. She spun off a curve and then hit a tree—head-on and going forty miles an hour. Her air bag deployed, but the seat belt had still snapped her collarbone in two like a hot wire though an icicle.

Bev couldn't be sure how long she'd been there, half-conscious, before two people ran to her car, opened the driver's side door, took her hand, and helped her out. When they'd walked her to the side of the road, she turned around and looked back. She hadn't had the car long; maybe it was only a scratch. Maybe it could be repaired.

It couldn't. Because it was on fire.

The same station that had sent the ambulance for Mary Lynn was only a few miles from the site of Bev's accident. By the time the fire truck and the ambulance arrived, Bev was sitting in the couple's van—they'd been on their way home when they'd found her—and her car had completely burned.

The experience had to have been terrifying, yet Bev never once said she'd felt afraid. She hurt; she was grateful to the people who'd helped her; and yes, that doctor really could have been more empathetic. Also, she did not know *what* the attorneys at her office were going to do without her for seven whole weeks. But she'd never once told me she'd been scared.

I hoped I would have been that brave and magnanimous, but I wasn't sure she would have been able to say the same if it had been me in that car, me squirming in pain while that bitch of a doctor exacted her torture.

In the following days, I did what I tried not to do, but often failed at when something terrible and beyond my control happened. I thought about it until I found someone to blame. In this case, that doctor. My complaint letter to the hospital's CEO didn't include her name, because I didn't know it. It did include a description I hoped would be helpful to the FBI if she ever went on the lam: Wiry arms, red Brillo Pad hair, big chin, no pulse.

During her recovery, Bev couldn't drive, and over the next few weeks I shepherded her to doctor's appointments, to pick up prescriptions, to buy groceries, and once, to make a beer run. The insurance company needed all kinds of paperwork filled out; there was another round of X-rays at the hospital's radiology department and a follow-up appointment with the orthopedist. On these errands I'd drive to her house and go inside so I could help her out to my car. Which was when I first noticed that the door of her kitchen cupboard was covered in sticky notes.

"Hey," she said a little defensively. "It's a lot to keep track of."

It was. And so besides that doctor, I was mad at her insurance company for not making the claims process easier to follow. Didn't they know the people trying to keep all their complicated forms straight had just been *injured*? That they were *traumatized*? That some of them couldn't even *use their hand to write*?

I offered to write a complaint letter to the claims adjuster, too, but Bev just laughed at my tirade. Then told me to cut it out, the up-and-down motion of all that laughing was making her shoulder hurt.

Maybe she wasn't frightened, but I was.

Yes, we'd lost Mary Lynn. And yes, it had been a terrible shock. But this was my best friend. My vivacious, brave, goofy, and irreplaceable best friend. And apparently, she was mortal, too.

What did that make me? What did that make any of us?

Bev's recovery was steady but slow. Even today, she can still press her finger into a small depression where the bone never fully repaired itself. And she still hurt. All the time. I only knew that because I asked her, though, and not because she complained about it.

Her accident made me take inventory of my own body, its idiosyncrasies, its muscle memory of insults and accidents past. The shoulder joint that had taken the brunt when my five-foot, eight-inch frame flew out of the saddle and into a tree stump during an ill-advised gallop down an unfamiliar trail on an unfamiliar horse. The C-section scar, long healed, that still sometimes throbbed its strange ghost-like pain. The way words now blurred on the page unless I extended my arms and held the book straight out, like some feminine interpretation of Moses on Mount Sinai. Thou shalt not covet thy neighbors' large-print edition.

I thought about some of the other girls' physical discords, too. Linda, Pam, and Jill spent so many hours on their feet I knew their legs and backs often ached. Susan battled insomnia, her quick mind often unwilling to power down after a stressful day at work. Andrea, a wealth of knowledge about holistic health, who ate organic and repeated good affirmations out loud, was at the mercy of her adrenal gland and frequent silent but judgmental self-talk, aka "The Committee."

Our once young and impervious bodies and minds had been aging all along, whether I'd noticed it or not. I'd felt a glimmer of that when Mary Lynn died, but it was Bev's accident that brought the passage of time into sharper focus for me. The seven of us may have acted like we believed there was a magical force Drummond Island exerted, rendering us immune from the effects of aging, but in truth time was a worthy adversary, relentless and cunning. It had finally found us, and the people we loved, too.

A humid Saturday morning in July and I half woke to the sound of the phone ringing. I opened one eye a crack and looked at my clock's glowing numbers. A seven, a zero, and a five. Too early for either a telemarketer or any of my friends feeling chatty. My mother and I were both early risers but even she wouldn't call that early.

Adrenaline surge—*where were my boys?* Then I remembered. Arguments. Paperwork. Lawyer. Except for the dogs and me, our home was empty because my sons had spent the night across the road at the house their father was renting now. The phone kept ringing, and once I was partially conscious I was sure it was him. Since we'd split up he'd developed the habit of calling at odd hours and always with some new grievance. I was selfish. I was unforgiving. I was stupid.

"What?" I snapped into the cordless.

"Um, Mardi?" A woman's worried voice. Familiar but I couldn't immediately place it.

"Yeah?"

"It's Tina? At Peegeo's?"

An image appeared in my still sluggish brain. Foul-mouthed prep cook, knife-blade skinny, hard worker, kids in foster care. Linda had hired me at Peego's again, but it had been temporary, just to get me over the hump. I'd shared some shifts with Tina, but I hadn't worked there for almost three months.

Why was she calling me so early on a Saturday?

Why was she calling me at all?

"There's cop cars and an ambulance at Linda's," she said, as if I'd asked my questions out loud.

Tina was as tough as they came, yet she'd sounded frightened. I could almost feel the telephone shaking in her hand. Taped to the wall next to the phone the cooks used to take carryout orders was a list of employees' telephone numbers. Once you'd been allowed into the Peegeo's family, you stayed there, and my number must have still been on it.

"I just...I didn't know who else to call," she said.

"On my way," I said.

I grabbed a pair of jeans from the floor and then drove straight for Linda's. The lake house she lived in with her boyfriend Kenny was less than two miles as the crow flies, but East Bay Township is dotted with lakes, forests, open fields, and illogically winding roads. So by car, the route isn't direct at all but a squared-off U of five excruciating miles.

I pulled into her driveway and saw a single police car and an ambulance. The vehicles were parked and idling. No lights, no sirens, which I thought was a good sign.

But when I got out of my car and headed for Linda's door, I saw her, and she was just getting into the passenger side of the ambulance.

"It's Kenny and it's bad," she said, breathing hard, her usually tan and healthy face bleached out and puffy. "Can you follow us to Munson?"

The whole way to the hospital, I felt completely out of it. Had Kenny had an accident? Or gotten into a fight? He worked in the oil fields as a troubleshooter, an industry that paid well but employed a lot of rough characters, so either was possible. Kenny was rough himself, not to mention big, so if it *was* a fight I was already feeling sorry for the other guy.

At the emergency room I walked through a wide atrium, gave Kenny's name to someone, went where they'd pointed, and found Linda in a dark hallway, sitting at the far end of a line of seats bolted to the wall. Across from her were a series of examination rooms behind heavy doors, all of which were closed.

Linda had her head in her hands, her hair draping almost to the floor, and she looked up when she heard me approach.

Usually, you didn't hug Linda. She'd never told us not to hug her, we just knew. But when she stood up I put my rangy arms around all five feet one inch of her anyway. I felt her chin heavy on my shoulder. She wasn't crying, not yet, but when she spoke her strong voice chipped apart.

"He's gone, Mardi," she'd said, barely getting the words out. "He had a heart attack and he's gone."

Linda and Kenny's first date had been nothing fancy. They'd met through a mutual friend and Kenny had invited her over to his house to watch some TV. By the time she'd met him, Linda had survived some difficult and abusive relationships. And so even though she met a lot of single men at Peegeo's, they all fell short of her expectations.

But then she'd met Kenny, and by the end of that first evening they were lying side by side, stretched out on his couch, watching a movie. He'd wanted to turn off the overhead light, but they were both so comfortable snuggled there together that he'd mumbled something about not wanting to get off the couch to do it. At the time, she'd thought that was incredibly romantic. This big, tough, muscular man liked her *that* much, and *that* soon, he couldn't bear to be away from her, not even for a few seconds.

As she was lying there, content and feeling lucky to have finally met her kind of man—edgy and a little tough but caring, too, and yes, even handsome—Kenny reached across her body with his long arm and felt around underneath his couch.

What is he groping for? she'd wondered.

And then she began to question her judgment. If it was a condom, she was going to be royally pissed off. Sure, she liked him already, a lot, but she hadn't given him an indication *that* was going to happen. At least, not yet.

Her suspicions were unwarranted. When Kenny pulled his hand back he wasn't holding a foil-wrapped square but a fishing rod instead. Strung with line and baited with a steel U-bolt. Without another word, he made a dead-eyed cast toward the switch plate on the opposite wall, releasing the line and sending the bolt sailing through the air. The curve of the U hit the switch just right, flicked off the light, and landed harmlessly on the carpet. Then Kenny reeled in the line, returned the pole to its resting place, and wrapped his arm back around Linda's shoulders.

Linda reassessed her date again. He was either really romantic or really lazy, but either way, he was definitely resourceful. What kind of mind put that much thought into getting out of such a mundane chore?

When he saw the expression on her face, it was the first time Linda heard his signature laugh. A deep "Huh, huh, huh." His was a playful, one-of-a-kind chuckle that first Linda, and then the rest of us, and soon everyone at Peegeo's, came to recognize and associate only with him.

And now that laugh was gone.

We waited for the emergency room doctor, saying little. When he came out of one of those doors, he provided official confirmation of what my friend already knew. Kenny had died in his sleep, probably instantly, of a time bomb that detonated inside his great and irreplaceable heart. He was forty-six.

What can you say about a man like that who'd just died? What can you say to the woman who loved him with everything she had in her? What can you say to your friend? There isn't anything. But you can be present; you can sit with her in those plastic chairs and press your shoulder into hers and put your hand on her knee while she cries.

Kenny had been all the family Linda had. Her parents were both dead; she didn't have any children and was estranged from her only sibling, a brother who lived on the other side of the world. Besides the Drummond Girls and Peegeo's, Linda was alone.

"What can I do?" I asked her.

"Just take me somewhere I can think," she said.

I was glad, then, that my sons were at their father's because I took her to my house, and we spent the next few hours on my front porch, me sitting and crying, and her pacing and smoking and crying. Later, she said she needed to call the girls. I offered to do it for her, but she said no. She wanted to do it herself. After each phone call, she'd seemed to feel both better and worse. She told the story over and over, and each time she did I'm sure it became more real. Maybe she even needed to tell it, just to convince herself.

"Take me back home," she said when she was through.

"Oh, Linda, no. Why don't you just stay here tonight? You can go back in the morning."

"Take me home," she said again in a voice that told me not to argue. "And when we get there, I'm just telling you now, I'm going in alone. You can come over tonight if you want, but I need to be by myself for a while."

When I'd made the drive to her house that morning, I'd been

confused. Now, I just felt empty. Pulling away and leaving her alone in her driveway like that felt wrong, and from my car's open window I told her so.

She was unyielding. I could come back later. I could bring the rest of the girls with me, she'd like that. But right then she wanted to be by herself. She and Kenny had lived in that little house on the lake together for fourteen years. His spirit was so large, so infused in the place, it was impossible for her to believe it was gone. It just couldn't be, not yet, and she wanted what was left of it all to herself.

"Do this for me," she said. "Please."

Without waiting for an answer she turned away, squared her shoulders, and walked into the house alone.

Later that night, most of the Drummond Girls, a few of Kenny's relatives, a couple of his coworkers from the oil fields, and the Peegeo's faithful all crowded into Linda's small living room. Drinks appeared, someone thought to bring a large order of Kenny's favorite Mexican chicken wings, and we shared stories about him until our voices got hoarse and there wasn't anything left to say anymore.

"You should have seen him in action," a rough-looking driller I'd never met told the crowd. "He'd climb up a well, without a harness or *nothing*, two hundred feet in the air. No fear. I mean it. None."

"I was working the day shift at Peegeo's once," I said. "And Kenny came in right before we opened with a big roaster pan in his arms. He set it on the bar, lifted the top, this amazing smell came out, and there was a whole cooked turkey inside, still warm. He tore off a piece of meat and handed it to me. I hadn't had time for breakfast and it was delicious. But I wondered why the whole thing was dark meat. So I asked him where it came from. He just said, 'Hammond.'"

At that word, the whole crowd broke out laughing. "Hammond" meant Hammond Road, a thoroughfare that cut through the fields and woods south of town, not too far from Peegeo's. The speed limit was a zippy fifty-five, but most people went at least sixty, making roadkill, especially the notoriously slow-moving wild turkeys, a constant.

"Sounds just like him," Andrea said, nodding. "And I'll tell you what else. Beware the Kenny pot. Linda, remember that year he rolled all those joints for us, and you didn't know it, and he hid them in your pack of smokes? And we found them on the way up to Drummond, and he'd written our *names* on them?"

"Yeah," Linda said, shaking her head at the memory. "In black marker!"

Her eyes were puffy and red but she was smiling. She'd had her alone time and seemed comforted by how many people just wanted to be in the same room with her. Kenny's favorite, Seagram's Canadian whiskey, was passed around and the stories poured out, one after another. The only person missing from that gathering was Kenny; I caught myself wanting to call him to tell him to come over.

It didn't matter anymore that I hadn't known what to say to comfort Linda. It didn't matter that none of us knew what to say. We were there in the same room with her, all remembering the fierce love the two of them had shared.

One Friday night on the island, our third or maybe our fourth year, it was raining steadily and already dark outside, but it wasn't late, maybe only ten or ten thirty. This was years before cell phones and we used a Michigan Bell phone booth under the lone streetlight near the island's hardware store to call home.

Our custom had been for us all to call our families as soon as we were on the island, so our husbands, boyfriends, and kids knew we'd arrived safely. We'd make it a point to call before we really started partying, because if we didn't do it right away, we might not remember to do it at all. Initially, Kenny didn't like the idea of Linda being away from him for the weekend, but once he realized Drummond wasn't negotiable, he'd actually made things easier for us by creating something he called the man phone tree.

It worked like this: Linda would pull up to the phone booth and call Kenny. Kenny would call George and Steve, then they'd each call someone, and so on, until every husband and boyfriend knew we were safe, knew we were on Drummond Island, and also knew they probably weren't going to hear from us for the next few days.

In the early years when none of us had a cell phone and even car phones were a novelty, the separation from us and home was an essential part of the Drummond experience. More than any other man, it was Kenny who understood that.

A month after he died, Linda turned fifty. To celebrate, all the girls took her on an overnight to a nearby hotel with a casino. Anytime I've looked back at the decision to escort our still very much–bereaved friend out of town for dollar slots and blackjack after just losing the love of her life, it has seemed bizarre. Linda wasn't much of a gambler even in happy times, and luck was obviously not something she was on good terms with in the summer of 2005. Whenever I'm tempted to pass judgment on our decision, I try to remind myself we really were only trying to help.

Linda was still so sad, and we just wanted to do something, *anything*, to take her mind off her heartache. One night away to mark a milestone birthday had seemed like a good way to do that. As far as the location was concerned, we were on a budget (as always), and hotel rooms at the Petoskey casino were inexpensive, even in the summer.

Plus, Petoskey was only about an hour north of Traverse City, so not an expensive trip gas-wise, either. Andrea did have to stop to fill up, though, and inside the station she bought each of us a pair of plastic sunglasses from a revolving carousel near the cash register. We put them on and pretended we were movie stars. Separately, we were adult women with jobs and responsibilities; together, we were just girls, even in the darkest times. Sometimes, like with those glasses, because of the darkest times.

Linda hadn't been at all excited about her big birthday and didn't even want a party, let alone an overnight trip. We'd insisted, though, and she tried to have fun, but for the most part, our hijinks didn't work.

"I'm Ali MacGraw," she'd said in a monotone, striking a somber pose from *Love Story*.

The rest of us didn't look much like the famous women we'd tried to impersonate—Susan Sarandon for Bev, Drew Barrymore for Jill, Diane Lane for Susan, Sandra Bullock for Andrea, and Julia Roberts for me—but Linda's long black hair and dark eyebrows were straight from that 1970 tearjerker.

"You could *be* her," Bev said, and we were all startled by how much Linda seemed like a tragic character from a movie.

When October came, Linda was still just trying to make it from day to day, but she wasn't the only one of us who was hurting. Bev's pain was physical—she still favored her shoulder, which remained weak and tender from the broken collarbone. Even nine months after the accident, she still couldn't bear the weight of her purse strap or even a heavy coat for more than a few minutes without wincing in pain. The rest of our aches were inside, hurts no doctor could mend. Pam's mother had been in and out of the hospital with a variety of serious maladies, and Andrea's mother, only in her sixties, had just been diagnosed with breast cancer. Jill and Tony's marriage hadn't worked out, and in February, they'd divorced. The split might have happened sooner if Jill hadn't been so fond of her stepson, something that made the end of the relationship even more painful for her.

"I think he was the one I loved all along," she'd said.

I thought of my bond with my own sons, my middle one about the same age as her stepson, and understood what she meant. I hadn't escaped the Drummond Girls' darkest year, either. The reason I'd been alone when Linda needed me, the reason my sons hadn't been at home, the reason their father was renting the little red house across the street was because we'd split. Two weeks before the girls and I left for Drummond, I'd had my husband served with divorce papers. After nearly twenty years of dark moods, I was tired of being his cheerleader. Our marriage had turned otherworldly, a place where two sleepwalkers occasionally bumped into each other, mumbled something nasty, then changed course.

No one was in any kind of party mood that fall, but we'd taken the pledge, and so we packed up, gassed up, and headed north anyway. Until now, we'd considered the island our place to let loose and celebrate; that year we just hoped it could be a place to heal. Or, if not that, then at least a place to rest up and forget everything that waited for us back home.

"I just can't see getting dressed today," Andrea said. "I mean, why?"

"I'm with you," Linda said.

It was three in the afternoon and Andrea was still in her robe. I looked around the house and realized the rest of us hadn't thought much about being properly clothed, either. Bev's ankles poked out of a pair of sweatpants that were too short, and on top she was wearing a plaid flannel shirt buttoned wrong. She couldn't wear anything that pulled over her head or pants that zipped because her arm still hurt too bad for either. Even buttons were a chore. Linda was wearing dark blue everything—pants, sweatshirt, socks—I supposed as an alternative to black. I had on ragged pajama bottoms and the T-shirt I'd slept in. An old pink one that read in loopy script "Barbie Dumped Ken."

All of the accoutrements of Mariner's Passage—the balconies, the tile kitchen, the view, even the pool table—didn't seem all that important anymore. Such luxuries were for happy people. Whole people. I pulled open the refrigerator door and considered my options. Orange juice, Diet Coke, beer. There was something soothing about drinking a can of Miller while still wearing your pajamas. The thin cool of that aluminum touching your lips even before a toothbrush did just said, "Fuck it."

Linda was usually the social one, the planner, the person who roused us in the morning and got us to commit to either this activity or that one. Two-tracking, Maxton Plains, Chuck's, or rock collecting could have been good options, but without another word, she'd headed outside to the deck, the sun, and the hammock; flopped down face-first; and took a nap.

Jill cooked eggs and toasted bagels, Pam read a *People* magazine, Bev and I played pool, Andrea played darts, Susan worked one of Linda's puzzles, and Linda napped. And napped. That evening, Andrea found a cabinet full of VCR tapes. Dave, the owner of Mariner's Passage, must have been a fan of dated action movies because there were three shelves of *Rambo*, *Dirty Harry*, and more *Death Wishes* than I'd thought existed.

On one shelf we found a few movies with women in the featured role, located the VCR, and hooked it up to the projection screen television. Andrea and I brought down pillows and blankets and lay on the floor. Jill and Pam took one couch, and Susan and Linda shared the other. Bev stretched out in the leather recliner, and for six hours we barely got up to go to the bathroom. Julia Roberts uncovered a conspiracy, Diane Lane eluded a plot to kill her, and Sandra Bullock drove a bus off one freeway and onto another just to impress Keanu.

Later, we would enjoy the elaborate kitchen and the big deck. We'd watch freighters pass on the St. Marys River and Bev and I would play marathon games of pool. Just not on that day. We could have watched six hours of movies back home—we didn't need to drive three hours and cross a bridge and ride a ferry to do that. We wouldn't have, though. If we'd been home, we would have been working, running errands, cooking, carting our kids somewhere, then somewhere else, or cleaning the house. Instead, we cheered on those actresses as they triumphed over bad men with bad aim and bad driving. The heroines' feats were impressive, yet seemed easier to pull off than the challenges we faced back home. The weekend would end; it always did, except there was no hero's welcome waiting in Traverse City to greet us upon our return.

"Anyone else up for a walk?"

"I'm not," Linda said. "But I'd be willing to go for a two-track if anyone else wants to."

That was the first glimmer of the old Linda we'd seen the whole weekend and perhaps the only thing that would have motivated us to get dressed. The ride from Mariner's Passage down Dix Point Road through town and out Maxton Cross Road toward Maxton Plains was a quiet one. At least inside Andrea's car it was, and we could imagine the same mood surely gripped the inside of Linda's Blazer.

None of us had lost a man we'd loved; the only thing that was going to bring Linda back was time. It was an odd feeling to hope the worst of her grief would pass quickly, yet to also want to slow time down while we were there together on Drummond.

Linda made her way to the Maxton Plains and parked. Although the Nature Conservancy had made the property open to the public, we'd visited three or four times over the years and had never seen anyone else there. We got out, stood together, and just looked for a while. The last time we'd been there, Mary Lynn had been with us. The last time we'd been there, Kenny was alive, I was married, no one we knew had cancer, and Bev was still whole.

Wind blew through the prairie grasses and poplar leaves, and it sounded as if they were speaking their own language, one we could all feel even if we couldn't translate the actual words. *You're here, right now, in this moment, in this place*, the voice seemed to say. *You're alive, and it's a gift, even when it hurts.*

Linda walked off on the alvar alone. Instead of following behind, we all went in different directions. Maxton Plains is a place where you can't help but look down while you're walking. Ancient evergreen roots claw their way over the flat rock. Moss grows in shallow depressions, and wildflowers somehow thrive in small holes where tiny bits of soil and rain collect.

Our walks felt timeless that day. As if Maxton Plains had been Maxton Plains before it had a name, before there *were* names or language or even people, and as if we knew it would still be Maxton Plains when all of us were gone.

It had been a hard year for us, but it had been a difficult one for Drummond Island, too. At least from our perspective it had. The Northwoods had been sold and the new owners had changed the name. At Chuck's, Garthalene and Missy were in a management feud, and when we'd lined up for the car ferry, we saw a big sign announcing more bad news. The Fogcutter had gone out of business. Worst of all, the Barb's Landing sign had been taken down. Frank's health wasn't good, we'd heard, and he'd moved to Florida.

"Feels like I should call home, but then I remember there's no one to call," Linda said.

We let that emotion sit for a while. If one of us had lost our husband, we'd still have people to call. Our children, our parents, perhaps a sibling. Linda had no one.

"It would make me feel good if you'd make your calls," she said. "Really. It would."

Susan, Pam, and Andrea all had cell phones then. They pulled them out of their pockets and purses and started dialing. No signal.

They tried walking around the alvar a bit but still nothing.

Kenny's man phone tree had gone the way of the pay phone and the phone booth. Linda didn't have a cell phone then, and even after years went by and we'd all had first TracFones, then flip phones and finally smartphones and tablets, none of us could ever talk her into getting one.

Who would she call? Everyone who mattered was on the island.

Back home, Linda's landline was still in Kenny's name. Years passed but she never took his name off the listing. Even today if you try to look her up, you won't find her in any telephone book. No, if you want to call Linda, you either have to know her number by heart, get it off the typed list probably still taped to the wall at Peegeo's, or you would have had to have known Kenny.

Every so often, the opposite happens. Someone trying to reach Kenny calls and gets Linda instead. She answers, the person on the other end of the line asks for him, and it's always someone selling something—a political party, a vacuum cleaner, and once even a medical alert system. When they begin their spiel, she usually just hangs up.

Sometimes, though, when she's not feeling too charitable, just for the shock value she tells the caller he's dead. In the silence that follows, Linda swears she can hear that laugh. "Huh, huh, huh."

CHAPTER TWELVE *2009*

*From left, Bev, Susan, Linda, Andrea, me, and Jill
with the Pigeon Cove geocache.*

A month or so before our sixteenth trip to the island, Andrea had asked for our T-shirt sizes and Linda wrote them down in her special Drummond notebook. Why? We didn't know, because as soon as we'd answered the two of them closed like a vault to all of our questions. Linda changed the subject—who was bringing hamburger buns for her sloppy joes?

Over the years we'd moved from the trailers at a fishing camp to a log mansion, from one rusty Jeep to two SUVs with satellite radio and heated leather seats, and our weekend kitty had grown from $300 to more than $2,500. Yet despite the years, despite the improvement of our fortunes, despite our (somewhat) more sophisticated palates, certain things never changed. And one of those was that we all still craved a Linda sloppy joe after a night at Northwoods or Chuck's. At least all of us but Bev, who couldn't eat beef because it aggravated her hiatal hernia.

When we met at Peegeo's to load up, Linda and Andrea handed us each a white T-shirt. A small medallion on the front read "D.I." and "2009." Underneath, they'd added our nicknames, and Wohelo, the Secretary of Defense, the Sheriff, Gamer, Jukebox Hero, Washycocky, and Pool Shark were island bound again.

It was still amazing to me how easily we slipped into our Drummond Island alter egos; how our shoulders relaxed, our eyes brightened, our step got bouncy. We became part of the island and the island's culture that year before we'd even left Traverse City. I suppose I was the one who'd initiated the launch sequence.

"Linda," I said, as we were getting into the cars, "did you tell everyone the news?"

"Yup," Linda answered, all business. "Everyone knows there's a cop on the island now. If there's a problem, we'll sic Jill on him."

"Well," Bev added matter-of-factly, "if he's at all good-looking, I'll do a washycocky on him."

We all burst out laughing. The image of a sixty-five-year-old woman—albeit an attractive, fit, aerobic bunny of a sixty-five-year-old woman—subduing a police officer with some version of her island nickname was quite a thing to try to imagine.

I'd been kidding (mostly) about whether a cop stationed on the island now was noteworthy. We did still go to the bars. We did stay out late and two-track. We played pool, and shared toasts, and hijacked the jukebox for hours at a time. We just did it all with a moderation unknown in the early years. I think we worried more about forgetting the hamburger buns, or that Mariner's Passage would be out of coffee filters, or even about getting enough sleep, than about being pulled over by the police.

But traditions were good. Traditions were what Drummond was all about. Sloppy joes and nicknames and no cops. And as we aged it was comforting to know some things stayed the same, year after year.

*   *   *

It had been a busy year, we hadn't seen as much of each other as we would have liked, and on the drive up, we got busy catching each other up on what had been going on in our lives. Kenny had been gone for more than four years, and I knew from talking with her about it that Linda had weathered the worst of her grief. She still worked at Peegeo's, and her take-charge personality had returned, though she'd still occasionally get quiet and need time alone. She hadn't dated anyone else; the longer he was gone, the more Kenny's legend grew. He was not just a hard act to follow; he was an impossible one.

Andrea had her second child, a girl, in 2003. Jill had been living with a man we all liked, Brett, and they'd had a baby, also a daughter, in 2006. Those little girls were in elementary school and preschool now, and our friends both said their families felt complete. Jill worked in shipping at a cherry processor and Andrea had closed the preschool in order to help her husband, Steve, with his automotive accessory business. Neither one planned to have any more children and wanted to focus on their careers.

Pam and her husband, Jim, had gone on several Caribbean vacations and had been discussing buying some vacation property nearby so they could relax closer to home. Susan and George had been married now for more than ten years, Peegeo's was thriving, and Susan had been given a promotion at the law office where she was a paralegal. She'd recently been assigned to more complex cases, some in federal court.

In contrast to how single-mindedly the rest of us pursued career success, Bev would be retiring at the end of the year. She'd been in the workforce for more than forty years, toiling away as a curb service waitress and short-order cook at the Dipsey Doodle Drive-In, then dispatching drivers for her father's cab service, answering phones, typing letters, and holding hands at various secretary and nurse's aide stints before becoming a legal secretary. For the past several years, she'd eagerly anticipated the day she'd no longer have to work for wages and was so excited by the prospect she could talk of little else.

"I'm going to travel, and learn to play the piano, and volunteer, and work in my garden, and go to the gym more, and get a new haircut, and—"

As for me, my life was in flux. I'd emotionally adjusted to being divorced, my sons had long been old enough to be in school all day, and I'd used the time alone to make my writing a priority. I was considering graduate school, my second book had been published, and I had won two regional awards. So I felt optimistic about my future, yet also unsure of my place in it. My sons were thriving, but my brother (and only sibling) had been in an ATV accident, suffered a brain injury, and struggled mightily to adjust to its lasting effects. I'd achieved my goal of being a working writer, yet was still recovering financially from the divorce and was barely making it month to month. Even coming up with $325 for Drummond that year had been a struggle. How was I ever going to pay for my own retirement someday? I had no idea.

As if all of that weren't enough for me to grapple with, there was a man.

A muscular and handsome, motorcycle-riding, cigarette-smoking, rum-drinking, salmon-fishing, politically aware, sharp-witted, and intelligent man. I was almost forty-eight years old, and yet, by "in love with him," I don't mean I felt some grown-up, reasoned, and mature affection. I mean I felt a giddy-up, lunatic-making, heart palpitation–causing, lost-my-freaking-mind kind of adoration.

When my divorce was finalized, my farmhouse had been in the middle of a remodel. Because of finances and emotional exhaustion, the project suffered a long hiatus. When I'd saved enough for the contractor to return, he arrived on a black Harley and I promptly fell in love with him. What a catch I must have seemed to him: a middle-aged woman with three kids, who was not only suffocating in debt, but gun-shy and hormonal, too. And yet, none of that must have mattered to him, because when we left for Drummond that year, I was wearing an impractically large pear-shaped diamond on my ring finger.

"Enough with the cell phone already!" Linda called after me.

She and I were sharing the master bedroom at Mariner's Passage that year, and she'd caught me *again* running up the stairs to check my messages. My fiancé (good Lord, the word gave me hives) had bought me a cell phone right before we'd left so that he and I could stay in touch. There was a time when the man phone tree had been more than enough contact with the outside world for me. Now I could think of nothing but that little rectangle of connection to him, even on Drummond.

"I love you, my Mardi," Pete's deep-voiced message reverberated from the speaker. "Be safe, don't do anything crazy, and get home to me soon, okay?"

But I *was* going to do something crazy. Not on Drummond Island, not anymore, but back at home. It was only fall, but when summer came back around I was going to marry that man.

"Hey lovebird," Linda said, calling up the stairs to me once more. "Get your ass down here. Gamer has a plan for our afternoon."

Gamer's—Susan's—plan was to spend the afternoon geocaching.

Just as the places we rented, the vehicles we drove, and our lives back home had changed, so had what we did for fun on the island. Modern Drummond Girls didn't just go to the bar, sit inside and play board games or watch old action movies anymore; they ran around outside in the woods, along the shore, or in our case in the swampy marsh of the DNR's Pigeon Cove Wildlife Flooding Area, and tried to find "caches" in a new kind of treasure hunt.

Susan explained geocaching was a worldwide phenomenon. The "treasure map" for this kind of hunt was digital. Latitude and longitude coordinates that had been logged into satellites by other geocache enthusiasts. They'd hidden treasures all over the world—including dozens on Drummond Island—and then uploaded their locations onto Geocaching.com. Satellites bounced the coordinates back down to an app on a smartphone or a fancy handheld GPS unit like the one Susan had. And *we* were going to go and hunt for one.

My own sense of direction was famously bad—I sometimes got lost in my own town—and I'd never heard of geocaching.

"Will we find *money*?" I wanted to know.

"Nah," Susan said. "Mostly just little knickknacks or doodads. You know, trinkets."

That made it seem less inviting to me. What was a treasure hunt without the treasure? I could find doodads at home in my kids' junk drawers. Still, we'd been to the island so many times by then, and I did like the idea of trying something new.

Susan thought the Pigeon Cove cache would be a good one to target for our first try. The coordinates were near a well-traveled spot on East Channel Road, about three miles from the ferry dock. A little creek flowed through the area, and on her GPS's map it looked like a seasonal marsh, with lots of wet-kneed cedar trees and rocks for someone to hide a cache behind.

We parked along a dirt crossroad and bounced into the high grass and cattails as if there really were piles of unclaimed cash to be found there.

All of us got our feet wet, but later when I'd had the chance to really look at a map, it awed me to think of where the water that had soaked through to my socks had been. And where it was going.

A culvert guided the tiny creek under East Channel Road where it emptied into Pigeon Cove, which later became Sturgeon Bay, then Potagannissing Bay. All those coastal bays of the island combined into the St. Marys River, and then the North Channel.

The North Channel emptied into the Georgian Bay, which flowed south into Lake Huron, then through the St. Clair River into Lake St. Clair. From there the water became the Detroit River, then Lake Erie, then Niagara Falls, Lake Ontario, the St. Lawrence Seaway, and finally, the Atlantic Ocean. If I looked at that map long enough, I could have traced the reverse route. I could have found how the Atlantic Ocean ended up as a wave lapping the shore of Drummond Island, then flooded the very marsh we'd been hunting in for treasure.

And I thought of how our trips to the island had been like that, too. A circle of friends and time, around the human calendar as the world rotated on its axis, whether the world meant literal geography or just our own cyclical lives. Youth and aging, experiencing and forgetting, driving home and then driving north, over the bridge and across the ferry, again and again.

Andrea was the one who found the cache, and when she did she whooped as loud as if she'd just captured a leprechaun. It was just a clear plastic jar, big, with a handle and a yellow screw-on lid. Inside was a lanyard, a pink stress ball (the kind an office worker might keep in their desk drawer), a tiny deer figurine, and a small spiral notebook.

The notebook functioned as a log and contained an entry from the maker of the cache as well as signatures of the other geocachers who'd found it before we had. That was Susan's favorite part. Reading through the log of any cache she found and then adding her name to it. She signed "The Drummond Girls" on the first blank page and then wrote a little note about us ("We're some fun girls from Traverse City up here on our annual trip!").

"When you find a cache, you can add something to it if you want," she explained, "and take something out."

We didn't take anything, but Susan wrote "GC" on the back of a cardboard coin good for one free drink at Peegeo's, and Linda added her Drummond Island key chain. The key chain never turned up again, but I now think people who put messages in bottles and toss them into the sea might improve their chances of getting them back if they added a drink offer. Because that coin did come back. At least, we've chosen to think it did.

Susan had dropped Peegeo's coins in a lot of geocaches that year (that's what the "GC" stood for), and a few of them did get cashed in. I like to imagine there was something of us embedded inside, and our essence worked on the finder the same way the currents worked on the water of that tiny creek, moving it south.

CHAPTER THIRTEEN
2011

Bev, Jill, me, Pam, Linda, and Andrea at my wedding reception, August 2010.

I did not Hula-Hoop at my first wedding. I did at my second, and while wearing my wedding dress, too. A lovely appliquéd, daisy-inspired, knee-length Lilly Pulitzer I'd bought on the Internet. Andrea and her daughters came to the reception, brought along their striped plastic tube, and I hula'ed the crap out of it. That activity alone explains anything anyone might want to know about the difference between my two marriages.

My second husband and I took our vows on my farmhouse's front porch while a poet presided; our sons witnessed; and my family, our friends, and all the Drummond Girls, along with their assorted husbands, boyfriends, children, looked on.

Bev was the first of them to hug me afterward.

"Be *happy*," she whispered into my ear.

A year later, my husband and I celebrated our first anniversary, not by doing anything special, but by doing something we did together all the time. We went fishing for salmon in the Grand Traverse Bay. He drove the boat and set the lines while I leaned back in the seat and felt the comforting hum of the motor vibrate down to my bones. When we came ashore, we had two big fish in the cooler and every organ inside my body felt swelled to bursting. Back at home, I picked up the phone and called Bev.

"I *am*," I told her, and even though there had been a yearlong break between her wish and my confirmation of it, she knew exactly what I meant.

My new husband could launch a boat, hook a fish, plow a driveway, build a china cabinet, glaze a roast, and tinker with the pieces of my jaded heart until they fit back together again. Not perfectly, not without a gouge here and a scratch there, but perfectly functional nonetheless.

When necessary, my new husband could also jerry-rig an ancient camper onto the back of his pickup truck. Which turned out to be a useful skill to have when you married into the Drummond Girls.

In 1959, the Midwestern-based Skamper Corp., known for its economic recreational vehicles and hardtop tent trailers, started manufacturing truck campers. My maternal grandpa Hain was an avid outdoorsman, and he liked the idea of being able to drive to remote backwoods locations while still having comfortable accommodations handily accessible. He was never one to cozy up to trends, though, and some serious time would elapse before he was convinced the Skamper engineers had worked out the kinks.

The hermit crab–ish lure of a real bed fitted inside his truck bed was ultimately too much for him, and in 1989, he purchased the thirtieth-anniversary edition—twelve feet of Skamper camper with the fetching side dinette design—and attached it to the bed of his Ford pickup. Many satisfying fishing, rock collecting, and wildflower identification trips followed.

When my grandfather died in 2008, my brother inherited the Skamper. But not too long after, he'd had his accident, and although he'd made an amazing recovery, his depth perception was no longer reliable enough for him to drive. And probably wasn't ever going to be. Accepting that took my brother two years, but in 2011, he gave the Skamper to Pete and me as a belated wedding present.

The timing of the gift was actually quite serendipitous—Pete had a new pickup truck (like my grandfather before him, my husband was a Ford man, too) and with a little adjustment, the Skamper would fit. The reason that mattered was because we'd just received Jill and Brett's wedding invitation in the mail. And there was going to be camping:

> *We wish to share our happiness with you,*
> *our family and friends.*
> *No gifts please.*
>
> *Camping is available*
> *at*
> *The Brown Campground*
>
> *Spend the weekend with us—*
> *Stay as long as you wish. Pets welcome.*

Jill had finally found a man worthy of her, and so on the appointed mid-June day, the plan was for a convoy of Drummond Girls, and some of our assorted spouses, children, and dogs, to meet at Peegeo's and embark together on the half-hour drive to the cozy home deep in the forest where Jill lived with her soon-to-be husband and their young daughter. The wedding was going to be in their side yard, with the surrounding forest as backdrop.

Jill and Brett's house wasn't exactly far away, but it was so remote and back in the woods that none of us had ever been there. The invitation included a map. Andrea and Steve and their two daughters led the way; Linda and Bev followed close behind them; Pete, me, our dog, and our Skamper were next; with Pam and Jim bringing up the rear.

The old three-quarter-ton Ford of my grandfather's had an eight-foot bed, perfectly matching the eight feet of camper floor designed to be inserted into it. Pete's truck was newer, shinier, lifted, with bigger tires, and far more stylish than my grandfather's. It was also two feet shorter. Once Pete removed the tailgate and attached the Skamper, twenty-four heavy inches of boxy white aluminum still protruded from the rear.

For this, our maiden voyage, he'd secured it with tow straps and commercial-grade bungee cords. It was locked on but good, though every time we'd hit a bump, the Skamper camper lifted off the pickup, then bounced back down.

"Back teeth all in one piece?" Pam giggled out her window when Jim pulled alongside us to check the directions.

We got back into formation, but then after a series of turns and a shuffle in line I heard Andrea call, "We lost Pam and Jim!" out her window. I checked the side-view mirror for their white Jeep and was rewarded with only a cloud of gravel dust. Up ahead, Andrea's hand, with her cell phone attached, was extended out her Jeep's window, exploring the backcountry air for service.

She was trying to phone the missing couple with our location when Steve hit a rock and Andrea's cell phone flew out of her hand and into the tall grass.

When Pam, Jim, and the cell phone were all finally located, we set out again and in due time came upon the first in a long series of hand-painted signs marking Jill and Brett's driveway. JILL LOVES BRETT, the first sign read, in pink script inside a red heart. The muddy two-track that was their driveway gently curved this way and that, and in another hundred yards we read, WEDDING, THIS WAY! then, KEEP GOING...More trees and underbrush, another curve, and YOU'RE ALMOST THERE!

The woods grew darker, the trees taller, the undergrowth thicker, the mud muddier, until finally the very last sign: I KNOW, RIGHT?

We parked in a sunlit clearing, got out of our cars, and walked en masse toward a woven twig arch in the distance, where perhaps sixty guests had gathered. The forest was eerily quiet for such a happy celebration and in half a minute we realized why. The ceremony was in progress. We'd missed the vows, barely catching the minister saying, "You may kiss the bride!" followed by hearty applause. In the distance, people whooped and laughed, but from within our ranks our shoulders slumped and Andrea's youngest daughter dissolved into tears.

She was only five. Missing a bridal kiss, deep within a fairy-tale forest, by only seconds was a tragedy beyond compare.

I wasn't a little girl and yet I'd felt like crying, too.

It'd been twenty years, but I'd still wished chance had brought me to Peegeo's a little sooner. Then I would have gone to Jill's first wedding and been with the girls on that first trip. But it hadn't, and I wasn't. None of us had been invited to her second wedding—it happened too fast—and now I'd missed her third one, too. The real one. The one I could tell was going to last.

Drummond Girls were supposed to be there for each other, wasn't that the whole point? "Being there" meant listening to each other's problems; knowing when to give advice and when to stay quiet; planning adventures together, protecting each other, sharing the grief of our lives, as well as the fun. "Being there" also meant literally being there. Having your body in the right place at the right time. And this had been one of those times.

What kind of friend was I, what kind of friends were any of

us, if we couldn't even manage to make it to a Drummond Girl's *wedding* on time?

We tried to make the best of it—we were finally there after all—and congratulated Jill and Brett, said hello to Jill's mom, and toasted the newly married couple. After the pig roast, after all the children went to bed and the dogs exhausted themselves and lay down, after the old people left in their old cars and the woods got dark and the bonfire got big, the reception turned into a party and the party got pretty crazy.

Pete lost his baseball cap when he jumped around inside the inflated bounce house, the one Jill and Brett had rented for the kids. A dirt bike was gassed up and, with a periodically changing cast of riders, went tooling through the forest at ridiculously high speeds, somehow missing every tree and rock. One of Brett's friends, an auto mechanic, had a dozen air bags he'd salvaged and he tossed them, one after the other, into the bonfire. The explosions reverberated through the forest and sent sparks fifty feet in the air.

A little while after that, I saw the outline of Jill walking toward the bonfire. She strode toward the last of her guests, looking thoroughly at home and content. She'd wanted a family of her own ever since she'd been barely out of her teens; it had taken twenty years, but she'd finally willed it to come true.

"Finally got Hannah down," Jill said, plopping into the empty lawn chair next to me. "She was so excited about the wedding, I didn't think I'd ever get her to sleep."

The rest of the Drummond Girls had gone home; my husband and I were anxious to try out the Skamper and so we were staying to camp.

"I'm so sorry we missed the ceremony," I told her, feeling my eyes sting. Perhaps they were already close to tears from the campfire smoke and the air bag gas, but the thought of Jill looking out at her guests just before she took her vows and not seeing a single one of her Drummond sisters made it impossible to hold them back. I could feel them rolling down my cheeks, and I didn't even try to wipe them away.

"Oh, honey!" Jill said, surprised. She leaned forward and put her small hands on both my knees, then cocked her head to the side. The golden flames of the bonfire reflected off her face and she looked...wise.

"I knew you were here with me. I felt you. Don't you understand that? Anytime anything big happens for one of us, we're *always* going to be there. Even if we're not there, we're *there*. You know?"

We'd been there with each other in the best of times—the weddings, the adventures, the successes, and the babies—but we'd been there with each other in the hard times, too. Even when we weren't there, when we were late or far away or blissfully ignorant of what was going on in each other's lives, we were still *there*.

When Jill found the strength to leave Marty and then Tony, we'd been with her.

When Andrea's mother died of cancer, we'd offered comfort.

When Linda found Kenny cold in his bed that morning, we'd felt her grief.

And when Mary Lynn got out of her bed in the early-morning hours, never to return to it again, I hoped she'd known we were right there, too, inside that house with her. I hoped pain hadn't really been the last thing she'd felt.

Jill hadn't meant our friendship was perfect or that it gave us the power to float around each other, invisible, like ghosts or spirits. She meant our friendship gave us the ability to transcend time and distance. Because we knew each other so well and loved each other so much, we could insert ourselves—and all of our love and hope—into the moments we'd missed.

The happiest ones, the hardest ones, it made no difference. In our hearts, we'd been there. Even if our bodies were doing something meaningless like crawling around in a patch of weeds looking for a lost cell phone.

"Hey, I've got something I want to show you," Jill said.

She ran into the house and came back a minute later with a photograph. It was of their woods—in the light of the bonfire I could see the same big tree trunk, but in the center of it was a dark blur. Even out of focus, the shape was unmistakable. A black bear standing on his hind legs.

I looked back at Jill, too surprised to say anything.

"We see bears all the time now," she said. "Our woods are full of them."

When I was just out of college, I'd always thought that by the time I reached a certain age, say fifty, my life would be pretty much set. I'd be in a mature marriage, my children would be in college, I'd have a couple good friends, a successful career, and my life would have settled into a comforting predictability.

But predictability was not something I valued in my twenties, so why did I think it would be desirable thirty years into the future?

Like that one, most of the assumptions I'd made back then turned out to be wrong. My "mature" marriage had been anything but, and in middle age I'd found myself a googly-eyed newlywed. My youngest son was more grown-up than I was, and his two older brothers had left college to work in restaurants. My writing career would not be a line angled consistently upward but rather a squiggle, with dramatic highs and lows.

Some marriages ended, some lovers died, all children grew up, parents aged, and most careers were fickle, especially creative ones. Sitting beside Jill and Brett's wedding fire, I could accept all of that uncertainty because I had seven constants in my life. I had the Drummond Girls. And they had me.

*   *   *

"C'mon, c'mon, read mine next!" Bev pleaded. "It's December ninth."

"I *know* when your birthday is, Bev," Jill said, flipping through the pages of the thick book. "We're both Sagittarius, remember?"

"And so is *Mar*-di," Bev sang out happily, putting her arm around my shoulders and squeezing. "So. What does mine say?"

Jill looked over the frames of her readers at Bev. I hadn't known Jill to wear glasses ever, but the print was pretty tiny. Even at forty-five, Jill looked like a teenager, especially with her new short haircut. Those tortoiseshell glasses looked funny on her, like she was back home with her daughter, playing dress-up.

Jill found the right page, scanned it silently for a minute, then grinned.

"You're the Day of Flamboyance, Bev," she said. "It says here, 'More than most, December ninth people must feel that they are the star of the show, the central character in the drama that is their life.' Oh, and check this out: Your planet is Mars and you share your birthday with Dick Butkus and Redd Foxx."

"Let me see that!"

Bev had been anxious for a reading, but now that she'd had her way, she didn't see how she could be connected to a smelly linebacker or a foul-mouthed comedian.

It was late, dark enough for the devil outside, and it'd been hours since we'd returned to the house from Chuck's. We were staying in a new place, the Paw Point Lodge, way out by Maxton Plains, and it was even more luxurious than Mariner's Passage. Bigger porch, better kitchen, more bedrooms. All seven of us were still up, even Pam who usually went to bed so early. It was Sunday—technically, the wee hours of Monday—and in the morning we'd be headed home, so no one was too anxious for the night to end.

"It says your tarot card is the Hermit," Jill continued. "And that you 'can learn the values of self-examination and thoughtfulness, but must beware of living in an isolated fantasy world.' Vigorous physical exercise is good for you—Look, it even says 'aerobics'! But"—and here Jill looked at Bev and recited in all seriousness the book's advice—" 'care must be taken in connection with martial arts.' "

Everyone, even Bev, laughed and laughed at that.

The book, *The Secret Language of Birthdays*, was Andrea's. She'd brought it along because she thought it would be fun to look up each other's birthdays, but, martial arts aside, the readings were proving to be eerily accurate. Still, the idea of Bev karate-chopping anyone was hilarious. And I couldn't help it, I pictured the year we were looking for Fort Drummond and she'd peed off of Andrea's back bumper, hitching up her Pepto-Bismol pants. Then I imagined her approaching that man driving the gravel truck, her hands in the attack position. I stood to demonstrate this—I guess because that's just the kind of thing Sagittariuses do—and the room cracked up.

"Dick Butkus? It does not say that!" Bev said. When she'd stopped laughing, she walked around the table and looked over Jill's shoulder. "Does it?"

"See for yourself," Jill said, lifting the heavy book up for inspection.

"Okay, just wait a minute," Bev said, strolling off. "I'll have to find my glasses."

While she searched the kitchen, Susan suggested we play a guessing game. Jill would read a birthday description for one of us out loud and the rest of us would try to guess who it was.

"Okay, here's an easy one," Jill said. "Whose birthday is—and I am *not* shitting you here—the Day of the Guiding Light. Who shares their birthday with Queen Elizabeth, and whose—"

"Linda!" we yelled in unison.

"—force of authority cannot be questioned," Jill finished.

Linda crossed her arms over her chest, shook her head, and smiled.

"You guys, this is crazy," Jill said, still absorbed in the book. "Listen to this part. 'Those born on August fourth are often the guiding light to whatever social group, political movement, family, or business they belong. They must remember to act in a responsible fashion since so many people are depending upon them.'"

Linda grinned and the rest of us looked around the table at each other in amazement. That was just *so* Linda.

"I found my glasses!" Bev said from the kitchen, holding them aloft like a trophy. "They were right inside the case. Right in my purse. Here on the counter! Right where I put them."

"Okay," Jill said, not looking up, "but we're on Linda now."

Bev retreated to the kitchen and began her standard cleanup routine. Although she was the oldest, Bev wasn't what you'd call maternal and had never been one to mother us. But she did have one care-taking attribute and it was to keep the kitchen, in whatever house (or trailer) we were staying, tidy. An early riser like me, sometimes she banged the pots and pans around in the kitchen before daylight, and we weren't always sure it was by accident. As Jill read on, Bev collected a few stray dishes and put them in the dishwasher.

Jill explained to everyone that the book also assigned a tarot card to each birthdate. Linda's was the Emperor.

"I can live with that," Linda said.

"That's good 'cause your planet is Uranus," Jill said, sticking out her tongue.

"Okay," Susan asked, "who else?"

Jill flipped through the book for a minute and eventually stopped on another page.

"Who do you think shares their birthday with Linda Ronstadt?" she asked.

"Andrea," Susan said automatically. "It has to be our Jukebox Hero."

"Yup," Jill said.

Andrea's July birthday made her influential, dynamic, and inspirational, with a magnetic personality. However, people born on that date also tended toward excess where alcohol was concerned and were materialistic in their youth, not moving toward a deeper sense of spirituality until they aged.

Next, we'd guessed Susan as the highly practical one, a person who always had her life well under control, but lacked patience for the pompous or the stuck-up. Incredibly, the book also said people with her November birthday were fascinated by illegal activities and borderline business shenanigans, but for study purposes only and not to participate in. (Susan was a paralegal, and she specialized in bankruptcy!)

I thought back to those dated walkie-talkies, the ones that had seemed so cool to me when Susan first brought them. We'd transmitted all sorts of clues about each other from car to car, but few guesses had been the correct ones. Now, all Jill had to do was read off a couple attributes and we recognized each other immediately. It was hard for me to believe the power was inside the book. I much preferred to think it was inside our friendship.

"All right, Miss Mardi," Jill said, arching an eyebrow at me, "how does it feel to be an *Empress*?"

"Oh, brother," Linda said, letting out a groan.

"Mardi's card signifies creative intelligence," Jill read in a voice suited to high tea. "She is the Mother Earth nurturer, who embodies our dreams, hopes, and aspirations."

"Yes," I said, leaning back in my chair. "That's definitely me."

"Yeah?" Jill countered, chuckling. "Well, don't get too excited, because it also says you're secretive and strange."

Secretive, I could buy—the girls were still mystified as to why I hadn't told them how tough things had been for me and the boys after my divorce. But *strange*? How was I strange?

"How am I strange?" I asked.

"You like school," Linda said, and everyone nodded, agreeing that was indeed strange.

"Okay, now what about you?" Susan asked, indicating Jill.

"I'm the Day of Mammoth Projects," Jill said a bit wearily. "Year after year, no matter what, I stick to what I'm doing. You know, that probably means hauling drywall. Painting. Sanding. Whatever."

"That's perfect!" Bev called from the kitchen.

"Perfectly nuts," Jill countered. "But as your Secretary of Defense, I'm also proud to say I share my birthday with a long line of military leaders. Oh, and Betty Grable."

Jill had worked so long and so hard to create a home for herself. Not just the actual house she lived in now, but the people who lived inside of it with her. She might have thought "mammoth projects" meant construction, but I thought Jill's true project had been creating a family.

Pam was the Day of the Direct Current, and the book said she was private and self-assured. Our Sheriff didn't aspire to any outlandish heroics, yet always exuded a sense of quiet valor.

"Does anyone know Mary Lynn's birthday?" Jill asked.

Susan did. It was June 2, and again Jill flipped back and forth until she found the date.

"The Day of the Problem Solver."

As soon as she said that, our teasing stopped and we all went quiet. In the coming years, I'd learn what Mary Lynn's boss had had to say about her, that she fixed printing mistakes and even fixed the machines themselves.

"Problems and difficulties abound for June second people," Jill continued, "and dealing with them is a way of life. They're usually social creatures so they may gain weight after too many parties and dinners out. But failure in no way dampens the enthusiasms of these hardy souls."

Jill read on and told us that Mary Lynn had shared her birthday with Charlie Watts, the drummer for the Rolling Stones. They were one of my favorite bands—I'd actually won a ticket to see them perform in the Pontiac Silverdome on my twenty-first birthday—and when Jill said the name I immediately pictured the drummer. The small but dapper white-haired guy, the band member who'd always seemed so proper to me, even though he'd spent his career surrounded by epic impropriety. He'd also seemed so old, even back in the 1980s.

We were silent for a long while, allowing our individual thoughts to conjure Mary Lynn. She had already been gone when we'd started renting Mariner's Passage, and now we were in another new place. She would have loved both of them.

Still, I was far too cynical to believe the day someone was born determined their personality. The authors were two men. How could they possibly know me and my friends so well? And yet, I couldn't deny some of the descriptions had been uncanny. Linda and Queen Elizabeth, Bev being the star of her own life, not to mention my need to be creative, and Jill's mammoth project.

Andrea and Jill both believed in what the rest of us called "woo-woo stuff," so I didn't want to say anything that would hurt their feelings. When neither of them was looking, I'd reached for the book, turned it over to read about the authors, and what I saw confirmed my suspicions. One man had been born on the Cusp of Energy, the other on the Cusp of Revolution. Oh, please. When I felt the cusp of something coming on, I ate more roughage and it passed within a couple hours.

But, I couldn't help myself. While everyone else's thoughts were on Mary Lynn, I ever so casually opened the book and turned to the page for my birthday, so I could read the full entry myself. I shared the date with Anna Freud (Sigmund's daughter) and heavy metal rocker Ozzy Osbourne. A thinker and a drinker. And then there was this: "December third people are not particularly devotional or religious; on the contrary, they tend to be highly rationalistic, perhaps even a bit cynical."

Good Lord.

"I'm tired," Linda said, looking around the table.

Until that moment, I'd been full of energy despite the hour. But Linda's words descended upon the room like a spell, and my limbs felt suddenly exhausted. ("December third people get carried away with their thoughts and neglect their health.")

Bev had finished cleaning the kitchen, and we gathered up our purses and our eyeglasses, our sweatshirts, extra blankets, and our Ambien. The smokers collected their cigarettes and lighters, and we said good night, sleep well, see you in the morning.

Maybe it had happened slowly, like the ice age's glaciers. Or maybe it occurred all at once like the big bang and I'd been having too much fun to notice. Either way, the pleasures of Drummond had changed for me.

It seems distant and far away to me now, but there was a time when the location of our trip hadn't mattered as much as the bars, the partying, and the freedom of being away from home, *anywhere* away from home. Once, Bev had even suggested we go somewhere else—Mackinac Island, Hilton Head, or the Caribbean. Now we couldn't imagine anywhere but Drummond. Part of who we've become lives on the island even though most of the time we're going about our lives hundreds of miles away. For us, there is safety in the very wilderness that some women our age probably fear. It is the reconnecting with that part of myself and of my friends that I look forward to. It's the sound of the ferry docking, the smell of cedar, the girls' aging voices, and their arms around my waist that I look forward to now.

Not that we don't still party. I do anticipate our over-the-bridge Jell-O shots—well, okay, *shot*, singular, because even though they're tempered with whipped cream, too many of those things can really tear up your stomach. I have a prescription for Xanax, just two pills once a year, for crossing the bridges on the way and back home. I can still take command of the pool table at Chuck's when I really want to and have energy to burn on the island the way I rarely do at home anymore.

"Sleep?" we still like to joke. "You can sleep when you're dead."

I think of the island as a her; as our ninth Drummond Girl, yet of course she's been with us all along. Watching over us. Growing us up. I've come to love a new ritual, one that's ordinary and has nothing to do with partying, winning at pool, or living through back-to-back all-nighters. The luxury of lingering.

I've always been one of the first people up, and ever since we moved to Paw Point Lodge, I've loved to take a steaming mug of fresh coffee out onto the big front porch. Still in my pajamas and often with a coat on against the early damp, I'll sit on those wide log steps, look out, and try to absorb Potagannissing Bay into every cell of my body. Not to take home anymore, but just to have inside of me for one more moment.

I'd been so focused on rearing my sons that for what had seemed like a lifetime my mornings back home were hectic. Scrambling for clean clothes, making their sack lunches, and getting them to the bus on time. When they became teenagers, it was new clothes, lunch money, and jump-starts on batteries in used cars.

My Drummond mornings were dominated by mythically sized hangovers, for which Jill's breakfasts were the only cure. Now, the mornings here are simpler. Waves on the water, the sound of wind through reed grasses, the smell of ancient pine trees, all surrounded by those timeless dolomite boulders.

Unless someone in a fishing boat happened by, there wouldn't be a single man-made sight or sound from me to the bay's distant horizon. Miles of just…nature. And I couldn't help wondering, how many such wild and remote places were left in the Great Lak—

"Hey! Anybody make the *decaf*?"

The exasperated voice coming from somewhere inside was as familiar to me as my own. Bev was an early riser, too, and she'd pushed open the screen door and stood in the doorway, looking like a baby bird the morning after a hard rain. Her short hair stuck straight out, and I could see the cords pulsing in her neck.

"Good morning, Bevy," I said, obnoxiously cheerful.

She quickly disappeared into the house, but not before I caught sight of her outfit. A pale pink corduroy shirt two sizes too big over tight lime-green stretch pants with flowers in odd places. The Day of Flamboyance was starring in the acclaimed contemporary drama, *Brewing Decaf.*

Then the morning opened the rest of the way, and all my Drummond sisters eventually found themselves out on the porch with me. Some, like Bev, were still in their pajamas, and some were already dressed, showered, packed up, and ready—physically at least—for the trip home.

"Why does it always have to be sunny the morning we leave?" Andrea asked. "Every stinkin' year?"

We still had a little bit of time, at least an hour, and I loved these last moments on the island, rain or shine. I wasn't ever quite ready to leave, but I also knew we'd be back. And that the island would be here for us a year from now, no matter what was happening in our regular lives.

Over at the edge of the porch, in the last chair, Bev reclined, arched her back, and stretched out her legs. She'd bought new slippers for the trip. Pale pink terry cloth slides. They matched her shirt and, compared to my raggedy flip-flops, looked cozy.

Bev was still beautiful, even though she'd gotten so thin since she'd retired. I often worried that she forgot to eat. But the steam coming from her mug looked like it had both awakened and warmed her, and there was a healthy glow in her cheeks. There was no tension in her face and even her shoulders, sometimes so tense, looked relaxed. Whatever funk had come over her earlier seemed to be gone.

"Enjoy it," she said slowly, thickly, as if the cold sun beaming upon her was a drug. She spoke quietly, and I'm pretty sure I was the only one who'd heard her. Her head rested against the back of the log chair and her eyes were closed.

"What'd you say, Bev?" Jill asked.

"The sun, the morning, the island," she said, louder this time. "Time. Just enjoy it."

Her tone was half weather prediction, half admonition. She didn't open her eyes or shift her position, just stayed in that languid pose until it was time to leave.

Soon we'd locked up the lodge, returned the key, and were in line for the ferry. It docked right on time, unloaded, and Susan and I drove onto it effortlessly, both of us parking exactly where the crewman indicated. The person directing us was young and slim—did they let teenagers work the ferry now?—and we did exactly as he instructed, with Susan first, me behind, tight against the railing.

Andrea's sunny forecast held, and the bright light made the white metal of the ferry gleam. Even so, all seven of us stayed inside the car for the ride back. The ferry wasn't novel anymore and up ahead of me I could see the girls in Susan's car chatting happily away, as if they'd just seen each other again after a long absence, instead of spending the whole weekend together, talking anytime they weren't sleeping.

The wind was light and I pushed the button opening the sunroof on my new Ford SUV. We'd parked facing toward home, and so I had to turn awkwardly in my seat in order to look back. The cold spray of DeTour Passage splashed through the opening and onto my face, but I didn't care. Whether arriving or departing I had loved that view from the first moment I saw it. Nothing but waves splitting onto man-sized dolomite and pudding stones, sugar maples and black poplars swaying in full fall color, and a hill dense with evergreens.

A woman could find herself in there, I thought. She and her friends could walk on in and find out exactly what they were made of.

EPILOGUE

Drummond Island's northern coastline.

It is sometime in the not too faraway future, October, and we are racing the dark.

In the twilight, an otherworldly glow seems to come from inside the sugar maples, the ones decorating the north shore of Lake Huron. Driving away from home, I felt nothing but anticipation. My sons are grown now and on to their own lives. My husband is happy for the time at home alone. He can fix the downriggers on his fishing boat and tinker with the oil pan on the snowplow, too, without me hovering nearby, offering advice. I have a lot of feelings inside of me for him, and not one of them is mechanical.

"Have fun, my Mardi," is what he exhales into my neck when he hugs me good-bye. I feel every muscle in his arms. It's unseasonably cold, and even through his thick canvas jacket, I feel them.

Whatever year this is, we've just crossed the Mighty Mac. The bridge authority's driver's report was "all clear," with visibility estimated at "one hundred miles plus." We are safely over.

There are no other cars on the road. No other headlights, no taillights, no lights at all save the nav screen and its blinking green arrow, pointing forever forward.

I'm driving, Bev's sitting in the passenger seat, Jill and Andrea are in the back messing with a playlist, when, from up ahead, Linda uses Susan's cell phone to call us and impart this detail: As a meteorological concept, visibility is not an exact science. It is simply an estimate of how far one thousand candles can be seen when illuminated against an unlit background. How cool is that, she wants to know.

We are not one thousand candles; we are only eight. Our background is just up ahead and we won't even need igniting. Just like those scarlet and gold maple leaves, we are lit from within. We hurtle toward Drummond, burning inside with love, adventure, shared memories, and *life*.

Linda has ideas. Tomorrow we can take a guided tour out to the Fossil Ledges or maybe even Marblehead, the remote and scenic cliffs on the island's northern shore. There's a man with a new touring business who will do the driving for us, sixty dollars a person but probably worth it. Or we could just hike there. Six miles through some pretty wild and dense woods but also probably worth it.

Bev likes the second idea. She's nearly seventy now, still has her same hiking boots from 1995, but even so, with her buoyant stride she'll be the first of us to the trailhead. Bears? No, she's not worried about bears. She's not worried about anything.

A grin takes over her face. "Remember that year we danced at the Northwoods?" she asks. "Remember how great that band was?"

I don't remember, and I glance out her window at the water, watch it pass by at highway speed, and then refocus on the road ahead. We are racing the dark.

Bev didn't volunteer or learn to play the piano after she retired, but she did travel. Alaska, New Zealand, Australia, Africa, and next, Spain. Sometimes I get to be the one who picks her up from the airport. I get to look into her eyes and see the lively person inside, still so engaged with the world. Often, when I'm with her and she is walking me around her garden, telling me about each plant, where she bought it, how much it cost, the environment it prefers, whether or not the deer will eat it, I find the face of the girl I imagine she once was. Alert, curious, happy. I wonder if she ever looks at my face, notices a new smile line, a new forehead wrinkle, and sees the girl *I'll* always be.

Just as we clear DeTour hill, the last bit of a red sun sinks into the tamaracks. We'll be first in line for the ferry this year because Drummond is waiting and we are racing the dark.

Susan calls again. Andrea puts her on speaker. Remember your ferry manners, she says, and then I hear Pam and Linda hooting in the background. Jill throws her head back and laughs out loud. Those girls are fired *up*, she says.

About this time, Bev will ask how many years it's been.

Then we'll drive onto the ferry, the island will come into view, and we'll all know the answer.

It's been always. It will always be always.

It is the first weekend in October and we are racing the dark.

ACKNOWLEDGMENTS

On my computer there is a folder titled "These Great Women," archiving the correspondence between my exceptional agent, Jane Dystel, and me. She knows how to be a friend, and that's why she knew eight waitresses bound for a wilderness hunk of up-north rock had a story to tell. And it sometimes felt like my editor, the kind and wise Gretchen Young, traveled back and forth to the island with me in this journey of memory. These two women do have a natural environment—Manhattan—and yet, take it from me, they are both Drummond Girl material.

My friend Kris Love said yes when I asked if she could draw a map. Then she presented me with the work of art on pages viii and ix.

My husband, Pete, and my son, Will, both endured my preoccupied state of mind with resignation, patience, and carryout dinners. While I disappeared into my pink-walled office, they carried on, building museum-quality custom furniture and graduating from high school, respectively. My parents did not raise me to kidnap police officers or bait nuisance bears, yet they've supported "this writing thing" both emotionally and financially, so please absolve them from any responsibility for my questionable judgment. It's a Drummond thing.

Would your best friends let you write a book about them? A book that included words like *washycocky*, *pot brownie*, *fish gut protocol, blow-up doll*, and *sissy la-la*? Mine did. There would be nothing to tell if Jill hadn't gotten married young, if Andrea hadn't said there was going to have to be a party for that, and if Linda hadn't loaded up her old Jeep Cherokee, told us to get in, and then headed north. There would be nothing to tell if they hadn't invited me along, and then Bev, Mary Lynn, Pam, and Susan, too.

They are my sisters, my true north, and to them I pledge with all my might.